Cowgirl Cuisine

# Cowgirl Cuisine

**RUSTIC RECIPES AND COWGIRL
ADVENTURES FROM A TEXAS RANCH**

## Paula Disbrowe

Photography by Shelly Strazis

WILLIAM MORROW

*An Imprint of* HarperCollins*Publishers*

FIRST EDITION

Designed by Leah Carlson-Stanisic

Library of Congress Cataloging-in-Publication Data

Disbrowe, Paula.
    Cowgirl cuisine : rustic recipes and cowgirl adventures from a Texas ranch / by Paula Disbrowe.
        p.   cm.
    Includes index.
    ISBN: 978-0-06-078939-8
    ISBN-10: 0-06-078939-5
    1. Cookery, American—Southwestern style.   2.   Cookery—Texas.
    3. Dude ranches—Texas.   I.   Title.

TX715.2.S69D58 2007
641.5976—dc22

                                                                2006046602

07 08 09 10 11 WBC/IM 10 9 8 7 6 5 4 3 2 1

FOR DAVID, WITH LOVE

# Contents

# Acknowledgments

*I* couldn't have written this book without the help and support of plenty of great people. I am lucky, and grateful, to have them in my corner.

Enormous thanks to my literary agent, Janis Donnaud, who believed in this outside-of-the-box book from the beginning, and who fought with her characteristic tenacity to make it a reality. Thanks for demanding my best work.

Thanks to the entire team at HarperCollins. I am extremely fortunate to have worked with Harriet Bell, a notoriously deft editor, on my first book. Thanks for helping it become the book I always wanted to write. Thanks also to Roberto de Vicq de Cumptich, for a knockout jacket; and to Leah Carlson-Stanisic for an insanely fun and sexy book design.

The stars also aligned when I crossed paths with Shelly Strazis, my talented photographer, soon after I moved to the ranch. I had a gut feeling she'd be the perfect person to shoot this book—and she was. We both love things a little quirky, a little sexy, and think there are few things finer than a great animal portrait. I am grateful for her talent, whimsy, generosity (schlepping cross-country props!), hard work, and the spectacular photographs that have made this book so fun to look at.

Photo shoots are always stressful endeavors, with countless details to juggle. The process is even more challenging in rural isolation, with no catered cappuccinos, and the nearest grocery store thirty miles away. We couldn't have pulled it off without Shelly's tireless assistants, Brad Rochlitzer and Andrea Gomez, and my friend Melissa Garnett who went above and beyond, as an official recipe tester, making last-minute shopping trips, ironing cowgirl shirts, and keeping us fed and laughing. David also took care of us with his great cooking, fire building, smart creative input, and basically keeping me calm. Thank you, Shelley Thomas, for zipping down from Seattle for the first shoot when I needed you—and hoisting straps, lending your abundant style, and keeping me laughing in front of the camera as I knew you would. Thanks to Brian Smale and Calvin and Charlotte Rose for letting her come. Thanks to Angela Romero for keeping the kitchen running smoothly and coffeepots full, and for your essential sweetness.

Thanks to Dorothy Winston, the owner of Julien's home store in Uvalde, for lending us many of the gorgeous plates, utensils, and linens in this book—you made this book more beautiful.

Thanks to Kit and Carl Detering for having the chutzpah to hire us, and to their children, Cassie and Carlos, for welcoming us into their spectacular corner of the world. Thank you for generously supporting our interest in raising animals and having a garden, and for enthusiastically sharing *your* Texas. Special thanks to Kit for the adventures that stretched from Mexican bingo parlors in Nuevo Laredo to the Plaza Athénée in New York, and for always being the first person to say "thank you" after a meal.

For lending their keen editorial skills as proofreaders, thanks to Peter Romeo, Clay Smith, Cate Conniff-Dobrich, Melissa Clark, and especially Amanda Hesser, who has been an encouraging and supportive friend. I am indebted to my friend Adam Sachs, who lent his sharp eye to the ranch vignettes. His suggestions tightened this book—and saved me from my most sentimental self.

Two friends provided a clean, well-lighted space to work when I needed a break from my beloved distractions. Thank you, Terry McDevitt (and Kathy Garza and Diego the cat), for sharing the beautiful refuge that is Casa Luna in Helotes, Texas. And thanks to Monica O'Toole for offering an urban escape in Chicago (and stocking the fridge with yogurt and sparkling water).

Love and gratitude to Craig and Melissa Garnett for friendship, flautas, and showing me that life can be a Fellini film anywhere you live. Our time in Texas has been infinitely richer because of you, and the other wonderful people you introduced us to, including Danny and Celina Leskovar, Buzz and Nancy Barton, Gina and Giovanni Piccinni, and David and Gabrielle Forbes.

Thanks to our friends in Rio Frio, especially George and Beverly Streib, Willis Springfield, and Sharon Purnell, for friendship, laughter, and beautiful horseback rides.

Thanks to Rebecca Rather for being such a generous friend and wonderful partner for many Texas adventures.

Thanks to our veterinarians for plucking out hundreds of porcupine quills, clipping Max's hooves, and patiently fielding my countless queries about cats, dogs, horses, sheep, and goats, including Dr. Teresa Coble, Dr. Tracy Colvin, Dr. "Salty" Arnim, Dr. John Barnes, and especially Dr. Pete Vaden for laughs, tall tales, and cold beer.

Thank you to the women in Europe who invited me into their kitchens, including Patricia Wells, Kathie Alex, and especially Janet Hansen and Maria Martinez Sierra.

Thanks to my many other friends and family, who helped David and me navigate Texas, tested recipes, or simply loved and encouraged me through this wild ride and tolerated that certain tone in my voice when I was trying to meet deadlines: April Sachs, Brenda Nelson and Tom Van den Bout, Danielle and Neil Teplica, Chip Wass, Babs Chernetz, Beth Traynor, Gabrielle Hamilton, Suzanne Goin, Dr. Mary Ann Flatley, Susie Morris and her extended family, Noel McKay, Hollin and JoCarol McKay, Angela King, Susan Spicer, Kristin Batson, Stefani Twyford, Ron and Peggy Weiss, Patricia Sharpe, Robb Walsh, Pam Blanton, Gretchen and Lance Lahourcade, and Jane and Milton Howe (especially for our first Terry Allen CD!).

Thanks to Fran Norman, Jana Norman, and Paul Turley for your warmth and enthusiastic support of this project.

Thanks to my sweet Grandma Millie for love, great cooking, and filling my life with a steady stream of cookies, brownies, and various other Scandinavian confections.

Much love and gratitude to my parents, Mike and Julie Disbrowe, for your love, support, and endless efforts to make our lives smoother. Our adventure has been richer (and houses and gardens neater!) because you shared it with us. Thanks, Mom, for being one of my official recipe testers, and Dad, for being an official taster. Thanks to my brothers, Tim and Tyler Disbrowe, for always being proud of their big sister.

Last, but far from least, I thank my husband, David Norman. You have been there for me at every step, from bringing me sandwiches while I was holed up writing my proposal to picking up kitchen shifts and literally shoveling more shit so I could finish this book. No one's feedback, or palate, has mattered more. Thanks for having the guts to move to Texas. This story would not be a story without you.

# Introduction
## A Door Opens

Switching it over to AM
  Searching for a truer sound
Can't recall the call letters
  Steel guitar and settle down
Catching an all-night station somewhere in Louisiana
  It sounds like 1963, but for now it sounds like heaven.

—SON VOLT, "WINDFALL"

*E*very now and then the stars align and an unexpected door opens. You find your-self in a quandary. Do you walk past the door and continue with what is familiar, or do you walk through the door and turn your world upside down? This is a story about walking through the door.

A little more than four years ago, I knew almost nothing about the Texas Hill Country. De-spite the fact that I had racked up plenty of frequent flyer miles as a food and travel writer, this unique part of the United States—a swath of rolling green nestled between the pines to the east and the *Giant* landscape to the west—had escaped my radar. There was really no excuse, given the fact that I spent a brief chapter of my childhood to the southeast, in Yoakum, Texas, picking bluebonnets and Indian paintbrush flowers, poking at possums (playing possum and ignoring me), and cheering armadillo races from my dad's shoulders.

There was a lot I didn't know about the Hill Country—the brisket and breakfast tacos, the fire ants and scorpions, the cactus blossoms and oak trees. And I certainly had no idea what it was like to live on a ranch. Now, as I reflect on how immersed our lives have become in this world, I'm amazed at the transformation that has ensued. Somewhere along the line, the Disney Texas that I first felt when I'd don a cowboy hat and pearl-snap-button shirt became more authentic. My jeans faded and my boots wore in, and I earned some legitimate cowgirl notches in my belt. More important, my inner dialogue quieted down. I used to find myself thinking, *Isn't this wild? I'm in a feed store buying bales of hay.* Soon the errand was just that—a task as familiar as hail-ing a taxi in New York once was.

As I write this we have a baby lamb sleeping in a box in our kitchen, a kid goat curled up on the porch with our three dogs, and a rooster imprisoned in the backyard on murder charges (two young roosters are dead and the hens aren't talking). And all this seems relatively normal. But I'm getting ahead of myself.

Before moving to the Texas Hill Country, I was a city girl. I lived in New York for ten years, with a two-year detour to Europe.

I first came to the Detering Ranch (aka Hart & Hind), a spectacular 5,250-acre property ninety miles west of San Antonio, in October 2001 to write a magazine article about a bakery in Fredricksburg. I penciled in a trip to Hart & Hind, a new guest ranch, hoping it might provide another story. It was then that I first met Kit, the owner and founder of Hart & Hind. I immedi-ately liked her irreverent humor and unassuming nature. We're both fast walkers, so we became acquainted on daily hikes.

Kit had been unimpressed with her experiences at trendy, of-the-moment spas, and wondered why she paid top dollar to leave her own spectacular setting. So she decided to create her own retreat—an "un-spa" inspired by the rugged landscape. The program would play up hiking, horseback riding, and good food, and leave the fluff-and-buff stuff to more frivolous destinations.

In turn, I told Kit that my boyfriend David Norman, then the head bread baker at Bouley Bak-ery in Manhattan, and I had been thinking about making a change. I had ten great years of New York under my belt, but I was getting older and weary of the same games. I was increasingly desperate to escape the land of beige office cubicles. I was tired of paying too much money for a tiny apartment. I wanted to spend more time outdoors and reconnect with the things that the city forced me to compartmentalize. My frequent travel was fun, but the freedom was deceptive. I spent too much time on airplanes, flying over homes with warmly lit windows.

David and I started talking about "what next." It was sport dreaming and it was cheap. Maybe Northern California or Tuscany? Maybe the Pacific Northwest? If no one had called my bluff, I would have continued to "think about a change" for another five years. New York is a famously difficult place to live, but it's an even tougher place to leave.

Kit had her own ideas. Her chef had just quit. "Why don't you two come down here and run this place?" she asked with her usual spontaneity. I was flattered, but my initial thought was a resounding *Yeah, right!* Where could I find Vietnamese takeout or Prosecco by the glass? Where would I meet girlfriends for cocktails and gossip? Perhaps most important, I saw myself as a writer more than a cook. I'd spent the last several years behind a keyboard, not a stove. I hadn't cooked full-time since living in France.

Yet the proposition was alluring. Despite myself, I started to get excited. The chapter I spent in Europe had made me a sucker for dramatic detours. I'd enjoyed several fun, frenetic years in New York, but I could predict the next few. The utterly new experience of living on a ranch—that was exciting.

Before I flew back to New York, I called David from the San Antonio airport. It happened to be his birthday. "I'm not going to give you any details," I said, "but as I fly home I want you to think about the job title 'ranch manager.'" Click. Later that night, over a mojito or three, he came around to my way of thinking. It was time for a change.

Just two months later, we loaded two apartments of stuff into a Penske truck and said many tearful good-byes. We pulled into the ranch on January 2 and haven't looked back since.

Our adventure unfolded quickly. With our first paychecks, we bought cowboy hats. With our second check came the leather boots. The horses, saddles, and pickup truck came months later. Both David and I share the sentiment that if you're going to live somewhere, you might as well *live* there. So we set about immersing ourselves in the unique culture of south central Texas. And we rolled up our sleeves and started cooking.

I wanted to make food that had a context, so I started cooking the kind of things I would want to eat in such a setting. The recipes are a confluence of people and places that have shaped my sensibilities, as well as the area's beloved cooking traditions and ingredients. You won't find sea urchins, truffles, squash blossoms, or candied violets in these recipes. While I love all those ingredients, I wanted to cook with ingredients I could find at local grocery stores.

South central Texas influences these recipes in many ways. I was living on a working cattle ranch, after all, so I served steak and other local favorites like venison and quail, citrus fruit (ruby red grapefruit, oranges, valley lemons), flour and corn tortillas, pinto beans, locally grown cabbage and broccoli, and fresh shrimp and snapper from the Gulf. I used local products whenever possible, be it homegrown pecans, honey from Uvalde (the self-proclaimed honey capital of the world), herbs from my garden, or our own fresh ranch eggs.

Most of our food is inherently healthy because we use good fresh ingredients, but this is not a diet book. This is about fresh, satisfying food that is easy enough to prepare while living life

(and juggling its demands) to the fullest. We created the menu with selfish motivations: We wanted to serve food that we'd be proud of, but we also wanted to be outside, participating in ranch life as much as possible. Based on feedback from our past guests, we succeeded.

Before we moved to Texas, I never had a taste for land, and certainly never dreamed of owning any. As we fell in love with ranch life, it was all I could think about. When I thought about what I wanted next, for the first time in my life I had a concise answer. I wanted to keep the best aspects of my days here: wide open spaces and room to raise animals, hills to hike, fresh eggs to gather, a garden and a pace that allowed time to cook good food and share it with the people I care about. Our adventure has been anything but predictable. But the biggest surprise of all was that when Hart & Hind closed last year, we decided to strike out on our own and stay. Choices are evolutionary. Sooner or later it's time to find a new place to love.

So we bought a ranch of our own in the Nueces Canyon—100 acres on a lonely highway in the shadow of Bull's Head Mountain. We packed up our menagerie of animals, ordered more chickens, and deepened our commitment to the Hill Country and this sort of living—and cooking.

I like living life in chapters because the days remain vibrant and dense with learning. The Hill Country has been, and remains, an incredible chapter—and we've eaten awfully well to boot. I am delighted to share both the food and the escapades that have happened along the way.

# Ranch Breakfasts

*I*f I haul myself out of bed early enough I can watch the sun break over the soft slope of hills that rise at the end of a field in front of our house. The light comes in two ways. When it's overcast, the sky is a wash of periwinkle before easing into cotton candy pink and then increasingly radiant shades of coral. On clear days the hills are a sharp silhouette backlit by a crisp, bright stroke of butter yellow. As the sky brightens, our morning rituals begin. The bedroom door is cracked open, and Flannery the cat darts past my foot to reclaim the bed. We let the dogs out of the laundry room; they step into the backyard to stretch and yawn. One of us fills two cups of coffee.

My sleepy-eyed drive to the lodge, where I cook for guests, often feels like a video game where I am a character on a mission. Along the way I hit several targets that trigger a specific reaction. As I pull out of the driveway and past the windmills, the blesbok, an exotic African antelope that escaped from a nearby ranch, snorts at the truck, territorially shaking his head and pawing the earth. I descend a small hill and pass a row of live oaks where three rabbits pop up from a warren, race alongside the truck, then disappear down into new holes. As I near the pond, the snapping turtles that rest on a partially submerged log slip seamlessly into the dark water. When I reach the creek, a gray heron takes flight, each day gliding along the same arc of air. I can't help but wonder if these animals anticipate me as I do them. I drive between my garden and the pasture of goats; they bawl and gallop along the fence for a few yards. Finally I park behind the lodge, flip on the lights and music, cinch an apron around my waist, and start cooking.

Some people pride themselves on skipping breakfast. I wake up hungry. Breakfast is the meal most evocative of ranch life, and in true Western tradition, ranch breakfasts are heartier and less harried. I've learned that a beautiful, thoughtfully prepared morning meal—whether it's a bowl of yogurt adorned with a drizzle of syrup and a scattering of toasted seeds or a plate of spicy Mexican eggs—can be as satisfying as anything I will eat that day. Because our days are long and active, everybody needs to be well fueled. The same can be said for the daily demands of any active person.

Cooking for guests, I've also discovered that breakfast is by far the most personal meal. Morning customs are particular and not to be tampered with (half-and-half is as crucial to one person's coffee as vanilla soymilk is to another's). For some, morning bliss is a bowl of crunchy, nutty granola or a warm Blackberry Blue Corn Muffin (page 31). For others, heaven is Eggs over Polenta with Serrano-Spiked Tomato Sauce (page 28).

In the spirit of true camp cooking, David makes a hearty campfire breakfast outdoors—a chuck wagon fantasy come to life. Eating fresh ranch eggs scrambled with green chiles, warm buttermilk biscuits drizzled with cane syrup, and homemade turkey sausage outside in the sweet morning air is one of the most beautiful ways I know to start the day. We sip thick cowboy coffee from tin cups and watch the goats and horses grazing in the distance. But even if you can't eat out on the range, make this breakfast (we prepare it inside as well!). You'll love the satisfying flavors that deliver an undeniable Texas kick.

# Canyon Granola

**Makes 11 to 12 cups**

One brisk and bracing morning, as I hauled buckets of sweet feed to the pasture, it occurred to me that I have a breakfast habit in common with my horses. We both like to start the day with crunchy, sweetened whole grains. Mercifully, I am able to keep more of them in my mouth while chewing. Oats, nuts, and seeds are essential to good health—but I crave this cereal because it's delicious. Pecans, an important local crop, are a natural for Canyon Granola—we have three orchards on the ranch. They nicely complement a few other favorite ingredients, like pepitas (green hulled Mexican pumpkin seeds, available in natural food or specialty stores) and sweet, chewy dried peaches and cherries. Scatter a few tablespoons of these crunchy, chewy nuggets over plain yogurt, enjoy them as cereal with milk, or simply tuck a serving into your bag (saddle or gym) as a snack. Clear bags of this granola, cinched tight with a few ribbons and paired with some tin coffee cups, make excellent hostess gifts.

1 cup pure **MAPLE SYRUP**

½ cup **DARK BROWN SUGAR**

⅓ cup **CANOLA OIL**

¾ teaspoon **SALT**

1 tablespoon pure **VANILLA EXTRACT**

4 cups old-fashioned **OATS**

4 ounces (about 1 cup) **PECAN HALVES**

2 ounces (about ½ cup) **PEPITAS**

2 ounces (about ½ cup) **SUNFLOWER SEEDS**

½ cup **WHOLE WHEAT FLOUR**

½ cup **NONFAT DRY MILK POWDER**

⅓ cup ground **FLAXSEED MEAL**

4 ounces (generous ½ cup) chopped **DRIED PEACHES** or **NECTARINES**

4 ounces (generous ½ cup) **DRIED CHERRIES** or **GOLDEN RAISINS**

**1.** Place the oven racks on the upper and lower thirds of the oven and preheat to 300°F.

**2.** Combine the maple syrup, brown sugar, oil, and salt in a small saucepan over medium heat. Cook, stirring occasionally, until the brown sugar is dissolved. Stir in the vanilla.

**3.** In a large bowl, combine the oats, pecans, pepitas, sunflower seeds, flour, milk powder, and flaxseed meal. Pour the warm syrup mixture over the dry ingredients and use a rubber spatula to combine well.

**4.** Divide the moistened oats evenly between two baking sheets. Bake for 20 minutes, then stir with a metal spatula and rotate the sheets to opposite racks to ensure even baking. Bake another 20 minutes, then stir and switch pans again. Bake until the mixture has a fragrant, toasty aroma, another 10 to 15 minutes. Cool the granola in the pans, breaking up any unwieldy clumps with a spatula. When the mixture is completely cool, mix in the dried peaches and cherries and store at room temperature in an airtight container.

# Breakfast Tacos 101

**Makes 4 tacos**

Served in *taquerias* and gas stations throughout the Hill Country, the breakfast taco is a beloved tradition and one of the first local food customs that I eagerly embraced. In the morning, they are as common as cornflakes. At just about any restaurant that serves breakfast, the menu will feature a roster of huevos scrambled with a choice of one or two other savory ingredients such as chorizo, bacon, fried potatoes, sautéed onions and poblanos, or grated cheese served in a warm fresh flour tortilla. The belt-busting bean and cheese taco, hefty with thick, creamy refried beans and grated cheese, is another favorite.

Breakfast tacos made with scrambled eggs are the perfect outlet for any ingredients that you might have on hand. I've given a standard recipe below, but feel free to add sautéed mushrooms, bell peppers, onions, tomatoes, or *nopalitos* (cactus paddles). You can also add any grated cheese, leftover meat (slices of smoked sausage are a favorite), or chopped fresh herbs. As with any dish of limited ingredients, the quality of each item is key. The best free-range eggs and tender, fresh tortillas transform this speedy breakfast into a sublime eating experience.

> 1 tablespoon **OLIVE OIL**
> 8 large **EGGS**
> **KOSHER SALT** and freshly ground **BLACK PEPPER**
> Dash of **HOT SAUCE**
> 1 bunch of **SCALLIONS**, thinly sliced
> ⅓ cup chopped fresh **CILANTRO**
> ½ cup **GRATED CHEESE**, such as Cheddar, jack, cotija, or queso fresco
> 4 flour **TORTILLAS**

1. Heat the olive oil in a large skillet over medium heat and swirl to coat.

2. In a medium bowl, use a fork to lightly beat the eggs with salt, pepper, and hot sauce.

3. Add the scallions to the skillet and cook, stirring, until softened.

4. Pour in the eggs and cilantro and use a spatula to push the edges of the eggs toward the center of the skillet, tilting the skillet as you go, until no liquid remains. Just before the eggs set, fold in the cheese.

5. Meanwhile, heat the tortillas (see "Warming Tortillas," opposite). Divide the eggs evenly among the tortillas and serve with your favorite red or green salsa or another dash of hot sauce.

**WARMING TORTILLAS** Store-bought tortillas become more flavorful and pliable when heated. Some of the freshest tortillas can even be a bit sticky when you buy them, from undercooking. I cook them a bit further by placing them directly on the grates over a gas flame (if your grates are particularly low, stack two on top of each other), turning as necessary, just until they darken and blister. If you don't have a gas range, heat them in a dry skillet (I use a well-seasoned cast-iron skillet) over medium-high heat.

**VARIATIONS:** Scramble eggs with any of the following combinations:

*Corn, scallions, and fresh ricotta*

*Sautéed shallots, tomatoes, and fresh mint*

*Sautéed cremini mushrooms, fresh thyme, and goat cheese*

*Chopped roasted vegetables or potatoes and chopped parsley*

# "COUNTRY GIRLS ARE ROUGHER":

## POST OFFICE AS GREEK CHORUS

*A*s soon as we moved into our new home, we immersed ourselves in the daily demands of getting settled and the completely foreign ranch chores that came with the job.

Each errand and presumably simple task took longer here. If we wanted something to eat, we had to make it, since there was no Chinese takeout or pizza delivery. The nearest grocery store was thirty miles away, so when it came to shopping, we had to be organized—not a strength of either of ours. Taking out the trash meant driving to the dump. Feeding the cows each morning meant driving a Mule (a Kawasaki ATV), opening cold and rusty gates, entering the mouse-filled feed barn, and hauling bales of hay and sacks of feed cubes. Sectioned-off flakes of hay reminded me of giant blocks of shredded wheat cereal. Clean clothes lasted a few minutes—muddy hoof and paw prints became tattoos on my trousers. For the first time in years, my clothes actually got *dirty*—and we're not talking about a splash of coffee or red wine.

Wrap dresses and heels stayed packed away and I began to dress from a box of old jeans, khakis, and T-shirts. My hair was usually in a ponytail, and I was mostly dusty, sweaty, and paint-splattered. There were prickly burrs in my shoelaces and strands of hay and dried corn, for the goats, in my pockets. When I took off my jeans each night, the kernels would dance across the wood floor.

It was a return to my tomboy heritage, and it was mostly great fun, but I can't deny that in

weaker moments the transition was unsettling. I could no longer rely on the validation of feeling pulled together. There was no one around to say "Cool shoes" or "You look nice today." Every once in a while I would feel the need to justify my disheveled appearance.

On one such morning I went to the post office in Rio Frio, a small rectangular building with bluebonnets planted in front and pungent goats out back. Sharon, the postmistress, had grown up in Rio Frio; her parents lived across the street and she lived next door with her husband. She was warm, friendly, and a fanciful dresser. I looked forward to seeing what she was wearing each day because she always looked great in her leopard prints, multicolored cat's-eye glasses, blinking holiday jewelry, Western fringe, and flecks of glitter.

I hadn't bothered to put in my contacts, so I peered at her through smudged glasses. "Don't look at me," I grumbled. "I'm a mess."

I thought she might politely object. I secretly hoped she would refute the notion I was going to pot, even find some charm in my haphazard ways. Instead she looked me up and down, frowned, shrugged, and with a bit too much resignation said, "Well, country girls are rougher."

Sharon shoots from the hip. She has continued to provide a running commentary on my appearance, weight fluctuations, haircuts, ranch life, and the contents of my mail. Hence, the post office came to serve as a Greek chorus of sorts to our time in Texas.

Stepping inside the Rio Frio post office is a bit of a time warp. The radio is set to an AM station, "where the legends of country live," so it is routine to hear old-time country-and-western singers like Johnny Conlee, Hank Williams, and Charlie Rich. On lucky days I'd catch Dolly Parton. Most of the time I'd catch Sharon mid-phone call. She would pop up when I came in—at least before she got to know me. One time I arrived to hear Tammy Wynette singing "D-I-V-O-R-C-E" and heard her whisper into the phone, "Well, isn't he just a blow hole . . ."

Sharon put admirable energy into making the space cheery. For each holiday there would be corresponding decorations: jack-o'-lantern napkins taped on the wall for Halloween, metallic cupid streamers in February, bunnies and plastic eggs for Easter. The counter featured a candy bowl filled with Double Bubble and Peanut Chews. There was often a candle that reeked of Nantucket breezes or snickerdoodles, and a few stems of carnations in a vase. Mysteriously, every once in a while there would also be crates of produce. "Do you want some cabbage?" she'd ask. The source was always vague ("Oh, they brought it from down yonder . . .").

Sharon was the central valve through which local news traveled. Certain folks seemed to spend a good portion of their day at the post office, for the air-conditioning and company. The ease and all-around pleasantness of going there couldn't have been more different than it was in Brooklyn, with its morose clerks and long, irritating lines. Rio Frio suited my lack of organization. I could have shown up with an armadillo and Sharon probably would have helped me package it and find the friend's address, lent me packing tape, and let me bring in the postage the next day. On lazy days, I would simply call from home to see if I had enough mail to warrant the drive. "Hey, it's me. Do I have anything?" I'd say, not bothering to tell her who it was.

"You got a check," she'd answer without looking. Sometimes she'd hand me a stack of envelopes, laughing, and say, "You got another postcard from that one friend . . . he is *funny.*"

We swapped stories about survival in the land of wild hogs and scorpions. "Killed one last night," she'd say.

"Scorpion?" I'd ask.

She'd nod and we'd both laugh nervously. One morning she held up a finger wrapped in a Band-Aid. "Take a guess," she said. She had been doing dishes and picked up a skillet only to be stung by a scorpion hiding underneath. "It drew blood and it *hurt,*" she said.

Once a wild hog chased Sharon and her dog up a tree. When the pig finally gave up and ambled off, she "climbed down and ran like a scalded dog" in the other direction.

Sharon's favorite adult beverage was a Flaming Doctor Pepper, a mixture of beer and Amaretto that was ignited before it was served. She enjoyed these in Ruidoso, where she and a girlfriend liked to sneak off for weekends. "They quit serving them," she sighed after one trip. "Someone got hurt, and there's, you know, liability . . ." We both shook our heads in disbelief.

# Salsa Verde

**Makes about 4½ cups**

Salsa verde is made from tomatillos, which resemble small green tomatoes encased in a papery husk. They are actually a member of the gooseberry family. Raw tomatillos are Granny Smith green; when simmered they turn the drab color of army pants. The cooking process is important—it transforms their raw tartness into a sweeter, more appealing flavor. You can assemble the components of this salsa in the time it takes for the water to boil to blanch your tomatillos. The avocado is optional, but it gives the salsa a luscious, creamy body. For a richer flavor and a bit more heat, roast and peel a couple of poblano chiles and add them to the blender.

Serve this salsa with Cowgirl Migas (page 25), chicken tacos, or cheese quesadillas. For an easy appetizer, pour a pool of the salsa onto an ovenproof platter, top it with slices of panela or another fresh Mexican cheese, and broil until bubbly (the cheese will soften but not melt). Serve warm corn tortillas on the side.

2 pounds **TOMATILLOS** (about 14 medium), husked

1 large **ONION**, coarsely chopped

2 to 4 **GARLIC CLOVES** (as desired)

2 to 3 **SERRANO CHILES** (or 2 to 4 jalapeños)

½ cup coarsely chopped fresh **CILANTRO** (about ½ bunch)

2 tablespoons chopped fresh **TARRAGON** and/or **MINT** (optional)

Juice of 1 large **LIME** or 2 to 3 **MEXICAN LIMES** (about 2 tablespoons)

1 tablespoon **OLIVE OIL**

½ teaspoon **KOSHER SALT**, plus more to taste

1 **AVOCADO** (optional)

Bring a medium saucepan of water to a boil. Add the tomatillos and simmer until they darken to drab green and soften, about 5 minutes. Drain and transfer to a food processor or blender. Cool briefly, then add the onion, garlic, serranos, herbs, lime juice, oil, salt, and avocado if using. Pulse to break down the tomatillos, then purée until smooth. Taste for seasoning and add more salt or lime as desired. Store in a sealed container in the refrigerator for up to 5 days.

PONY EXPRESS: Canned tomatillos are not my first choice, but in a pinch and with the help of a few other ingredients (the avocado becomes more essential here), they make a tasty substitute. Drain two 10-ounce cans of tomatillos. Place in a blender with the serranos, onion, garlic, cilantro, and 1 avocado. Purée until smooth. Season to taste with salt and lime.

**BLISTERED TOMATILLO SALSA** Another way to make green salsa is to char and blister the tomatillos and vegetables under the broiler, which creates a more complex roasted, smoky flavor. When I make this version, I add 3 or 4 long, light green Hatch chiles (also called Anaheim). To prepare the salsa, place the tomatillos (they'll need to be rinsed, since they are not being blanched), onion, unpeeled garlic, serranos, and Anaheim chiles on a baking sheet. Drizzle with a small amount of olive oil and toss well to coat. Place the baking sheet under the broiler and cook, turning as necessary, until blistered on all sides. The peppers will darken first, followed by the tomatillos and then the onions and garlic (remove them from the oven in batches if necessary). Stem the chiles (it's not necessary to seed them), peel the garlic, then transfer all ingredients to a blender or the bowl of a food processor. Purée until smooth, taste, and season with salt and lime.

## FRESH CHILE PEPPERS

he following varieties are the ones I use most often. They appear in recipes throughout the book.

**Hatch/Anaheim:** A long, pale green, and tapered chile with a vegetal flavor that ranges from slightly warm to medium hot. Also called New Mexico Green Chile and Chimayo. Hatch chiles hail from around the town of Hatch in southern New Mexico.

**Poblano:** Fatter and wider than the Anaheim with a thick skin (making them perfect to stuff for chiles rellenos), poblanos are dark green with a rich flavor. The dried form is ancho. They are medium-hot, and usually roasted and peeled or sautéed with onions to form rajas, a popular condiment for fajitas and tacos.

**Jalapeño:** Green and bullet-shaped, jalapeños are the most famous hot chile in the world. Pickled jalapeños are the classic Tex-Mex condiment.

**Serrano:** Hotter and slimmer than jalapeños, serranos have a fuller, more herbaceous flavor with a nice, clean heat. This is my favorite for fresh salsas and guacamole.

**Habanero:** Also known as Scotch bonnet, this is the world's hottest pepper. It has a pretty lantern shape and wonderful fruity aroma, but treat it with respect! Use habaneros in small quantities and wear gloves when slicing.

**Pequín Chile:** This tiny chile, which grows wild throughout Texas and northern Mexico, looks like a small jelly bean on a thin stem. (Local lore says that wild turkeys eat them and acquire a spicy meat!) I use fresh pequíns when I roast vegetables, and crumble the dried chiles as a garnish over pasta and salads. They have a bright heat, like cayenne, and a more interesting flavor than crushed red pepper flakes.

## DRIED CHILE PEPPERS

*I* use these peppers in countless salsa and sauces. I also toast a mix of them (my favorite combination is ancho, pasilla, and New Mexico) on a baking sheet in a 350°F oven for 7 to 8 minutes. After they cool, I stem and seed the chiles and finely grind them in a food processor to create a complex, smoky seasoning that I leave on the table next to the salt and pepper.

**Pasilla (also called Negro):** Long and skinny with a purplish-black, wrinkled skin and medium heat, pasilla is Spanish for "raisin," named for the wrinkled skin, but it also suggests the flavor (along with notes of coffee and tobacco).

**Guajillo:** Long and tapered with a glossy reddish skin, it has a tart, fruity flavor and medium heat.

**Chile de Arbol (literally, "tree" chile):** A small and shiny bright red to orange chile with tapered body, it has a bright, high heat and a subtly sweet and toasty flavor. It's delicious when simmered with tomatoes to make a hot table sauce.

**Ancho:** The dried form of a poblano, ancho (meaning "wide") chiles are a deep reddish brown color. They're most aromatic when the skin is soft and leathery (as opposed to dry and brittle). The flesh is slightly bitter, with smoky notes of prunes, raisins, and chocolate.

**New Mexican:** Long, smooth, and tapered with a deep cabernet color, this is a workhorse chile, good in countless sauces and stews, with rich tomato and dried-fruit tones.

**Chipotle:** The dried form of a smoked jalapeño. I buy them canned in adobo sauce (prepared by cooking the dried chiles with vinegar, onions, and tomato). My favorite brand is San Marcos.

# Smoky Red Chile Salsa

**Makes about 2 cups**

Whereas salsa verde is light and herbaceous, this salsa, which relies on dried red chiles, is thick and jammy, smoky and intense. As the chiles and garlic toast atop a cast-iron skillet, they darken slightly and begin to smell like chocolate, raisins, and prunes. The chiles are soaked until they soften and are puréed with the roasted garlic and blistered tomatillos, which provide a tart, juicy base. A bit of honey softens the chiles' slightly acrid edges, and onion macerated in lime juice provides an acidic balance. Serve this salsa with fajitas, roasted chicken, breakfast tacos, or cheese quesadillas. It's also delicious alongside grilled tuna or sausage or mixed with mayonnaise to create a spicy condiment for burgers.

$\frac{1}{2}$ large **RED ONION**, chopped

2 tablespoons **LIME JUICE** (2 Mexican limes or $\frac{1}{2}$ large lime)

5 **ANCHO** or **PASILLA CHILES** (about $2\frac{1}{2}$ ounces)

4 large **GARLIC CLOVES**, unpeeled

10 large **TOMATILLOS** (about 22 ounces), peeled and rinsed

$\frac{1}{2}$ teaspoon **SALT**

1 tablespoon **DARK HONEY** or **CANE SYRUP**

1. Combine the onion and lime juice in a small bowl and set aside.

2. Line the bottom of a large cast-iron skillet with foil. Place the chiles and garlic on the foil and place over medium-high heat, turning as necessary until evenly blackened and blistered. Remove from the heat; set the garlic aside and transfer the chiles to a small bowl of hot water. Place a small saucer on top of the chiles to keep them submerged and soak for 30 minutes, or until completely soft.

3. Meanwhile, place the tomatillos on a foil-lined baking sheet and place under the broiler until evenly blackened and bubbly, turning as needed. Set aside to cool.

4. When the chiles have softened, stem and seed them. Peel the garlic cloves. Combine the chiles, garlic, tomatillos, salt, and honey in a food processor and purée. The salsa will have a fairly thick, jamlike consistency. Add the onion-lime mixture and pulse to combine (do not purée). Taste and adjust the flavors, adding more salt, honey, or lime to taste.

**NOTE:** Like apples, tomatillos contain naturally occurring pectin, so this salsa will thicken upon standing. If it's too jellylike when you take it out of the fridge, feel free to stir in a tablespoon or two of hot water to thin it.

# Horse Trader Salsa

**Makes about 3 cups**

This is the perfect salsa to make when your garden is heavy with peppers that have been baking and intensifying in the late-summer sun. If you buy them at the store, go for a mix of varieties and colors (I use red, green, and yellow jalapeños whenever possible); the results will be prettier and the flavor more complex. My friend George Streib first made this salsa for me. He learned the recipe from one of the Mexican laborers who work for him. He said the secret to getting it just right is that you have to crush the peppers with a heavy can. The first time I made this salsa I followed his instructions, then realized that a potato masher would work much better. Don't purée this salsa—the rough flecks of chile pepper are part of the appeal. The thyme is my touch; it provides a faint herbaceous flavor through the heat, which is significant. Feel free to substitute other varieties of milder chile peppers, such as yellow Hungarian wax or red Fresno, into the mix.

> 20 ounces fresh red, green, and yellow **JALAPEÑOS** and/or **SERRANOS**, stemmed but not seeded
> 1 large **TOMATO** (7 to 8 ounces), chopped
> 1 medium **ONION**, chopped
> 3 to 4 **THYME SPRIGS**
> 1 teaspoon **SALT**, plus more to taste
> 1½ teaspoons **RED WINE VINEGAR**

1. Place the chile peppers, tomato, onion, thyme, salt, and red wine vinegar in a large pot or Dutch oven. Add about 2 cups of water (it should come about halfway up the vegetable mix). Bring to a boil over medium-high heat, then cover and reduce the heat to low. Simmer vigorously for about 25 to 30 minutes, stirring occasionally and adding more water if the pot gets too dry.

2. When the peppers are completely soft, cool, remove the thyme sprigs, and use a potato masher to blend. Taste for salt and serve with tortilla chips. Stored in the fridge in a sealed container, this salsa lasts 7 to 10 days.

# Huevos with Ranch Hand Red Sauce

**Serves 4 to 8**

Just about every cook in Texas has his or her own method of making huevos rancheros, or eggs served atop a fried tortilla with spicy red sauce. For me it's all about a balanced, fresh-tasting tomato sauce, the freshest eggs, and a full-flavored cheese melted on top. This recipe makes enough sauce for 8 servings, but it keeps well, so simply cook the eggs and tortillas to order and serve it throughout the week.

Partner this eye-opening breakfast with black beans or refried pintos and sliced avocado. As an alternative, try the Blistered Tomatillo Salsa (page 9) instead of the red sauce. For a brunch party (margaritas, anyone?), the sauce can be made a day or two in advance. Then all you need to do is fry the tortillas (they can be done earlier in the morning), assemble the garnishes, and cook the eggs to order.

6 medium **TOMATOES** (about 2½ pounds)

3 to 5 **SERRANO CHILES**

4 **GARLIC CLOVES**, unpeeled

1 cup coarsely chopped fresh **CILANTRO**

1 teaspoon **SHERRY WINE VINEGAR** or **RED WINE VINEGAR**

¾ teaspoon **SALT**

1 tablespoon **OLIVE OIL**

1 **GREEN BELL PEPPER**, chopped

½ **RED ONION**, chopped

**VEGETABLE OIL**, for frying

1 **FLOUR TORTILLA** per serving

1 to 2 **EGGS** per serving

**GRATED WHITE CHEESE** (such as jack, asadero, or cotija),
   for garnish

**CILANTRO SPRIGS, AVOCADO SLICES**, and **LIME WEDGES**
   for garnish

**1.** Heat a large cast-iron skillet covered with foil over medium-high heat. Place the tomatoes, serranos, and garlic on top of the foil and heat until blackened on all sides, turning as necessary (you can also place the vegetables on a foil-lined baking sheet and cook them under the broiler). Allow the vegetables to cool, then stem the serranos, peel the garlic, and transfer to a blender. Purée with the cilantro, vinegar, and salt.

**2.** Heat the olive oil in a large nonstick skillet over medium-high heat. Add the green pepper and onion and cook, stirring, until softened, about 5 to 7 minutes. Add the tomato purée, reduce the heat to medium-low, and cook, stirring, for an additional 5 minutes.

**3.** To serve, heat ½ inch of the vegetable oil in a large skillet over medium-high heat. When the oil is hot but not smoking, fry the tortillas, one at a time, until puffed and golden brown on each side. Transfer the tortillas to a plate lined with paper towels. Cover each tortilla with an additional paper towel. Repeat as needed with the remaining tortillas.

**4.** Heat a tablespoon of the vegetable oil in a medium nonstick skillet over medium heat. Fry 1 to 2 eggs per person, as desired. To serve, top each tortilla with eggs, a generous ladleful of red sauce, grated cheese, and cilantro. Garnish with avocado slices and lime wedges.

## FOUR FRESH WAYS TO EAT YOGURT

*U*ntil I started buying the good stuff and adding a few embellishments, yogurt was something I had to force myself to eat. But with the great organic varieties available and these quick preparations, I look forward to eating it almost every morning.

**Maple Syrup and Pepitas:** This is my most common breakfast. Top yogurt with a drizzle of maple syrup and a scattering of raw or toasted pepitas.

**Melon Cup:** Use a knife to trim the peel from a small (softball-size) honeydew or cantaloupe. Then use a paring knife to slice small, slanted slits around the middle of the melon, so the melon eventually splits open like a cracked egg. Use a spoon to gently scrape out the seeds. Fill the melon cup with yogurt and top with fresh berries.

**Citrus-Mint:** Use a knife to trim the peel from a grapefruit, orange, and Meyer (or Valley, as the variety grown in South Texas is called) lemon. Feel free to add lime or regular lemon as well, if you want a tarter taste. Holding the peeled fruit in your hand, trim the fruit into segments, allowing both the juice and segments to fall into a bowl. Toss the fruit with chopped fresh mint and serve atop yogurt. (For sweeter results, stir a little honey into the citrus juice.)

**Berry Compote:** Simply simmer a pound of fresh or frozen berries (my favorite combination is blackberries and raspberries) with a generous drizzle of maple syrup; ½ fresh vanilla bean, split; a pinch of salt; cinnamon; and ground ginger (or a couple tablespoons chopped candied ginger). Simmer over medium-low heat, stirring occasionally, until the berries break down and the juices thicken. On cold mornings, I serve this compote warm as a topping for oatmeal. Stored in a sealed container in the refrigerator, this compote will last about 10 days.

# Texas Tofu Scramble

**Serves 4**

Many of our guests at Hart & Hind had unshakable Texan tastes. They like their steaks "flipped" (rare enough that a good vet could still save it), their iced tea sweet, and jalapeños on just about everything. Needless to say, I was leery of serving tofu. So I didn't say a word before I presented this fragrant, colorful scramble. I simply disappeared into the kitchen and listened. "How does she get these eggs so creamy?" I heard one of them say.

Chalk one up for the chameleon powers of tofu.

For a heartier breakfast, serve this scramble with black beans in a whole wheat tortilla, with a dollop of plain yogurt and salsa. I heat up leftovers with chopped fresh tomatoes for a quick, healthy lunch. Whether you tell anyone it's tofu is up to you.

1 tablespoon **VEGETABLE** or **OLIVE OIL**

1 medium **ONION**, diced

1 **RED** or **ORANGE BELL PEPPER**, diced

1 **SERRANO CHILE**, stemmed, seeded, and minced

One 12-ounce package firm or soft **TOFU**, drained (see Note)

1 teaspoon **TURMERIC**

1 teaspoon **RED WINE VINEGAR**

1 teaspoon **SOY SAUCE**

½ teaspoon crumbled dried **BASIL** or **MEXICAN OREGANO** (optional)

¼ cup chopped fresh **CILANTRO**

**SALT** and freshly ground **BLACK PEPPER**

1. Heat the oil in a large skillet over medium-high heat until hot but not smoking. Add the onion, bell pepper, and serrano and cook, stirring, until softened and slightly browned, about 8 minutes.

2. Meanwhile, drain the tofu and place on a cutting board, then pat dry with a paper towel. Slice into ½-inch squares. Add the tofu to the browned vegetables along with the turmeric and cook until heated through. Add the vinegar, soy sauce, basil if using, and cilantro and stir to combine. Taste and season with salt, black pepper, and additional vinegar or soy sauce. Serve immediately.

NOTE: Soft tofu will result in a looser, creamier texture that really does resemble scrambled eggs. Firm or extra-firm tofu will hold its cube shape.

# MAIL-ORDER CHICKS

*U*pon reflection, I think it was the possibility of raising chickens that clinched my decision to relocate. Fresh eggs to gather for huevos rancheros! Plus what is prettier than a bunch of hens picking around the yard? Over the past four years, I've raised dozens of chicks, ducklings, goslings, and guinea hens, and I can't imagine not having my own fresh eggs. But when my first chicks arrived, I was unaccustomed—romantic notions had overruled the logistics of how things would come together.

For my first batch, I leafed through a mail-order catalog from a hatchery in Iowa, picked up the phone, and ordered a batch of thirty chicks as casually as I might select a sweater from J. Crew. The process was similar, after all. I could select just about any color, size, and breed imaginable, each promising a particular flourish. Black Rosecombs were noted for a "stylish body and alert personality." Anconas promised "lustrous black plumage" and Pearl guinea hens would "reduce the number of bugs and ticks." I wanted *Aracaunas*, the chickens that lay pastel-colored eggs in shades of blue, olive green, and peachy pink.

The chicks were to be sent via airmail and were scheduled to arrive on Presidents' Day—a Monday and national holiday when the post office was closed. Assuming *those who knew best* would take this into account, I expected them to arrive on Tuesday. That Monday, I busied myself preparing their new home. I swept out the "aviary," a stuffy old cabin that once housed migrant workers and now served as a makeshift birdhouse, based on the basic instructions that I'd read in the catalog. I hauled in a deep metal tub that would shelter the chicks from drafts, lined the tub with wood shavings, then placed a few sheets of newspaper on top. The paper would prevent the chicks, dazed and confused from their journey, from eating the shavings instead of their feed.

I found an old heat lamp in the barn, fitted it with a new red bulb, and secured it over the tub. The cord just reached a weathered socket in the ceiling, so everything seemed to be fitting into place. I filled the feeder with food, which resembled pale gray Grape Nuts. Pleased with my efforts, I headed up to the lodge for a glass of water. On a whim, I checked the answering machine, only to hear a panicked voice. "Paula, this is Sharon at the post office. Your chicks are here, and they're not going to live through the night." Click.

Mail-order chicks are shipped a few hours after hatching. They're nestled into a perforated cardboard box small enough to reserve body warmth. Then they endure what must be a nerve-racking journey and arrive jostled, confused, and thirsty. Surely they feel adrift in an unkind world. I considered these things as I sped along the road.

The minute I opened the door to the post office I heard a frantic peeping. "They're all alive," Sharon screamed with no small amount of drama. "I checked."

I grabbed the noisy, alarmingly light box and headed for the truck. I could feel the scratch and scramble of tiny claws through the cardboard. To calm the chicks, I started singing. It was a high-pitched hum really, which basically morphed into the word *baaaaabeeeeeeees* over and over again. To my surprise, the peeping stopped. The chicks grew quiet and listened to the fluctuating pitch of my voice. When they'd start to chatter again, I'd change tones and that would do the trick for a few more minutes.

At the ranch I rushed the box into the aviary. Desperate peeping resumed. It was a cold morning, and I was eager to get the chicks under the heat lamp, but first I had to mix them a drink of vitamins and electrolytes with a few tablespoons of sugar, which I poured into the water dispenser. Then I tore off the cardboard lid and took a good look at the downy balls of charcoal gray and yellow buzzing around on a thin layer of straw. They looked like wind-up toys.

According to instructions, I was to catch each chick and dip its beak into the water so it would be able to locate its drink source. I carefully scooped up a chick, lowered it into the tub, and used my index finger to gently push its beak into the water. I released it and watched it stagger around on the newspaper. I continued this process as fast as I could. When I had unloaded about half of the box, I paused and looked into the red bulb of the heat lamp. Then it exploded.

There was a bright flash and I felt the sting of shattered glass on my face. Because I had been staring directly into the light, I saw stars. Unfortunately, so did the chicks. I could hear their panicked peeps, and when I was finally able to focus I saw one of the chicks, flat on its back, beak pointed up, knocked out like a boxer in a cartoon.

Just then David arrived. He found me on my knees, surrounded by broken glass and frantic chicks. "The bulb blew up," I sobbed. "That one is dead." I pointed to the knockout. David picked up the bird, cupped it in the palm of his hand, and stroked it. "It's not dead," he said calmly. "It's just in shock." Sure enough, the chick was starting to come around and so was I. David found another bulb, plugged it into an extension cord that led to a more trustworthy socket, and picked up the mess. Sniffling, I baptized the remaining chicks.

When they were fully feathered at two months and able to venture outside, I would sit outside their pen and watch them buzzing around. There was a relaxing rhythm to their scurry, and I loved the sound of their chatter, as soft and buoyant as rushing water.

Chickens start laying eggs in five to seven months. The act of searching for and finding an egg must satisfy an impulse left over from the playground—the process made me giddy. Often the eggs would still be warm in my hands when I carried them into the house. Our hens foraged for green things all day, and feasted on my vegetable trimmings and food scraps. As a result, their yolks were saffron-colored and richly flavored.

To raise chickens for the first time is to learn by a painful process of trial and error. Predators were numerous and unyielding. Who knew that a raccoon, with its crafty, tenacious paws, could skillfully work through a wire fence? Skunks, snakes, and barn cats were just as persistent. David and his shotgun made frequent midnight trips to the barn.

It was dangerous to get too attached to any given chicken, and naming one seemed like a death sentence. We coddled one hen while she sat on eggs until she hatched two chicks. Then on Christmas morning, just as I poured each of us a glass of champagne, Tex, the golden Lab, showed up at the screen door, proudly wagging his tail with the hen in his mouth.

# Scrambled Eggs with Hatch Green Chiles

**Serves 4**

These eggs get their kick from plenty of chopped green chiles. This scramble is so simple that we cook it for outdoor campfire breakfasts (partnered with fluffy biscuits) and inside on the range to serve with warm flour tortillas and beans. If you can find fresh or even canned Hatch chiles (from Hatch, New Mexico), they will create a particularly tasty scramble. However, in a pinch any canned green chile will work just fine. Feel free to add shredded Cheddar or jack cheese to the eggs just before they finish cooking.

1 tablespoon **OLIVE OIL**

1 tablespoon **BUTTER**

8 large **EGGS**

¼ cup **MILK** or **LIGHT CREAM**

**KOSHER SALT** and freshly ground **BLACK PEPPER**

Dash of **HOT SAUCE**

2 **HATCH** (also called Anaheim) **CHILES**, roasted (see below), peeled, seeded, and chopped (or one 4-ounce can fire-roasted green chiles)

1. Heat the olive oil and butter in a nonstick skillet over medium heat, and swirl to coat.

2. Whisk together the eggs and milk or cream in a medium mixing bowl. Add the salt and pepper, hot sauce, and chiles. Pour into the skillet and use a spatula to push the edges of the eggs toward the center of the skillet, tilting the skillet as you go, until eggs are just set, about 4 to 5 minutes, and serve.

## ROASTING CHILES

To roast chiles, place them directly over the grate on a gas range and heat over the flame, turning as necessary, until they are evenly charred and blackened. Transfer chiles to a large bowl and cover with a dish towel. This will steam the chiles a bit longer and make it easier to remove the skins. When the chiles have cooled, slice off the stems, remove the skins with your fingers (or a paper towel or paring knife), slice them open, and scrape out the seeds and discard. Alternatively, you can place the chiles on a baking sheet and roast them under the broiler, turning as necessary until they are evenly blackened. Transfer chiles to a large bowl, as directed above.

# Cowgirl Migas

**Serves 4**

Migas (Spanish for "crumbs") is a beloved Tex-Mex breakfast scramble with two familiar ingredients: eggs and fried corn tortillas that have been crumbled into bits. Traditional recipes are rich and heavy, laden with greasy tortilla strips and an avalanche of yellow cheese. I typically lighten mine by adding more egg whites than yolks, charred (not fried) corn tortillas, vegetables and fresh herbs, and a dusting of a more flavorful aged cheese such as Cotija or queso añejo. If you want a heartier version (a good idea the morning after a particularly enthusiastic fiesta), use whole eggs, your choice of breakfast meat, and more grated cheese.

Nopalitos, or pickled cactus paddles, are common partners with eggs in this area and a delicious addition to migas. Sold in jars in the condiment or Mexican section of grocery stores in most of the country, they have a mild green flavor that resembles a well-cooked green bean (which can be used as a substitute). Leftover grilled veggies, blanched asparagus, or sautéed zucchini, spinach, or mushrooms are good additions to migas. Substitute or add vegetables as you please, adjusting the amount of eggs, as necessary, to suspend the extra ingredients. Serve this dish warm from the skillet with a wedge or two of lime and some red or green salsa.

3 **CORN TORTILLAS** (or 4 small maseca tortillas, if available)

6 **EGG WHITES** plus 2 whole **EGGS** (or 8 eggs)

**KOSHER SALT** and freshly ground **BLACK PEPPER**

**HOT SAUCE**

1 tablespoon **OLIVE OIL**

1 small **RED ONION**, chopped

1 **YELLOW, ORANGE,** or **RED BELL PEPPER**, chopped

2 **SERRANO CHILES**, seeded and sliced into half-moons

3 **PLUM TOMATOES**, seeded and diced

½ cup **NOPALITOS**, rinsed, patted dry, and coarsely chopped (see Note)

⅓ cup chopped fresh **CILANTRO** (leaves and tender stems), plus additional sprigs
    for garnish

2 ounces (about ½ cup) finely grated **COTIJA** or other aged cheese

**LIME WEDGES** and **SALSA** (optional)

1. Toast the tortillas over a gas flame until charred and blistered but not too dark. If you don't have a gas range, toast them in a dry skillet over medium-high heat until slightly darker and fragrant. Cool the tortillas slightly, then coarsely chop into ½-inch squares.

2. Combine the egg whites and eggs into a small bowl, season with salt, black pepper, and hot sauce, if desired, and beat lightly with a fork. Heat the olive oil in a large skillet over medium-high heat, and swirl to coat. Add the onion, bell pepper, and chiles and sauté

until softened, 4 to 5 minutes. Add the tomatoes and cook until they begin to break down, about 4 minutes. Add the tortillas and cook, stirring, until they are moistened and have absorbed any juices. Add the eggs, nopalitos, and chopped cilantro and cook, stirring with a rubber spatula, just until the eggs set. Serve immediately with a dusting of cotija, lime wedges, salsa, and cilantro sprigs, if desired.

NOTE: If you want a hotter scramble, don't seed the serrano chiles. A microplane is the easiest way to grate the cheese over the hot migas. If you can find fresh no-palitos (they will be vacuum-packed in plastic bags in the produce section), by all means use them. They will have a more vibrant color, fresher flavor, and an asparaguslike texture. To prepare fresh nopalitos, empty the packet into a colander and rinse (the paddles will be coated in a gooey okralike liquid). Blanch the no-palitos in boiling water, then rinse again. Pat dry with paper towels before adding to the migas.

PONY EXPRESS: For a quicker migas, simply sauté the onion, then stir in a drained 10-ounce can of RO*TEL® tomatoes and green chiles. Cook a few more minutes to reduce the juices, then stir in the eggs and a cup of crushed tortilla chips; garnish with cheese. If you don't have salsa, douse with your favorite hot sauce.

## MASECA TORTILLAS

*Y*ou'll have a hard time finding these tortillas if you don't live in an area with a Hispanic community. If you do, seek out a Mexican grocery to find these tortillas, which are made from coarsely ground masa. They have an appealing pebbly texture, and are more flavorful than other varieties. They are my choice for enchiladas as well, because they become tender (not chewy or soggy) when baked with a sauce.

## MEXICAN CHEESES

*T*ypically on the mild side, Mexican cheeses fall into two basic categories. Fresh cheese (*queso fresco*) is supple and moist, and dried cheese (*queso añejo*) has a concentrated flavor and crumbly texture. The following cheeses are available in most grocery stores and Mexican markets.

**Crema:** Not really a cheese, but a thick, tangy dairy condiment used to enrich sauces and as a topping for tostadas, tacos, and enchiladas. I love a drizzle on soups, black beans, and hot fruit cobblers. Sour cream, crème fraîche, or even whole milk yogurt can be used as a substitute.

**Cotija:** Think of it as Mexican Parmesan. This pleasingly salty, pungent cheese has a lightly moist crumb. It's typically sold in a square brick shape. Since it's a firm, aged cheese with a stronger flavor, this is the cheese I use most often as a garnish for salads and enchiladas. Pair it with milder asadero for a great cheese quesadilla. Crumbled feta, ricotta salata, or even pecorino or Parmesan can be substituted, although the latter will be drier and not as milky tasting.

**Asadero:** Also called "queso quesadilla" because it's an excellent melter, it's the best choice for nachos, burgers, *queso flameado* (literally "flaming cheese," a popular appetizer of melted cheese and salsa or chorizo), or even a Mexican-inspired panini made with spicy puréed beans. Whole milk mozzarella, provolone, mild, Cheddar-like Chihuahua cheese, and Muenster are good substitutes.

**Queso Fresco:** The catchall name for "fresh cheese." Most versions are soft, moist, mild, with a coarse crumble, for sprinkling over enchiladas, black bean soup, or a salad. It's not a good melter.

**Panela:** A light, milky fresh cheese typically crumbled over tacos, salads, and enchiladas. In the morning, it's a nice breakfast cheese with a drizzle of honey. I like to place slices over a pool of red or green salsa, broil it, and serve with fresh corn tortillas. The cheese softens with heat, but it does not fully melt.

**Queso Añejo:** An aged cheese with a dry texture and salty, nutty flavor, it's an excellent garnish for tostadas and beans.

# Eggs over Polenta with Serrano-Spiked Tomato Sauce

**Serves 4**

I first had this combination of eggs, polenta, and tomato sauce at a bistro in New York's West Village, where it was flavored with red wine and prosciutto. Now I add Mexican flavors. This satisfying breakfast makes for a welcome Sunday brunch—it holds friends through the afternoon and their travels home (a consideration when you live in a remote setting!).

The sauce and polenta can be made in advance (hold the latter in a water bath in a larger pot). For a crowd, I pre-poach the eggs and re-warm them at the last minute; for a smaller group, I poach them to order. If time is of the essence, feel free to use instant polenta or even quick-cooking grits.

1 cup coarsely ground **ITALIAN POLENTA**, or **YELLOW CORNMEAL**

1 teaspoon **KOSHER SALT**, plus more as needed

2 fresh **BAY LEAVES**

1 tablespoon **OLIVE OIL**

1 medium **ONION**, chopped

1 **BELL PEPPER**, chopped (optional)

1 or 2 **SERRANO CHILES**, thinly sliced into half-moons

One 28-ounce can **TOMATOES** in their juice (preferably San Marzano)

Chopped fresh **CILANTRO**

Juice of 1 medium **LIME** (about 2 tablespoons)

1 teaspoon **APPLE CIDER VINEGAR**

4 large **EGGS**

$\frac{1}{3}$ cup **GRATED COTIJA** or other **WHITE CHEESE** (such as ricotta salata, pecorino, or crumbled feta) for garnish

1. In a medium saucepan, bring 4 cups of water to a boil over medium-high heat. Slowly whisk in the cornmeal, then use a wooden spoon to stir in the salt and bay leaves. Bring to a boil, then reduce heat and simmer, stirring occasionally, for 45 minutes, or until the polenta begins to pull together and away from the sides of the pan.

2. Meanwhile, make the sauce. Heat the olive oil in a large nonstick skillet over medium-high heat. Add the onion and cook, stirring, until softened, about 5 minutes. Add the chiles and cook another 2 minutes. Add the tomatoes, reduce the heat, and simmer for

about 2 minutes, until thickened. Stir in the chopped cilantro and lime juice and taste for seasonings.

3. Bring a small saucepan of water to a boil. Add the vinegar, then use a spoon to stir the water in a clockwise direction, creating a whirlpool current. Crack the eggs into a small cup and add them, one at a time. The current should pull the whites around the yolk. Poach until they are just set (since you'll be heating them again), about 5 minutes. Using a slotted spoon, transfer the eggs to a bowl of ice water. Keep the hot water over low heat so you can reheat the eggs, by plunging them into simmering water, before serving.

4. When you are ready to serve, plunge the eggs back into the barely simmering water. Place a generous pool of the polenta into the serving dish. Top with a poached egg, a spoonful of sauce, and a sprinkle of grated cheese.

COWGIRL CUISINE

# Blackberry Blue Corn Muffins

**Makes 16 muffins**

These muffins have a rustic texture and they're not too sweet. They're also heavy on the fruit, which means big bites of warm, juicy blackberries. The blue corn, which has a sweet, nutty flavor, gives them a pretty lavender color, but yellow cornmeal can be used as well. For the best results, make this batter the night before. If the batter chills overnight, the leaveners get a chance to do their thing and the muffins really pop up in the hot oven. Feel free to use blueberries or raspberries as well.

2 cups **ALL-PURPOSE FLOUR**

1 cup **BLUE CORNMEAL**

½ cup **LIGHT BROWN SUGAR**

1 tablespoon **BAKING POWDER**

1 teaspoon **BAKING SODA**

¾ teaspoon **SALT**

1½ cups **PLAIN YOGURT**

⅓ cup **CORN OIL**

3 tablespoons **MAPLE SYRUP**

2 teaspoons pure **VANILLA EXTRACT**

3 **EGGS**

1 pound fresh or frozen (see Note) **BLACKBERRIES** (2 generous cups)

1. Preheat the oven to 375°F. Grease two standard 12-cup muffin tins.

2. Whisk the flour, cornmeal, sugar, baking powder and soda, and salt together in a large bowl. In a medium bowl, stir together the yogurt, oil, syrup, vanilla, and eggs. Using a rubber spatula, fold the wet ingredients into the dry ingredients until just mixed. Fold in the blackberries. (If you are going to chill the batter overnight, wait and add the blackberries just before baking.) Fill 16 of the muffin cups just to the top and bake for 10 to 15 minutes. Rotate the tins and bake for an additional 10 to 12 minutes, until puffed and slightly golden and a toothpick inserted into the center of a muffin comes out dry.

3. Allow the muffins to cool in their tins for 5 minutes before inverting onto a cooling rack.

**NOTE:** If using frozen berries, stir them in frozen just before baking so the batter doesn't become too streaky. For even baking, fill the empty cups in the second tin halfway with water.

# Spiced Pumpkin Muffins with Pepitas

**Makes 12 muffins**

Warm holiday spices give these muffins an inviting, homey fragrance. Dried dates are the secret ingredient. They add chewy, caramel-like nuggets of sweetness. Pumpkin purée keeps the muffins moist, so they freeze particularly well. Chopped toasted walnuts and pepitas create a pretty topping and add a satisfying crunch. For the best results, use your fingers to gently press the nuts and seeds into the top of the batter before baking.

$\frac{1}{2}$ cup (1 stick) **UNSALTED BUTTER** plus more to grease the tins

1 cup **PUMPKIN PURÉE** (pure canned pumpkin, not pumpkin pie mix)

$\frac{1}{2}$ cup **BUTTERMILK**

2 **EGGS**

1 teaspoon pure **VANILLA EXTRACT**

3 tablespoons **MOLASSES**

$1\frac{1}{2}$ cups **ALL-PURPOSE FLOUR**

$\frac{1}{2}$ cup **WHOLE WHEAT FLOUR**

$\frac{1}{2}$ cup **DARK BROWN SUGAR**

2 teaspoons **BAKING POWDER**

$\frac{3}{4}$ teaspoon **SALT**

1 teaspoon ground **CINNAMON**

$\frac{1}{4}$ teaspoon **NUTMEG**

$\frac{1}{4}$ teaspoon ground **CLOVES**

$\frac{1}{4}$ teaspoon **BAKING SODA**

$\frac{3}{4}$ cup chopped **DATES**

$\frac{1}{3}$ cup toasted **PEPITAS** (pumpkin seeds)

$\frac{1}{3}$ cup toasted **WALNUTS**

1. Preheat the oven to 400°F.

2. Grease a 12-cup muffin tin with butter or nonstick spray. Melt the butter and place in a medium bowl with the pumpkin, buttermilk, eggs, vanilla, and molasses. Stir with a fork to blend.

3. In a large bowl, whisk together the flours, brown sugar, baking powder, salt, spices, and baking soda. Using a rubber spatula, fold the wet ingredients into the dry ingredients until just mixed. Fold in the dates and half of the pepitas and walnuts.

4. Divide the batter among the muffin cups and top with the remaining pepitas and walnuts (use your fingers to gently press them into the batter). Bake for 10 minutes, rotate the tins, and bake another 10 minutes, or until puffed and firm and a toothpick inserted into the center of a muffin comes out clean.

5. Allow the muffins to cool in their tins for 5 minutes before inverting onto a cooling rack.

# Pear-Rosemary Bread with Pine Nuts

**Makes two 8 × 4½-inch loaves**

On a crisp fall afternoon, my friend Melissa and I picked pears at a small orchard north of the ranch. The pears were a unique local variety, wonderfully misshapen and gnarled with mottled pale green skin. That same afternoon I trimmed my garden and gave a few unwieldy rosemary plants a much-needed haircut. A pile of the fragrant stems and the crate of aromatic pears inspired this moist quick bread.

Use any variety of pear for this recipe. After my local variety, my choices would be Comice or Anjou, because they cook down to a particularly creamy texture. This recipe makes two loaves: one is eaten all too quickly, and the other can be frozen or given as a gift.

> 2 cups **ALL-PURPOSE FLOUR**
> 1 cup finely ground **YELLOW CORNMEAL**
> 2 teaspoons **BAKING SODA**
> 1 teaspoon **SALT**
> 2 teaspoons finely grated **LEMON ZEST**
> ½ cup (1 stick) **UNSALTED BUTTER**, at room temperature, plus more to grease pan
> 1 cup **SUGAR**
> 2 large **EGGS**
> ½ cup **PLAIN YOGURT** (low-fat is fine, but do not use nonfat)
> 1 recipe **QUICK PEAR-ROSEMARY PRESERVES** (recipe follows)
> 1 cup toasted **PINE NUTS** or sliced **ALMONDS**

1. Preheat the oven to 350°F. Grease loaf pans with butter or nonstick spray.

2. In a medium bowl, whisk together the flour, cornmeal, baking soda, salt, and lemon zest. In the bowl of an electric mixer fitted with the paddle attachment, cream the butter and sugar at medium-high speed about 2 minutes, until smooth. Add the eggs, one at a time, and beat until light and fluffy. At a lower speed stir in the yogurt, then the pear preserves. Add the dry ingredients and stir until just combined, then fold in the nuts.

3. Evenly divide the batter between the prepared pans and bake for 35 to 45 minutes, or until lightly golden and a toothpick inserted in the center of the loaf comes out mostly clean. Cool the loaf in the pan for 10 minutes, then run a knife around the rims of the pans and invert onto racks; cool completely. The loaves can be wrapped in foil and stored for up to 3 days or frozen for up to 1 month.

# Quick Pear-Rosemary Preserves

**Makes about 1½ cups**

Pears and rosemary might seem like unusual partners, but the cool, piney fragrance of the herb melds beautifully with the honey sweetness of the fruit. I jar big batches of these preserves, then spoon them over yogurt and warm biscuits, and serve them alongside aged cheeses (or even foie gras).

3 medium **PEARS** (about 1½ pounds), peeled and cored
Juice of 1 medium **LEMON**
¼ cup **HONEY**
1 tablespoon plus 1 teaspoon chopped fresh **ROSEMARY**
1 teaspoon **BRANDY** or **PEAR LIQUEUR** (optional)
Pinch of **SEA SALT**

Peel and core the pears, dropping the fruit into a bowl of water that has been acidulated with the juice of 1 lemon. When you are finished, transfer the pears from the water to a small, heavy-bottomed saucepan. Add the honey and rosemary, bring the mixture to a boil, reduce the heat, and simmer until the pears break down and soften and the juices have thickened, about 30 to 45 minutes. Stir in the brandy and sea salt, cool the mixture, then use a potato masher to help break down the softened fruit. For a smoother texture, purée in a blender or food processor. Refrigerate until needed, or up to a week.

**VARIATION:** As an alternative to the fresh rosemary, consider flavoring the preserves with a tablespoon of fresh grated ginger (or chopped candied ginger) and a clove of star anise (remove after cooking).

# Banana Bread with Almonds and Orange Essence

**Makes two 8 × 4½-inch loaves**

Whenever I have a surplus of overly ripe bananas, I throw them in the freezer where they turn even darker, and then use them to make banana bread. I always make two loaves at a time, since the first is gone in a flash. The other freezes beautifully, making this a great thing to pull out when we have houseguests. Plus baking two loaves helps me get rid of some of those bananas.

3 cups **ALL-PURPOSE FLOUR**

1 teaspoon **BAKING SODA**

1 teaspoon **SEA SALT**

½ cup (1 stick) **UNSALTED BUTTER**, at room temperature

1 cup **SUGAR**

1 cup **HONEY**

1 tablespoon plus 1 teaspoon **ORANGE ZEST**

4 large **EGGS**

5 medium, very ripe **BANANAS** (about 2½ cups)

1 teaspoon **ORANGE OIL** (or 2 tablespoons orange liqueur; see Note)

1 cup **SLICED ALMONDS**

1. Preheat the oven to 350°F. Grease two loaf pans with butter or nonstick spray. In a large bowl, whisk together the flour, soda, and salt; set aside.

2. In the bowl of an electric mixer fitted with the paddle attachment, cream the butter and sugar until smooth. Add the honey and beat at medium-high speed until creamy and light, about 2 minutes. Add the orange zest and eggs, one at a time, then add the bananas and orange oil and mix slowly until the batter is smooth and uniform. Stir in the dry ingredients until just combined, then fold in the almonds.

3. Bake for 1 hour, or until a toothpick inserted into the center of the loaf comes out mostly clean. Cool the loaves on a rack for 10 minutes. Run a knife around the rims of the pans and then invert onto rack and cool completely. The loaves can be wrapped in foil and stored for up to 3 days, or frozen for up to 1 month.

**NOTE:** Orange oil is much stronger than orange liqueur, so a little goes a long way. It's available at most specialty food stores and baking supply shops.

# CAMPFIRE BREAKFASTS AND

## DAVID'S BURNIN' RING OF FIRE

*D*avid embraced ranch life with gusto. In fact, you might say that he discovered his inner cowboy. This came as a bit of a shock to me. In New York, David worked in a fancy four-star restaurant, baked sophisticated breads and pastries that rivaled the best in Paris, and adopted the urban preference for wearing mostly black. But on the ranch, he learned to drive a tractor and plow a field. He used the bulldozer to uproot cedar trees (which usurp water from native hardwoods) and to smooth the road. Whenever we had a break for an hour or so, I'd head out for a hike and David would get on a horse. As a result, he quickly grew confident in the saddle. His cowboy hat suited him. "David looks like he was born here," people would remark. It was true: The physical work had made him fit, he was tanned, and his brown eyes sparkled. He was happier than I'd ever seen him.

But at times I worried that things were getting out of hand. He spent an increasing amount of time in the backyard throwing a lasso. He bought spurs and ordered a bedroll. In the evenings,

he'd sip whiskey from a shot glass purchased at the Houston rodeo. His nightstand held shotgun shells, a tattered copy of *Lonesome Dove,* and a lamp that featured a John Deere tractor as its base. On most nights, a rifle leaned in the corner of our bedroom. "Careful," I warned, "you're a hairsbreadth from Bandera [the self-proclaimed cowboy capital of Texas]." Worried that I'd come home and discover a camouflage bedspread, I hid the Cabela's catalog.

This enthusiasm for all things Western spilled into the food David wanted to prepare. "It would be neat if we had a chuck wagon," he said. *If I don't keep a handle on this,* I mused, *we're headed for a future of chili cook-offs, Texas Ranger reenactments, and period costumes.*

Since we both wanted to be active and outdoors as much as possible, we kept our menus simple and tag-teamed kitchen duties. David took on a few meals as his own. On Fridays he'd make pizzas in the bread oven for an alfresco lunch on the patio. And one morning a week, I'd get to sleep in and David would prepare a campfire breakfast, served after the sunrise hike, when guests came back famished.

We'd been talking about doing an outdoor breakfast for some time, but the meal didn't come together until David stopped at a flea market and met a guy selling a grill of his own invention. The base was a large fire ring (which sheltered the flames from drafts), fitted with a grate. Above the ring was a vertical bar attached to two horizontal posts, called fire irons, used for suspending pots over the fire. There was a swinging arm with two grate shelves and a hook for suspending a coffeepot over the flames. On one side of the ring, the fellow had built a fire box that could be covered with a grill or flat iron plate and used as a griddle. It was David's camp-cook fantasy realized, so he wrote the guy a check.

David cleared and leveled the campfire site as best he could. Eventually the space was enclosed by a corral made of rough cedar posts (handy when the horses got curious about cooking smells). He dug a pit next to the Ring of Fire, as it was named, and surrounded it with smooth white stones to keep the fire from spreading. He seasoned cast-iron pots and skillets with bacon grease, and a meal was born. The night before his breakfast, he placed a couple scoops of pinto beans in a pot and covered them with water.

The next morning, David and our dog Slidell slipped out of the house well before dawn. He needed plenty of time to build a fire in the pit and allow it to burn down into coals that would be used under and on top of the Dutch oven to bake biscuits. After the first fire was lit, he'd light another in the ring so he could make campfire coffee—a cup or so of grounds boiled in a tin pot of water. The coffee was so thick it was almost chewy. For the breakfast, he suspended one pot of beans and another of grilled tomatoes from the fire irons. He'd fry turkey sausage patties in a cast-iron skillet and scramble eggs and green chiles in a speckled blue tin pot.

I'd head up before the guests returned so we could enjoy a bit of the morning together. It was a luxury to arrive at a warm, crackling fire and have my first cup of coffee outdoors. On some days, we'd get to spend a few minutes sitting on a horse blanket on a bench, watching the dogs wrestle and listening to the fire pop.

Something about an outdoor meal strips away pretenses and is a great equalizer. People fully relax and lighten up, in a summer camp sort of way. "This is *delicious*," guests would inevitably say.

David would smile shyly and say, "I enjoy doing it."

"Oh, come on," I'd say later, when we were alone. "Do you *really* enjoy doing that? Getting up before dawn? It's a ton of work!"

He would laugh and swear that he did. "Well, sometimes it is hard to leave a warm bed," he admitted. When he asked if I would care if he slept outside by the campsite one night so he could try out his new bedroll and simply wake up and start the fire, I believed that he did enjoy it. And I wished him a good night.

# Buttermilk Biscuits

**Makes 12 biscuits**

David loves to bake these flaky buttermilk biscuits outside in a Dutch oven under hot coals. They're much easier to bake inside. Truthfully, I prefer them baked separately on a cookie sheet, rather than nestled together in a Dutch oven, because more of the biscuit gets golden brown and crispy.

Biscuits, like piecrusts, simply require a bit of practice. This recipe is easy and foolproof. Pat out the dough and use a biscuit cutter to create neat rounds, or just use your hands to shape them. Serve them hot with butter, honey, or my favorite—a drizzle of cane syrup (a dark, molasseslike sweetener from Louisiana that has an appealing bittersweet flavor). If you're lucky, you'll have leftovers for egg sandwiches the next day.

3 cups **WHITE LILY** or **ALL-PURPOSE FLOUR** (see Note)

1 tablespoon **BAKING POWDER**

2 teaspoons **BAKING SODA**

1 teaspoon **SALT**

$\frac{1}{2}$ cup (1 stick) **UNSALTED BUTTER**, cold, cut into chunks

1 cup well-shaken **BUTTERMILK**

1. Preheat the oven to 450°F. In a large bowl, whisk together the dry ingredients. Using a pastry blender or your fingers, cut the butter into the flour until the mixture is coarse and crumbly. Add the buttermilk and mix with a fork until just combined. Do not overmix or knead. The dough should be moist and slightly sticky; add a little buttermilk if it is too dry.

2. Scrape the batter onto a lightly floured surface. Use your fingers to pat it out to about $\frac{1}{2}$ inch thick. Using a $2\frac{1}{2}$-inch biscuit cutter, cut into rounds. (You can also simply form into individual balls of batter and flatten them gently with your hand.) Arrange the biscuits on two baking sheets, leaving plenty of room between them (each sheet can hold 6 biscuits). Bake for 12 to 15 minutes, rotating the baking sheets halfway through the baking process, until golden brown. Serve immediately.

**NOTE:** White Lily is our preferred flour for biscuits. It's made from soft winter wheat and ground extra fine. As a result, it makes incredibly light, tender biscuits.

# Turkey Sausage with Marjoram

**Serves 4 to 6 (about 8 patties)**

This is a lean, healthier breakfast sausage that can be made in minutes with ground turkey. Don't use a grind leaner than 15 percent or the patties will be dry. The flavor of fresh marjoram or oregano goes well with the turkey—but sage is delicious as well.

1 pound ground **TURKEY** (15% fat)

½ medium **ONION** or 1 large **SHALLOT**, minced (optional)

½ teaspoon crushed **RED PEPPER FLAKES**

2 tablespoons chopped fresh **MARJORAM**

1 teaspoon **SALT**

½ teaspoon freshly ground **BLACK PEPPER**

Using your hands, gently combine the ingredients in a medium mixing bowl—do not overwork the meat. Shape the turkey into 8 even 3-inch rounds. The patties can be covered and refrigerated until needed or cooked immediately. To cook the patties, place them in a large nonstick skillet over medium heat. Sear the patties until browned and just cooked through, about 3 to 4 minutes on each side.

# Spicy Seared Tomatoes

**Serves 4**

For a campfire breakfast, we grill these tomatoes, so that they have a deliciously smoky taste, and then keep them warm in a pot over the fire.

4 **PLUM TOMATOES**
**OLIVE OIL**
**CHILE POWDER**
**SALT**

Halve the tomatoes and rub the cut sides with oil. Sear the tomatoes, cut side down, on a hot grill pan or skillet. Transfer to a baking dish, sprinkle the tops with pure chili powder (such as ancho or New Mexico) and salt, cover, and heat in a low oven until the rest of breakfast is ready.

# Big-Hearted Salads

*I* tend to miss the foods my favorite people cook, not just the people themselves. With my mom it's her cinnamon rolls; my Grandma Millie, her perfectly crisp and buttery cookies. When David is not baking, I miss his bread. People tell me they miss my salads. I can't think of a compliment that would please me more—I've always been a salad freak. My perfect meal would always include a big pile of pretty greens (forget the skimpy salad plate).

A good salad is a deceptively simple thing to make. There are a few key details to get it just right. The first is lettuce: Go out of your way to seek out the freshest and prettiest varieties. I often combine store-bought baby greens with a head of frisée, leaf lettuce, or butter lettuce for added texture. The vinaigrette requires real Dijon mustard (which has a sharper, hotter taste than more refined American mustards), kosher salt, and freshly ground pepper. A good ratio of acid (citrus juice and vinegar—I prefer a combination of both) and olive oil is also paramount. I almost always use extra virgin olive oil, though I sometimes finish a vinaigrette with a drizzle of really good walnut oil.

The following combinations are inspired by my favorite flavors and our Hill Country locale. There are simple green salads to stimulate your appetite and kick off a meal, pretty vegetable compositions that make a great first course, and heartier salads that create a satisfying lunch or light dinner. Many of my salads are driven by color (like Ruby Salad, which is a hot pink tangle, or emerald green broccoli couscous). I love bright, beautiful combinations of vegetables, and the results are all the more nourishing. I hope you will be inspired to hit the produce aisle, or your local farmer's market, and have fun.

# My Favorite Green Salad

**Serves 6**

In my opinion, the best vinaigrette is made with two acidic ingredients. Lemon juice adds a sunny brightness, while good-quality wine vinegar adds sweetness and depth. The best-quality Dijon mustard makes the dressing sing. This is a salad I've been making for years, yet when I'm able to bring all these ingredients together, it still tastes incredibly special.

2 tablespoons fresh **LEMON JUICE**

2 teaspoons **DIJON MUSTARD**

2 teaspoons **RED WINE VINEGAR**

**KOSHER SALT** and freshly ground **BLACK PEPPER**

3 tablespoons **EXTRA VIRGIN OLIVE OIL**

8 ounces mixed **BABY GREENS** (preferably a mix that includes frisée)

½ cup mixed fresh, **SOFT HERBS**, such as chervil, mint, basil, flat-leaf parsley, dill, cilantro, and tarragon leaves

2 medium **SCALLIONS**, very thinly sliced

1 **AVOCADO**, peeled and thinly sliced

In a large bowl, whisk together the lemon juice, mustard, vinegar, and salt and pepper. Whisk in the olive oil until the dressing has pulled together and emulsified. Add the greens, herbs, and scallions to the bowl and toss gently until evenly coated. Divide the salad into equal portions and top with the avocado slices.

# Spinach and Hearts of Romaine with Walnuts and Eggs

**Serves 2 for lunch or 4 as a first course**

One day after I'd worked through lunch, I found myself completely ravenous. I had some nice greens and a packet of chives on hand. There were eggs in the fridge and walnuts in the freezer, so this salad was born. It's a perfect combination—bright and refreshing with sweet, crunchy hearts of romaine, crisp spinach leaves, and a sharp mustard dressing, yet satisfying with rich toasted nuts, egg, and cheese. Crispy herbed croutons or chewy lardons (bacon cubes) would be delicious additions to this salad.

2 large **EGGS**

2 teaspoons **DIJON MUSTARD**

2 tablespoons good-quality **RED** or **WHITE WINE VINEGAR**

2 tablespoons **EXTRA VIRGIN OLIVE OIL**

2 tablespoons good **WALNUT OIL**

**SALT** and freshly ground **BLACK PEPPER**

1 head **ROMAINE LETTUCE**, trimmed of outer leaves and chopped

2 generous handfuls (about 4 ounces) **BABY SPINACH LEAVES**

2 tablespoons fresh **CHIVES**, chopped into 1/2-inch lengths

4 ounces fresh **CHÈVRE** (optional)

1/2 cup **WALNUT HALVES**, toasted and coarsely chopped

1. Bring a small saucepan of water to a boil over medium heat. Boil the eggs and simmer (reducing the heat if the boil becomes too lively) for 9 minutes. Remove from the heat, drain, and rinse with cold water until the eggs are cool enough to handle; set aside.

2. Meanwhile, whisk together the mustard, vinegar, oils, and salt and pepper to taste in a large mixing bowl. Peel the eggs and separate the yolks, which should be slightly creamy, from the whites. Crumble the yolks into the vinaigrette and whisk until fairly smooth. Chop the whites and set aside.

3. Add the lettuce and spinach to the vinaigrette and toss well. Add the chives, chèvre, walnuts, and egg whites and toss again until all the ingredients are evenly coated. Finish with a final grinding of black pepper and a pinch of salt, making sure you season the egg whites.

# Ranch Dressing

### Makes about 1¼ cups

Living on a ranch was a good excuse to come up with my own version of ranch dressing, which has always been a guilty pleasure of mine. Buttermilk and mayonnaise provide the creamy base. Good Dijon mustard, scallions, and fresh herbs make this dressing brighter and more sophisticated than commercial varieties. This recipe calls for five of my favorite fresh herbs. It's not essential to use them all (individual packets of herbs can be expensive). If you only want to use a couple, go for dill and chives.

Because ranch dressing has plenty of personality, keep the salad simple. I like to pour it over hearts of romaine or Bibb lettuce, halved cherry tomatoes, sliced cucumber, and crispy cubes of thick-sliced bacon. For best results, make the dressing a few hours in advance and store it in the fridge to allow the flavors to bloom.

½ cup **MAYONNAISE**

½ cup well-shaken **BUTTERMILK**

1 tablespoon **DIJON MUSTARD**

2 tablespoons **APPLE CIDER VINEGAR**

4 **SCALLIONS** (using only the white and light green parts), minced

1 **GARLIC CLOVE**, minced

2 tablespoons chopped fresh **DILL**

2 tablespoons snipped **CHIVES**

1 tablespoon chopped fresh **TARRAGON**, or ½ teaspoon dried

2 tablespoons fresh **CHERVIL** (optional)

2 tablespoons chopped **PARSLEY** (optional)

Dash of **WORCESTERSHIRE SAUCE**

Dash of **HOT SAUCE**

½ teaspoon **SALT**, plus more to taste

Freshly ground **BLACK PEPPER**

Whisk together the ingredients in a medium bowl and refrigerate until needed. To serve, toss the greens with enough dressing to lightly coat the salad.

# THEN ALONG CAME GILDA

Gwendal the kid goat has spotted me inside the house and she's not taking no for an answer. I do my best to ignore her as I make the bed, fold clothes, wash dishes, and check e-mail. But she's a clever girl. She races around the house, leaping from one window ledge to the next (each dismount punctuated by an impressive 360-degree spin), finding me in each and every room. When I make eye contact, she taps the glass with her hoof and bawls. The cry of a baby lamb or goat is alarmingly childlike. As a result, each *baaaaaah* makes a knot in my stomach and is hard to ignore. Gwendal's problem is that she feels it's an injustice to be locked out of the house, and who can blame her—it's where she was raised.

There is perhaps no greater nuisance than a bottle-fed goat or lamb, or "bottle baby" as they're called in these parts. They are always underfoot (getting in and out of the house without allowing a ruminant to race through the living room becomes a daily negotiation). They will destroy just about everything you own, and they will break your heart.

In any ranching community, orphan kid goats and lambs are common. A mother who has two or three offspring often rejects one of them. The choosing is the cruel and timeless law of nature—the weakest baby, the one that doesn't have the strength to fight for the nipple and suck, will be left behind. If not rescued, the orphan will starve, not be able to keep warm, or be picked off by a predator, like a coyote or mountain lion. But as long as the baby receives just one good drink of its mother's colostrum, it can survive on bottled formula. Few ranchers have time for such coddling—the babies need to be fed every four hours or so. Which is why Gwendal and others like her end up in a giveaway box at the feed store or given to suckers like us. Being more tenderhearted than practical, we developed quite a menagerie.

Our first baby was Gilda, a capricious cinnamon-colored goat. We inherited her from a friend in Uvalde, who wisely passed her on when Gilda started feasting on her flower beds.

Gilda had enough personality to host her own talk show, and she came to think of me as her mother. She knew my voice and responded enthusiastically whenever I called her. (I favored a high-pitched *goateee!* that sounded a bit like a yodel.) If I crouched down beside her, she would walk behind me and delicately place two front hooves on my back—a sign of trust and perhaps the highest compliment a goat can give. She daintily nibbled dry leaves as though they were potato chips. She followed me everywhere, and even joined David, me, and the dogs for our evening hikes.

Always eager to dart through an open door, Gilda occasionally rode in the passenger seat of the pickup. She learned to open the door handle at the lodge with her hooves, so it wasn't uncommon for her to burst in and find her way onto my lap.

I witnessed these antics with blind affection, the way a lovesick mother smiles obliviously while her child wreaks havoc in someone else's home or terrorizes waiters in a restaurant. The older Gilda got, the more destructive she became, and others found her less charming. Gilda leapt onto the hoods of cars, ate the colorful cactus blossoms, and cheerfully digested a misplaced straw hat. One day she went too far. When I returned from a morning hike, I was met by a frantic, infuriated housekeeper. "She's been everywhere!" she seethed. "That goat made a terrible, terrible mess." While I was away, Gilda had let herself into the lodge and had a delightful time, leaping onto the couch, running across the dining room table, racing around the kitchen, and leaving a trail of pellets, cloven hoofprints, and chaos.

It is nearly impossible to teach a bottle baby who has become quite comfortable as a member of the immediate family that it is time to become a goat. With a heavy heart, I tried leaving Gilda in the pasture with the others, but she protested. She was still small enough to squeeze through gaps in the fence and would inevitably come running after me. Eventually, David mended the fences and Gilda was at last confined. Life moved forward.

At first I visited Gilda every day, but it was sad for both of us and the leaving was brutal. Gradually, I went less and less, partially out of laziness—it took more effort to open gates or climb fences—and Gilda adapted to life in the pasture. Since she was a goat, after all, even a bawl at my passing truck was cut short by her eagerness to take another bite. At least there was plenty of good grass to distract her. It was probably worse for me. Ultimately, the real reason I avoided the pasture was because it made me sad that she wasn't our pet anymore. I didn't like the way things had changed. I would go on to learn this lesson many times over, and the truth is, it never got any easier.

# Celery Root Rémoulade with Arugula

**Serves 4**

Though it won't win any beauty contests, the gnarly brown bulb known as celeriac or celery root is the main ingredient in this salad, which is one of my favorites. I love the crunch and faint parsley flavor of the vegetable, especially when it's paired with a creamy mustard dressing. When celery root appears in the market in San Antonio, I can't wait to make this salad. I lighten the traditional version with a few handfuls of arugula and add a sprinkling of celery seed. This salad is a great first course, but it's also delicious alongside any kind of grilled meat, especially steak.

1 large **CELERY ROOT** (about 1 pound, 3 cups grated)
Juice of 1 **LEMON**
$\frac{1}{2}$ cup **MAYONNAISE**
2 tablespoons **MEXICAN CREMA**, **SOUR CREAM**, or **CRÈME FRAÎCHE**
1 tablespoon plus 1 teaspoon **DIJON MUSTARD**
2 tablespoons **LEMON JUICE**
$\frac{1}{2}$ teaspoon **CELERY SEED**
$\frac{1}{2}$ teaspoon **SALT**
Freshly ground **BLACK PEPPER**
6 ounces **BABY ARUGULA LEAVES**

1. Use a paring knife to trim the peel away from the celery root, then use a chef's knife to cut the root into quarters. Place the quarters in a bowl of water that has been acidulated with the lemon juice.

2. Whisk together the mayonnaise, crema, mustard, the 2 tablespoons lemon juice, celery seed, salt, and pepper in a large mixing bowl.

3. Remove the celery root quarters from the water and pat dry with paper towels. Grate each quarter in a food processor fitted with the grating attachment (trimming the quarters as necessary to fit into the chute). Alternately, use a chef's knife to thinly slice the quarters, and then cut them into matchsticks.

4. Toss the grated celery root with the dressing. Add the arugula and toss again until the ingredients are evenly coated with dressing. Taste for seasoning and add more salt or pepper as desired.

# Golden Beet, Celery, and Chèvre Salad

**Serves 4**

Celery is too often relegated to uninspired crudité plates. In this striking salad it's the star, thinly sliced and tossed with a mustard vinaigrette that enhances its sweetness. This salad is all about contrasts: clean, fresh-tasting celery, sweet, earthy beets, and creamy goat cheese. If the beet stems and/or greens are in good shape, feel free to blanch and chop them and add them to the salad. (If the greens and stems are too wilted, discard them.)

On the ranch I made this salad with Mexican mint marigold (also called Texas tarragon), an herb that is more tolerant to heat. Up north you can make it with French tarragon.

### TO PREPARE BEETS

1 bunch (3 to 4) **GOLDEN BEETS** with nice greens attached
2 fresh **THYME** or **ROSEMARY SPRIGS** or 3 fresh **BAY LEAVES**
Coarse **SEA** or **KOSHER SALT**
**OLIVE OIL**

### FOR THE VINAIGRETTE

2 tablespoons **LEMON JUICE**
1 tablespoon **CHAMPAGNE VINEGAR**
2 teaspoons **DIJON MUSTARD**
4 tablespoons **EXTRA VIRGIN OLIVE OIL**
2 teaspoons chopped fresh **TARRAGON** or **MEXICAN MINT MARIGOLD**
**KOSHER SALT** and freshly ground **BLACK PEPPER**
Pinch of crushed **RED PEPPER FLAKES**

1 large bunch **ORGANIC CELERY**, cleaned and trimmed (see Note)
6 ounces **CHÈVRE**

1. Trim all but $\frac{1}{4}$ inch of the stem from the beets. Trim the leaves from the stems and set aside. Scrub the beets in a sink of clean water, rinse, and pat dry. To roast the beets, preheat the oven to 400°F. Line a rimmed baking sheet with foil. Put the beets, herbs, salt, and a drizzle of oil in the center; toss the beets to coat. Fold the foil into a loose-fitting but tightly sealed packet around the beets. Roast the packet on the baking sheet until the beets are tender, about 1 hour and 15 minutes. Let the beets cool completely in the foil.

When cool, use a paring knife to peel and slice the beets into rounds. The beets can be roasted up to 2 days ahead and refrigerated.

2. Meanwhile, wash the beet greens. Bring a medium pot of generously salted water to a boil and blanch the greens. Shock the greens in ice water, then drain in a colander. Use paper towels or a dish towel to squeeze excess moisture from the leaves, then coarsely chop and set aside.

3. To make the vinaigrette, whisk together the lemon juice, vinegar, mustard, olive oil, and tarragon in a large mixing bowl. Season to taste with salt, pepper, and crushed red pepper flakes.

4. Just before serving, use a Japanese mandoline or chef's knife to thinly slice the celery at a slight diagonal. Toss the celery and reserved beet greens with half the vinaigrette. Toss the beet rounds with the remaining vinaigrette. Divide the celery among four salad plates and top with equal portions of beets. Top each salad with a round slice of chèvre and an additional grinding of black pepper.

**NOTE:** If the celery has particularly tough, stringy veins, peel them off with a vegetable peeler.

# Ruby Salad with Crumbled Feta and Spicy Pepitas

**Serves 8**

Several friends have told me that I'm the only person who can get them to eat beets. Since beets are one of my favorite ingredients, I consider this a major victory. Part of the trick is tempering their earthy sweetness with sharp and tangy flavors. In this salad, I rely on spicy pepitas, pungent feta cheese, and a sherry wine vinaigrette. The results are crunchy, vibrantly colored, and satisfying. For a wild color, toss the beets with the slaw and dressing ahead of time. The beet juice will stain the cabbage and onion a spectacular fuchsia. Leftovers make a very good lunch when eaten in warm corn tortillas.

### TO PREPARE BEETS

1 bunch small **BEETS** (4 to 5), trimmed and scrubbed

2 to 3 fresh **THYME** or **ROSEMARY SPRIGS** or 3 fresh **BAY LEAVES**

$\frac{1}{2}$ teaspoon **KOSHER** or coarse **SEA SALT**

**OLIVE OIL**

### FOR THE VINAIGRETTE

1 tablespoon **DIJON MUSTARD**

2 tablespoons **SHERRY WINE VINEGAR**

2 tablespoons fresh **LEMON JUICE**

**KOSHER SALT** and freshly ground **BLACK PEPPER**

$\frac{1}{4}$ cup **EXTRA VIRGIN OLIVE OIL**

### FOR THE SALAD

4 cups very thinly sliced **RED CABBAGE** (1 very small head)

1 medium **RED ONION**, very thinly sliced

4 ounces (4 cups) mixed **BABY GREENS**

6 ounces **FETA CHEESE**, crumbled (about $\frac{1}{2}$ cup)

6 ounces **SPICY PEPITAS** (1 generous cup; recipe follows)

1.  To roast the beets, preheat the oven to 400°F. Line a rimmed baking sheet with foil. Put the beets, herbs, salt, and a drizzle of oil in the center; toss the beets to coat. Fold the foil into a loose-fitting but tightly sealed packet around the beets. Roast the packet on the baking sheet until the beets are tender, about 1 hour and 15 minutes. Let the beets cool com-

pletely in the foil. When cool, use a paring knife to peel and slice the beets into wedges (6 to 8 per beet). The beets can be roasted up to 2 days ahead and refrigerated.

2. In a small bowl, whisk together the mustard, vinegar, lemon juice, $\frac{1}{4}$ teaspoon salt, and a few grinds of pepper. Slowly whisk in the oil.

3. To assemble the salad, combine the cabbage and onion in a medium bowl and set aside. Up to an hour before serving, add the beet wedges to the cabbage and onion and gently toss with half the vinaigrette.

4. Just before serving, add the baby greens, half of the feta, and half of the pepitas; toss with the remaining vinaigrette. Arrange on a big serving platter and garnish with the remaining feta and pepitas.

**SPICY PEPITAS:** Toss 6 ounces pepitas with 1 teaspoon corn or peanut oil, 1 teaspoon pure chile powder (such as New Mexico or ancho), and $\frac{3}{4}$ teaspoon kosher salt. Spread evenly on a rimmed baking sheet and roast at 375°F until golden and fragrant, 6 to 8 minutes (you'll hear them popping). Cool completely on the baking sheet. If making ahead, store in an airtight container.

# Lean and Green Broccoli Couscous

**Serves 4 to 6**

Broccoli is an important crop that flourishes in South Texas during the winter. Locally grown and fresh from the field, it's deeply colored and particularly sweet. In this salad, a generous amount of broccoli turns the salad bright green. Finely chopped broccoli has an appealing texture and better absorbs the lemony dressing. Feel free to add chopped red pepper, radish, carrots, or even olives to the mix.

One 10-ounce box **COUSCOUS** (scant 2 cups)
1 bunch **BROCCOLI** (florets and peeled, chopped stems), about 4 cups
**KOSHER SALT**
1 pint **CHERRY TOMATOES**, halved
4 **SCALLIONS**, minced
1 **SERRANO** or **JALAPEÑO CHILE**, seeded and minced
1 tablespoon **CAPERS**
2 teaspoons finely grated **LEMON ZEST**
Juice of 1 medium **LEMON**, plus more as needed
4 tablespoons **EXTRA VIRGIN OLIVE OIL**
½ cup chopped fresh **CILANTRO**
2 tablespoons chopped fresh **MINT** (optional)
Freshly ground **BLACK PEPPER**

1. There are two ways to prepare couscous. Follow the package directions (adding couscous to boiling water and covering until cooked) or Malika's method, which takes more time. Malika was the Tunisian chambermaid at the château where I cooked in France. Place the couscous in a large bowl and drizzle it with a small amount of very hot water. Then use your fingers to mix the couscous with the water, cover it with a dish towel for several minutes, and allow the grains to absorb the moisture. Add more hot water every 15 minutes or so, mixing the grains with your fingers each time, until the couscous is tender and fluffy. This method results in tender pebbles of couscous that have a more toothsome texture. It's easy to do if you're going to be in the kitchen for a while.

2. Bring a medium saucepan of water to boil. Add a generous pinch of salt and the broccoli. Cook 4 to 5 minutes, until the broccoli is just tender. Drain in colander and briefly rinse with cold water. Finely chop the broccoli.

3. Combine the cooked couscous and remaining ingredients in a large mixing bowl and toss to combine. Taste for seasoning and add more lemon juice, salt, or olive oil as desired.

# Chicken and Citrus Slaw Tostadas

**Serves 6**

Sweet, crunchy cabbage has an affinity for a creamy, spicy dressing and bright citrus flavors. In this Mexican-inspired salad, the slaw mingles with chicken atop a crispy tostada shell. You can fry your own corn tortillas or purchase them. In this dressing, tofu fills in for mayonnaise, offering creaminess with less fat. This recipe calls for roasted, shredded chicken meat, but it's also delicious with slices of grilled chicken. Serve this salad with additional lime wedges and a bowl of chopped chipotle chiles as a garnish.

**VEGETABLE OIL**, for frying

Six 6-inch **CORN TORTILLAS**

3 ounces firm **TOFU**, diced

$\frac{1}{4}$ cup fresh **LIME JUICE**

2 tablespoons **RED WINE VINEGAR**

1 tablespoon **HONEY**

1 tablespoon **DIJON MUSTARD**

1 canned **CHIPOTLE CHILE** in **ADOBO**

2 teaspoons finely grated **ORANGE ZEST**

1 teaspoon finely grated **LIME ZEST**

**KOSHER SALT** and freshly ground **BLACK PEPPER**

$\frac{1}{2}$ small **GREEN CABBAGE**, finely shredded (3 cups)

$\frac{1}{4}$ small **RED CABBAGE**, finely shredded ($1\frac{1}{2}$ cups)

1 small **RED ONION**, thinly sliced

1 large **CARROT**, coarsely grated

3 tablespoons finely chopped fresh **CILANTRO**

$3\frac{1}{2}$ cups shredded **ROAST CHICKEN** (from 1 medium roast chicken, skin removed)

**LIME WEDGES**, for garnish

Additional chopped **CHIPOTLE CHILES IN ADOBO**, for garnish

1. In a small skillet, heat $\frac{1}{2}$ inch of oil over moderate heat until hot but not smoking. Add 1 tortilla and fry until golden and crisp, turning once, about 2 minutes. Transfer the tostada to paper towels to drain. Repeat with the remaining tortillas.

2. In a food processor or blender, combine the tofu with the lime juice, vinegar, honey, mustard, and chipotle and process until smooth. Add $\frac{1}{4}$ cup oil in a thin stream and pro-

cess until creamy. Transfer to a bowl. Stir in the orange and lime zests and season the dressing with salt and pepper to taste.

3. In a large bowl, toss the cabbages, onion, carrot, and cilantro; season to taste with salt and pepper. Add all but 3 tablespoons of the dressing and toss. Set the tostadas on plates and mound the slaw on top. Add the chicken to the bowl, toss with the reserved 3 tablespoons of dressing, and mound on the slaw. Garnish with lime wedges and additional chipotle peppers in adobo, if desired.

# Cumin Chickpeas

**Serves 4 to 6**

Having a can of chickpeas on hand is meal insurance–they are one of my pantry staples. Earthy, satisfying, and high in protein, they create a nourishing meal in a flash when tossed with pasta, canned tuna, or this cumin vinaigrette. I often partner this salad with Smoked Turkey Wraps with Chipotle Cream (page 134), and fresh fruit for picnics. You can substitute an equal amount of Spanish Pequillo peppers (sold in jars) for the roasted red pepper–their smoky flavor permeates the dressing and complements the smoked paprika.

1 **GARLIC CLOVE**, finely chopped

2 teaspoons **DIJON MUSTARD**

2 tablespoons **LEMON JUICE**

2 teaspoons **RED WINE VINEGAR**

⅓ cup **PLAIN YOGURT**

2 tablespoons **OLIVE OIL**

Dash of **HOT SAUCE**

1 teaspoon **CUMIN**

¼ teaspoon **SMOKED PAPRIKA**

¾ teaspoon **KOSHER SALT**

Freshly ground **BLACK PEPPER**

Two 19-ounce cans **CHICKPEAS**, drained and rinsed

1 medium **CARROT**, finely chopped

1 **RED BELL PEPPER** (fresh or roasted and peeled), finely chopped

4 **SCALLIONS**, thinly sliced

¼ cup chopped fresh **CILANTRO** or **PARSLEY** (or a combination of the two)

Whisk together the garlic, mustard, lemon juice, vinegar, yogurt, oil, hot sauce, and seasonings in a large mixing bowl. Add the chickpeas, carrot, red pepper, scallions, and cilantro and toss to combine. Serve immediately or refrigerate up to 4 days.

**MEXICAN LIME SALAD** I use a variation of this dressing to make a refreshing green salad that's great before enchiladas or a bowl of chili. Simply replace the lemon juice with lime juice, and skip the paprika and hot sauce. Toss the dressing with about 8 cups mixed greens, lime segments, thinly sliced radish, and red onion.

# Wild Rice and Chickpea Salad with Smoked Ham

**Serves 6**

I love the earthy palette of this salad, and the flavors are just as satisfying. Smoked ham and golden raisins add intrigue to the wild rice and chickpeas, as does the faintly sweet vinaigrette flavored with a touch of curry. To make this a vegetarian salad, replace the ham with toasted sliced almonds.

1½ cups (10 ounces) **WILD RICE**

**KOSHER SALT**

2½ tablespoons fresh **LEMON JUICE**

2 tablespoons **RED WINE VINEGAR**

2 tablespoons **DIJON MUSTARD**

1 tablespoon **HONEY**

1 teaspoon **CURRY POWDER**

1 teaspoon **GROUND CUMIN**

Pinch of **CAYENNE PEPPER**

¼ cup **EXTRA VIRGIN OLIVE OIL**

One 19-ounce can **CHICKPEAS**, drained and rinsed

¼ pound **SMOKED HAM**, diced

6 **SCALLIONS**, thinly sliced

¼ cup **GOLDEN RAISINS**

Freshly ground **BLACK PEPPER**

**HOT SAUCE**

1. Fill a large saucepan three quarters full of water and bring to a boil. Add the wild rice and 1 tablespoon salt and simmer over moderate heat until the rice is tender and most of the grains have just split, about 50 minutes. Drain and rinse the rice under cold water, then drain again.

2. Meanwhile, in a large bowl, whisk the lemon juice, vinegar, mustard, honey, curry powder, cumin, and cayenne. Add the olive oil and whisk until combined. Toss in the chickpeas, ham, scallions, raisins, and wild rice. Season the salad to taste with salt, pepper, and hot sauce. Transfer to a bowl and serve. The salad can be refrigerated overnight. Bring to room temperature and toss before serving.

# Sardinian Rice Salad

**Serves 6**

The first time I tried this salad (on a summer vacation in Sardinia), I knew it was a combination I'd make again and again. Eggs and oil-packed tuna make it rich and satisfying, while lemon, crisp vegetables, and intensely flavored ingredients like capers, olives, and cornichons brighten up the mix. Served chilled or at room temperature, it's a perfect warm-weather lunch. I call for celery, which is more traditional, but shaved icicle radishes and/or carrots also make nice, colorful additions. If you can get your hands on a Sardinian white wine, such as a Vermentino, it's just the thing to drink.

2 cups (14 ounces) **TEXMATI** or **BASMATI RICE**

**KOSHER SALT**

⅓ cup fresh **LEMON JUICE**

¼ cup **EXTRA VIRGIN OLIVE OIL**

8 small **SCALLIONS**, thinly sliced

⅓ cup **CORNICHONS**, thinly sliced

⅓ cup pitted **KALAMATA OLIVES**, coarsely chopped

½ cup finely chopped **FLAT-LEAF PARSLEY**

2 large **CELERY STALKS**, thinly sliced

2 tablespoons drained **CAPERS**

1 teaspoon finely grated **LEMON ZEST**

Two 6-ounce cans **TUNA** in olive oil, drained and left in chunks (my favorite is bonito tuna from Spain)

2 **HARD-COOKED EGGS**, thinly sliced

Freshly ground **BLACK PEPPER**

1. In a large saucepan, bring 6 cups of water to a boil. Add the rice and 1 teaspoon salt and cook over moderately high heat, uncovered, until tender, about 12 minutes. Drain the rice, shaking off the excess water. Let the rice cool slightly.

2. Meanwhile, in a large bowl, whisk the lemon juice with the olive oil. Stir in the scallions, cornichons, olives, parsley, celery, capers, and lemon zest. Add the rice, tuna, and eggs and toss gently. Season the salad with salt and pepper to taste, transfer to a bowl, and serve immediately, at room temperature, or refrigerate.

# Quinoa Salad with Tomatillo Vinaigrette

**Serves 6**

Quinoa, a high-protein grain, pairs with colorful sliced vegetables and a vinaigrette that tastes like your favorite green salsa. The small amount of creamy cheese balances the tartness of the dressing. If you can find it, red quinoa makes a beautiful salad. I've suggested a variation for an ancho vinaigrette that plays up its brilliant color below.

2 cups (¾ pound) **QUINOA**

8 medium **TOMATILLOS** (½ pound), husked

1 medium **YELLOW ONION**, chopped

½ cup chopped **CILANTRO**

7 tablespoons fresh **LIME JUICE**

⅓ cup chopped **PARSLEY**

⅓ cup **EXTRA VIRGIN OLIVE OIL**

2 tablespoons **CHAMPAGNE VINEGAR**

1 **SERRANO CHILE**, seeded and minced

1 **GARLIC CLOVE**, minced

1 tablespoon finely grated **LIME ZEST**

**KOSHER SALT** and freshly ground **BLACK PEPPER**

½ large **CUCUMBER**, thinly sliced

1 bunch (¾ pound) **RADISHES**, thinly sliced

1 small **RED ONION**, thinly sliced

1 **ORANGE** or **RED BELL PEPPER**, thinly sliced

10 ounces (2 cups) cooked **CORN KERNELS**

4 ounces **QUESO AÑEJO**, thinly sliced

1. Preheat the oven to 350°F. Toast the quinoa on a baking sheet for 8 minutes. Bring 3 cups of water to a boil in a saucepan. Add the quinoa, cover, and simmer until the water is absorbed, 15 minutes; cool.

2. In a medium saucepan of boiling water, blanch the tomatillos for 3 minutes. Drain and rinse under cool water.

3. In a blender, purée the tomatillos with the yellow onion, cilantro, lime juice, parsley, oil, vinegar, chile, and garlic. Transfer to a large bowl and stir in the quinoa and lime zest. Season to taste with salt and pepper. Garnish with the cucumber, radishes, red onion, bell pepper, corn, and queso añejo; serve.

**ANCHO VINAIGRETTE** This brick-colored vinaigrette is a nice color alternative, and particularly appealing with the red quinoa. Consider adding Spicy Pepitas (page 57) and the finely grated zest from 1 medium orange to a salad made from the latter. Toast 1 ancho chile, 2 garlic cloves, and 1 medium tomato on a foil-lined cast-iron skillet, turning as necessary to darken evenly. Soak the chile in warm water for 20 minutes, until softened, and allow the tomato and garlic to cool. Remove the softened chile from the water, stem, and seed. Combine the chile, peeled garlic, tomato, 4 tablespoons orange juice, 2 tablespoons red wine vinegar, 3 tablespoons fresh oregano or parsley, $\frac{1}{3}$ cup olive oil, $\frac{1}{2}$ teaspoon salt, and freshly ground black pepper to taste in a blender. Purée until smooth. Taste the dressing and add more salt or acid, as desired.

# Tuna and Haricot Vert Salad

**Serves 4 to 6**

When preparing this salad—kind of a quick-fix Niçoise—splurge on the tuna (buy imported albacore packed in pure olive oil; my favorite is bonito tuna from Spain) and green beans (go for the slender and delicate haricot vert). This salad is so simple it barely requires a recipe, but it's incredibly satisfying. Feel free to add a few chopped anchovies, oil-cured black olives, or a hard-cooked egg. A plate of this salad, along with fresh sliced tomatoes and some crusty bread, is my idea of a perfect lunch.

12 ounces **HARICOTS VERTS** or **GREEN BEANS**, stem ends only trimmed
1 large **SHALLOT**, finely chopped
2 teaspoons **DIJON MUSTARD**
2 tablespoons **LEMON JUICE**
2 teaspoons **RED WINE VINEGAR**
¼ cup **EXTRA VIRGIN OLIVE OIL**
**KOSHER SALT**
Freshly ground **BLACK PEPPER**
Two 6-ounce cans **TUNA IN OLIVE OIL**, drained

1. Bring a medium pot of generously salted water to a boil. Blanch the haricots verts for 2 to 3 minutes (green beans for 3 to 5 minutes), until just cooked through. Drain, shock in ice water, drain again, and then lay on a baking sheet topped with a few paper towels to dry.

2. Meanwhile, make the vinaigrette. In a large bowl, whisk together the shallot, mustard, lemon juice, vinegar, and olive oil and season with salt and pepper to taste. Transfer the beans to the bowl and toss well to combine. Add the tuna and toss gently, leaving it in large chunks. Taste for seasoning and add more salt, pepper, or lemon as desired.

# Ranch Panzanella with Avocado

**Serves 4**

With David turning beautiful loaves from the oven, I frequently have a surplus of day-old bread, so this Italian-inspired salad was born. I prefer to toss cubes of the bread with oil and fresh rosemary and then toast them in the oven–they take on a nice flavor and hold their shape in the salad. Gently heating the tomatoes with oil and vinegar, then allowing them to marinate, coaxes out their flavor. I toss the bread cubes at the last minute with the fresh salad and slices of ripe, creamy avocado.

For a Texas touch, garnish the salad with a few crumbled dried pequín chiles.

8 cups cubed **DAY-OLD BREAD** (ciabatta or another rustic peasant bread)

½ cup **EXTRA VIRGIN OLIVE OIL**

2 tablespoons chopped **FRESH ROSEMARY**

**KOSHER SALT** or flakes of **SEA SALT**

1 pint **SWEET 100** (or cherry or grape) **TOMATOES**, halved

1 medium **RED ONION**, thinly sliced

3 tablespoons **RED WINE VINEGAR**

1 large **CUCUMBER**, peeled and diced

2 tablespoons **CHIFFONADE OF BASIL**, plus extra whole leaves for garnish

2 tablespoons chopped fresh **CILANTRO** or **MINT** (optional)

Freshly ground **BLACK PEPPER**

Dried **PEQUÍN CHILES** (or other red chile), crumbled

1 large **AVOCADO**, peeled and thinly sliced

1. Preheat the oven to 375°F. In a large mixing bowl, toss the bread cubes with ¼ cup olive oil, rosemary, and a pinch of salt. Transfer the bread to a baking sheet and bake until golden brown, about 10 minutes (use a spatula to toss the cubes every few minutes for even toasting). Set aside to cool.

2. Warm the tomatoes, red onion, vinegar, and remaining oil in a deep skillet over medium heat. As soon as the tomatoes become fragrant (but before they sizzle), remove from the heat and set aside to marinate for at least 30 minutes.

3. When ready to serve, gently toss the toasted bread cubes with the tomato mixture, cucumber, and herbs. Season with salt, black pepper, and crumbled chile pepper to taste. Divide the salad among four plates and top with sliced avocado and basil leaves.

Nourishing Soups

slow-simmering pot of soup is an elixir that makes a house (or lodge) more homey and people more content. I often have a pot of soup on the stove when guests arrive because the smells greet them in a friendly way and make them feel that they've come to just the right place.

Soups and feisty, full-flavored chilis also allow me to showcase some of the best local ingredients like poblanos, habaneros, pumpkins, sweet onions, fresh herbs, avocados, and lime.

A few of these soups require a bit of advance planning, but the benefits are worth it: Your house will smell delicious as the poblanos blister or the garlic or tomatoes roast and sweeten. However, many of them can be assembled quickly, creating a stockpile of healthy meals to last throughout the week. Making time to prepare a pot of soup is a gift in itself. It's a sensual process, the vegetable chopping is relaxing, the colors are inspiring, and your efforts smell good. So pull out your knife and a cutting board, cue up some good music, and pour yourself a glass of wine. It's time to treat yourself, and your favorite people, to a soothing pot of soup.

# Roasted Tomato Soup

**Serves 8**

Even the most lackluster tomatoes improve and deepen in flavor when they are slow-roasted in the oven for several hours at a low temperature. The juices concentrate and sweeten, resulting in the deepest flavor imaginable. Don't be put off by the roasting process. It takes just a few minutes to prepare the tomatoes, and then you get to enjoy the fragrance that permeates your home while they roast. My favorite thing to do is to put them in the oven before bedtime, so I spend the night having tomato dreams and wake up to their rich aroma.

This soup can be garnished to suit your mood or menu. I frequently top it with a scattering of fresh herbs (such as basil, dill, or fresh oregano), thin, crispy Parmesan toasts, or a dollop of plain yogurt, crème fraîche, or Mexican crema. Simmering a dried chile with the soup doesn't make it overly spicy but adds depth and complexity to the stock.

### FOR ROASTED TOMATOES

3 pounds (about 20) **PLUM TOMATOES**, halved

**OLIVE OIL**

**KOSHER SALT**

**HERBES DE PROVENCE, DRIED THYME,** or **BASIL**

### SOUP

2 tablespoons **OLIVE OIL**

1 large **LEEK**, thinly sliced (about 1 cup)

1 large **ONION**, chopped

1 large or 2 medium **CARROTS**, chopped

2 **CELERY STALKS**, chopped

**KOSHER SALT**

2 **GARLIC CLOVES**, finely chopped

2 **BAY LEAVES**, preferably fresh (see Note)

1 tablespoon chopped fresh **THYME** (or 1 teaspoon dried thyme, basil, or herbes de Provence)

Pinch of crushed **RED PEPPER FLAKES** (optional)

¼ cup **WHITE WINE** (optional)

6 cups **CHICKEN STOCK** or **WATER**

One 28-ounce can **PLUM TOMATOES** in juice (preferably San Marzano)

1 **DRIED CHILE** (such as ancho, pasilla, or New Mexico)
Freshly ground **BLACK PEPPER**

1. Preheat the oven to 200°F.

2. The morning (or night) before serving the soup, place halved tomatoes, seed pockets facing up, on a baking sheet. You do not need to skin or seed the tomatoes. Squeeze the tomatoes lengthwise to open up the seed pockets. Drizzle the tomatoes with a small amount of olive oil (a few drops per tomato), then sprinkle with salt and the dried herb of your choice. Use your fingers to rub the seasonings evenly over the tops of the tomatoes.

3. Roast the tomatoes for 8 hours (or about 6 hours at 250°F). The tomatoes will shrivel and concentrate but they should remain meaty and moist—not completely dry. They can be roasted up to 2 days in advance and stored in the refrigerator until you're ready to make the soup.

4. Heat the oil in a large pot or Dutch oven over medium-high heat. Add the leek, onion, carrots, celery, and a pinch of salt and cook, stirring, until softened, about 5 minutes. Add the garlic, bay leaves, thyme, and red pepper and cook for 2 to 3 more minutes, until fragrant. Add the wine and scrape up any vegetables sticking to the bottom of the pot (they should not brown). Add the canned tomatoes with their juice, breaking them apart with your fingers or a wooden spoon. Add the dried chile and bring the soup to a boil. Reduce the heat and simmer for 10 minutes, stirring occasionally.

5. Add the roasted tomatoes (be sure to include any rich red tomato oil that has accumulated on the baking sheet) and simmer, partially covered, for 30 to 40 minutes. Remove the chile and bay leaves and cool the soup briefly. Transfer the soup to a blender, in batches if necessary, and purée until smooth.

6. Return the soup to the pot and season to taste with additional salt and freshly ground pepper. If the soup seems too thick, thin it with a little water or stock. Garnish as desired and serve.

**NOTE:** When using fresh bay leaves in a stock or soup, tear them in a few places to better release their fragrance.

## USING ROASTED TOMATOES

*I* roast pans of these tomatoes even when I'm not making this soup—whenever plum tomatoes look good in the store—because they are delicious with so many things. I chop the tomatoes and toss them with hot cooked penne (and a little extra virgin olive oil and vinegar), fresh basil, and grated ricotta salata. I serve them on turkey sandwiches made with crusty bread. I place the sweet, meaty tomatoes atop green salads and on antipasti platters (with olives, artichoke hearts, and slices of hard dried sausage). Chopped roasted tomatoes are also incredibly delicious stirred into white bean soup that has been made with a ham hock and all the other usual suspects. There's always bruschetta, omelets with Parmesan, or fresh ricotta—you'll find plenty of ways to enjoy them.

# Carrot Habanero Soup

### Serves 8 (Makes about 8 cups)

Habaneros are an underused chile pepper. They are famous for their heat—and they are undeniably fiery—but they also have an intriguing, apricotlike aroma that enhances other ingredients. This vibrant, sunny purée makes a great lunch when paired with Chicken and Citrus Slaw Tostadas (page 59) or a cheesy grilled panini with bitter greens. I love the play of the three orange flavors—carrots, habaneros, and fresh orange juice. Sweet potatoes create a silky body.

Even though this soup is made with orange juice, sometimes I finish it with just a bit of fresh lemon juice—particularly on the second day—to brighten the slightly sweet flavors.

2 tablespoons **GRAPESEED** or **OLIVE OIL**

1 large **LEEK**, thinly sliced (about 1 cup)

1 medium **ONION**, diced

1 pound **CARROTS** (preferably organic), chopped

1 **GARLIC CLOVE**, minced

1 tablespoon peeled minced fresh **GINGER**

1 to 2 **HABANERO CHILES**, seeded and finely chopped (see Note)

$\frac{1}{4}$ cup **DRY WHITE WINE**

6 cups **CHICKEN STOCK** or **WATER**

1 medium **SWEET POTATO**, peeled and cubed (about 1 cup)

$\frac{1}{4}$ cup fresh **ORANGE JUICE**

1 teaspoon ground **CUMIN**

$\frac{1}{2}$ teaspoon ground **CORIANDER**

1 tablespoon **HONEY**

$\frac{1}{2}$ teaspoon **KOSHER SALT**, plus more as desired

**MEXICAN CREMA, SOUR CREAM,** or **PLAIN YOGURT**, for garnish

**CILANTRO LEAVES**, for garnish

**1.** Heat the oil in a large pot or Dutch oven over medium-high heat. Add the leek, onion, and carrots and sauté 7 minutes, or until tender. Add the garlic, ginger, and habanero chile and sauté for an additional 2 minutes. Stir in the wine, scraping up any browned bits.

**2.** Add the stock or water and the sweet potato and bring to a boil. Reduce the heat, partially cover, and simmer 30 minutes, or until the vegetables are tender. Stir in the orange juice, cumin, and coriander.

**3.** Let the soup cool slightly. Place half of the carrot mixture in a blender and process until smooth. Pour the puréed mixture into a medium bowl or pitcher and repeat the procedure with the remaining carrot mixture. Press the purée through a large, fine sieve into the pot and discard any solids that remain. Stir in the honey and salt and cook over medium heat for 5 minutes, or until thoroughly heated. Ladle into bowls and top with yogurt and cilantro.

**NOTE:** I suggest wearing plastic or rubber gloves when working with any hot pepper, but particularly habaneros. If you skip the gloves, don't try to put in your contacts after working with chiles—no matter how many times you've scrubbed your hands. I learned that lesson the hard way. For a milder soup, you can pierce the whole habanero chile and let it steam in the cooking liquid, then dispose of the chile before puréeing the soup.

# Potato Poblano Soup with Cheese

### Serves 8 to 10 (Makes about 12 cups)

Few aromas are as alluring as poblano peppers blistering over a flame. A puréed soup is one of the best uses for roasted poblanos, because their smoky green heat permeates every bite. Potatoes and poblanos are easy allies—the earthy starch of the potatoes tempers the heat of the roasted chiles. I call for a range of peppers—four create a respectable (but not mild) heat while six, the number I use at home, makes for a downright feisty bowl. The heat of this soup tends to increase overnight, so plan accordingly. (You'll also want to keep in mind that heat levels in fresh chiles tend to vary quite a bit.) A generous amount of parsley plays off the green notes of the pepper and results in a more vivid soup. Cubes of cheese that begin to melt in the hot soup are the perfect garnish.

2 tablespoons **UNSALTED BUTTER**

1 tablespoon **OLIVE OIL**

2 large **LEEKS**, thinly sliced (about 2½ cups)

**KOSHER SALT**

3 pounds (about 6 medium) **YUKON GOLD POTATOES**, peeled and cubed

4 to 6 **POBLANO CHILES**, as desired

¼ teaspoon **NUTMEG**

⅛ teaspoon **WHITE PEPPER**

1½ cups **FLAT-LEAF PARSLEY LEAVES**

**ASADERO** (or other white melting cheese), cubed into ¼-inch dice (about ¼ cup per serving)

1. Heat the butter and olive oil in a large soup pot or Dutch oven over medium heat. Add the leeks and a sprinkling of salt and stir. Cover the leeks for a few minutes to allow them to steam, then remove the lid and cook a few minutes more, stirring. The leeks should not brown. Add the potatoes, stirring briefly to coat with oil, then add 8 cups of water. Bring to a boil, reduce the heat, and simmer until the potatoes are tender, about 25 minutes.

2. Meanwhile, roast the peppers. For gas ranges, place the chiles directly on the burner and char over a medium flame. Do this in batches if necessary. Alternately, you can broil the peppers, turning once, until they are blistered and evenly charred. Place the chiles in a medium bowl and cover with a dish towel until cool. Remove the charred skins (reserving as much of the chile juices as you can), stem, seed, and coarsely chop.

3. When the potatoes are tender, add the poblanos, nutmeg, and pepper and simmer for an additional 5 minutes. Add the parsley, cool slightly, then purée the soup in a blender until smooth. Return the soup to the pot. Taste for seasoning, adding more salt or pepper as desired.

4. To serve, scatter the cheese cubes into warmed bowls and ladle the soup over the top.

# Roasted Pumpkin Soup with Red Chile Cream

### Fills 6 individual pumpkins, with leftovers

It's hard to imagine a prettier or more inviting way to serve pumpkin soup than in an individual roasted pumpkin—it's the perfect first course for an autumn dinner party. However, if you are short on time, skip this step and roast just two of the pumpkins. This soup is enhanced by several garnishes. Try the Red Chile Cream or Cilantro Cream described opposite, a drizzle of good-quality pumpkinseed oil, or a scattering of Spicy Pepitas (page 57). No one would complain about a dollop of crème fraîche or Mexican crema and a pinch of ground chipotle chile either. Pair the soup with a pinot gris from Oregon or sauvignon blanc from New Zealand.

This soup tends to thicken upon standing. You may need to add more water or chicken stock to reach the desired consistency.

8 small **SUGAR PUMPKINS**, about 2 pounds each
1 tablespoon **OLIVE OIL**, plus more to rub in the roasted pumpkins
**KOSHER SALT**
1 tablespoon **BUTTER**
1 large **ONION**, chopped
1 large **LEEK**, thinly sliced
2 **CELERY STALKS**, chopped
2 teaspoons chopped fresh **THYME**
1 large **YUKON GOLD POTATO**, peeled and chopped
1 tart medium **APPLE** (such as Granny Smith), peeled and chopped
8 cups **CHICKEN STOCK**
2 teaspoons ground **CORIANDER**
½ teaspoon **SPANISH SMOKED PAPRIKA** (also called *pimentón*)
Freshly ground **BLACK PEPPER**

1. Preheat the oven to 375°F. If you plan to serve the soup in individual pumpkins, select the 6 smallest of the bunch and prepare them as though you were making jack-o'-lanterns. Cut out the top (a 4- to 5-inch circle for the easiest serving) and trim the underside of stringy fibers; reserve. Use a melon baller to scoop out the seeds and fibers from inside the pumpkin. This will take a bit of time, but the cleaner you get the pumpkin, the more pleasurable it will be to eat. Rub the inside of the cavity with a light coating of olive oil

and salt. Return the top to each pumpkin and roast on a baking sheet for 30 to 40 minutes, or until the inside flesh is tender when pierced with a knife. Set aside.

2. Carefully split the 2 remaining sugar pumpkins in half horizontally. Clean with a melon baller as described above. Coat the pumpkin flesh lightly with olive oil and sprinkle with salt (use your fingers to spread evenly). Roast the pumpkins for 30 minutes, until very tender when pierced with a knife. Remove from the oven, cool, then use a spoon to scoop out the flesh from the pumpkin. Transfer the flesh to a bowl and set aside.

3. To prepare the soup, heat 1 tablespoon of the olive oil and the butter in a large pot or Dutch oven over medium-high heat. Add the onion, leek, and celery and stir until evenly coated. Cover the pot (to steam rather than brown the aromatics), reduce the heat to medium-low, and cook for about 4 to 6 minutes, lifting the lid to stir once or twice, until softened and fragrant. Remove the lid, stir in the thyme, potato, and apple, and cook for 2 additional minutes. Add the chicken stock, bring to a boil, then reduce the heat and simmer for 20 minutes, stirring occasionally. Add the roasted pumpkin flesh and spices and simmer for another 10 minutes.

4. Allow the soup to cool slightly and then transfer to a blender, in batches if necessary, and purée. Taste for seasoning and add salt and pepper to taste.

5. To serve the soup in individual pumpkins, use the melon baller to scoop out a dozen or so balls from the bottom two-thirds of the six pumpkins (be careful not to scoop so deeply that you puncture the outside skin and leak soup!). Ladle the purée into the shell and over the pumpkin balls and garnish as desired.

## TWO GARNISHES

Cilantro Cream: Using a mini food processor or blender, purée ½ cup plain yogurt, sour cream, or Mexican crema with ½ cup cilantro, 2 serrano chiles, stemmed and seeded, and a pinch of salt.

Red Chile Cream: Toast an ancho chile on a hot, dry skillet, turning as necessary, until slightly darkened and aromatic. Soak the chile in hot water for 20 minutes, or until completely soft. Stem and seed the chile, then coarsely chop. Using a mini food processor or blender, purée the chile with ½ cup plain yogurt, sour cream, or Mexican crema and a pinch of salt. Alternately, you can also purée the cream with 2 red jalapeños, stemmed and seeded.

# Creamy Corn and Mushroom Soup with Fresh Herbs

**Serves 6 to 8**

This is one of my favorite soups. An intoxicating mix of warm spices and fresh herbs create a flavor that is both gentle and exotic. Crisp sautéed cremini mushrooms add a layer of earthiness that mingles nicely with the sweet corn; the soup is finished with three kinds of herbs and scallions, heated just long enough to release their perfume. Consider serving this soup with quesadillas made with a Mexican white cheese (like asadero and cotija, or queso fresco) and corn tortillas, black bean tacos, or whole grain bread and a simple spinach salad.

4 whole **CLOVES**

8 **PEPPERCORNS**

$\frac{1}{2}$ teaspoon **CORIANDER SEEDS**

3 tablespoons **OLIVE OIL**

1 medium **RED ONION**, diced

2 large **RIPE TOMATOES**, stemmed, seeded, and chopped

2 young **ZUCCHINI**, chopped

1 **YELLOW CROOKNECK SQUASH**, chopped

2 **SERRANO CHILES** (or 1 to 2 jalapeños), stemmed, seeded, and finely chopped

**KOSHER SALT**

4 cups **CHICKEN STOCK**

$3\frac{1}{2}$ cups **CORN KERNELS** (cut from 6 ears of corn) or 1 pound **FROZEN CORN**

2 cups **MEXICAN CREMA** (or heavy cream or half-and-half)

8 ounces **CREMINI MUSHROOMS**, stemmed and thinly sliced

Freshly ground **BLACK PEPPER**

8 **SCALLIONS**, thinly sliced

$\frac{1}{3}$ cup chopped fresh **CILANTRO**, leaves and tender stems

$\frac{1}{4}$ cup chopped fresh **MINT**

3 tablespoons **CHIFFONADE OF BASIL** (about 3 sprigs or 10 to 12 leaves)

1. Toast the cloves, peppercorns, and coriander in a dry skillet over medium-high heat until fragrant and slightly darkened, about 2 to 3 minutes. Crush the spices with a mortar and pestle or finely grind in an electric coffee grinder used for spices; set aside.

2. Heat 2 tablespoons olive oil in a large soup pot or Dutch oven over medium-high heat. Add the onion and cook, stirring, until just softened, about 5 minutes. Add the tomatoes, zucchini, yellow squash, serrano chiles, ground spices, and a pinch of salt and cook 5 more minutes. Add the chicken stock and bring to a boil. Reduce the heat and simmer about 15 minutes, until the vegetables are cooked through but not mushy. Add the corn and cream and heat another 5 minutes (do not boil).

3. Heat the remaining tablespoon of olive oil in a large nonstick skillet over medium-high heat until the pan is very hot but not smoking. Add the mushrooms (in batches, if necessary, so you don't overcrowd the pan) and a pinch of salt and sauté until brown and crisp, about 3 to 4 minutes. Scrape the browned mushrooms into the soup pot and repeat the process with the remaining mushrooms. Taste for balance and seasoning, adding salt and pepper as desired.

4. Add the scallions and fresh herbs and allow the soup to steep for 2 to 3 minutes, until they release their perfume. Serve in warmed bowls.

# Mexican Lentil Soup with Roasted Garlic

**Serves 6 to 8**

I've been simmering lentil soups, prepared in various guises, since college. Here in Texas, I give them Mexican flavors, so I add fresh epazote, a Mexican herb that is readily available in my local supermarket. Epazote has a unique flavor. I think of it as a cross between fresh parsley, oregano, and tarragon (it has a faint anise perfume), and it also makes beans easier to digest. If you can't find fresh epazote, use one of the above-mentioned herbs or a combination of all three (I'm not a fan of dried epazote). I call for black beluga lentils (so named because they resemble caviar) because they create a particularly rich stock. However, you can also use small green or brown lentils. I purée a portion of this soup with an entire head of roasted garlic and spices, which creates a luscious texture and incredible depth of flavor.

1 head **GARLIC**

2 tablespoons plus 1 teaspoon **OLIVE OIL**

1 large **ONION**, chopped

2 **CELERY STALKS**, chopped

2 **CARROTS**, chopped

**KOSHER SALT**

2 fresh **BAY LEAVES**

2 cups **BLACK BELUGA LENTILS**, rinsed

8 cups **WATER** or **CHICKEN STOCK**

½ cup chopped fresh **EPAZOTE**

1 tablespoon ground **CUMIN**

1 teaspoon ground **CORIANDER**

1 to 2 tablespoons **ADOBO SAUCE** from canned chipotle chiles or **HOT SAUCE** to taste

Freshly ground **BLACK PEPPER** (optional)

**SHERRY WINE VINEGAR**, for garnish (optional)

Chopped fresh **CILANTRO**, for garnish (optional)

1. Preheat the oven to 325°F. Hold the garlic by its stem end and trim off the top fourth from the opposite end. Place the garlic, cut-side up, on a square piece of aluminum foil. Drizzle the garlic with the teaspoon of olive oil and tightly seal in a loose-fitting foil envelope. Place the foil packet on a cookie sheet and roast in the oven for 1 hour.

2. Meanwhile, heat the remaining 2 tablespoons of olive oil in a large soup pot or Dutch oven over medium-high heat. Add the onion, celery, carrots, and a pinch of salt and cook, stirring, until softened and fragrant, about 5 minutes. Add the bay leaves, lentils, chicken stock, and epazote and bring to a boil. Reduce the heat and simmer until the lentils are tender, about 25 minutes.

3. Remove the roasted garlic flesh from the paper skin. To do this, grip the stem end of the garlic and squeeze the flesh out through the cut end. Set aside.

4. Remove the bay leaves. Transfer 2 cups of the soup to a blender, along with the roasted garlic flesh, cumin, coriander, and adobo sauce or hot sauce. Purée the mixture until silky smooth and return to the pot. Stir well to incorporate and simmer for an additional 5 minutes. Taste again for seasoning, adding salt, pepper, hot sauce, or a few drops of sherry wine vinegar as desired. Remove the bay leaves and serve, garnished with fresh chopped cilantro, if desired.

NOTE: The flavors in this soup deepen and intensify after a day or two, and it will thicken up on standing. When reheating, you may need to add water to reach the desired consistency and a drop or two of vinegar to perk up the flavor.

# The Best Vegetable Chili

**Serves 8 to 10**

You might think that I am pressing my luck serving vegetable chili in the land of beef and big belt buckles, but I crave lots of vegetables when I'm on a health kick. This satisfying chili, chock-full of colorful peppers and beans, has plenty of flavor from pure ground chile and spices. This makes a big batch, but the chili keeps for several days and freezes well. I put bowls of the various garnishes on the table and let people embellish their chili as they please—that's part of the fun, after all. This chili is delicious with Corn Bread with Scallions (page 222).

2 tablespoons **OLIVE OIL**

2 large **ONIONS**, diced

3 **BELL PEPPERS** (preferably 1 orange, yellow, and red), diced

1 **POBLANO PEPPER**, diced

2 large **CARROTS**, sliced into 1/2-inch half-moons

**SALT**

6 to 8 **GARLIC CLOVES**, minced

2 fresh **BAY LEAVES**

3 tablespoons ground **NEW MEXICO CHILE**

1 tablespoon **MEXICAN OREGANO**

1 teaspoon ground **CHIPOTLE CHILE**

1 teaspoon **FENNEL SEEDS**

1 teaspoon **DRIED BASIL**

1 **CINNAMON STICK**

Freshly ground **BLACK PEPPER**

64 ounces **LOW-SODIUM TOMATO JUICE**

Two 26-ounce cans or boxes chopped **TOMATOES** in juice

2 small young **ZUCCHINI**, chopped

1 cup frozen **CORN**

One 15-ounce can **CHICKPEAS**, drained and rinsed

One 15-ounce can **KIDNEY BEANS**, drained and rinsed

**FOR GARNISH**

Shredded **CHEDDAR** or **JACK CHEESE**

**SOUR CREAM, PLAIN YOGURT,** or **MEXICAN CREMA**

Thinly sliced **SCALLIONS**
Chopped **CILANTRO**
**LEMON** or **LIME** wedges

**1.** Heat the olive oil in a large pot or Dutch oven over medium-high heat. Add the onions, peppers, carrots, and a pinch of salt and cook, stirring, until the vegetables are slightly softened, about 5 to 7 minutes. Add the garlic, bay leaves, and remaining herbs and spices and continue to stir until the vegetables are coated, about 4 minutes. Add the tomato juice and chopped tomatoes and bring to a boil. Reduce the heat and simmer for 30 minutes, or until the carrots are just tender.

**2.** Add the zucchini and corn and simmer another 5 minutes. Add the beans and simmer until just heated through, about 5 more minutes. Serve garnished with cheese, sour cream, scallions, cilantro, and lemon or lime, as desired.

**NOTE:** For the best-looking chili, be sure to trim the pale ribs that hold the seeds from the inside of the peppers.

# Turkey Chili with White Beans and Sage

**Serves 8 to 10**

This is a delicately seasoned chili with a thinner, fragrant broth (if you want a thicker texture, purée a cup of beans with a cup of broth). Fresh sage and Mexican oregano are delicious partners for ground turkey. Warm spices like cumin, coriander, smoked paprika, and allspice add warmth and depth to the stock. As with most stews, this is even better on the second and third days.

2 tablespoons **OLIVE OIL**

2 medium **ONIONS**, chopped (about 3½ cups)

2 medium **POBLANOS**, chopped

2 **CELERY STALKS**, chopped

2 medium **CARROTS**, chopped

**KOSHER SALT**

3 pounds ground **TURKEY** (15% fat)

Freshly ground **BLACK PEPPER**

4 **GARLIC CLOVES**, minced

2 **JALAPEÑOS**, seeded and minced

24 fresh **SAGE LEAVES**, chopped

1 tablespoon plus 1 teaspoon pure **CHILE POWDER** (such as New Mexico or ancho)

1 tablespoon crumbled **MEXICAN OREGANO**

1 tablespoon plus 1 teaspoon ground **CUMIN**

2 teaspoons ground **CORIANDER**

1 teaspoon **SPANISH SMOKED PAPRIKA** (also called *pimentón*)

½ teaspoon ground **ALLSPICE**

2 **BAY LEAVES**, preferably fresh

1 cup chopped **TOMATOES**, with their juice

8 cups **CHICKEN STOCK**

Two 15-ounce cans **CANNELLINI** or other **WHITE BEANS**, drained

**SOUR CREAM** or **PLAIN YOGURT**, for garnish

**SCALLIONS**, thinly sliced, for garnish

1. Heat the oil in a large nonstick skillet over medium-high heat. Add the onions and sauté for about 8 minutes, until softened. Add the poblanos, celery, carrots, and a pinch of salt and sauté another 10 minutes. Reduce the heat or add a small amount of water, if necessary, to prevent the vegetables from sticking or becoming too brown.

2. Place the turkey in a large pot or Dutch oven and heat over medium-high heat. Season with salt and pepper to taste and cook, stirring, until no longer pink (about 5 to 6 minutes). Add the garlic, jalapeños, spices, and bay leaves and continue cooking until the meat is well coated and the spices begin to form a paste.

3. Add the sautéed vegetables, tomatoes, and chicken stock and bring the mixture to a boil. Reduce the heat and simmer, partially covered, for about 45 minutes. Add the beans and simmer 5 minutes more. Serve immediately, garnished with sour cream and scallions, or refrigerate overnight.

# *Nuevo Laredo Tlalpeño Soup*

**Serves 8**

The ranch was two and a half hours from the Mexican border at Laredo and Nuevo Laredo, its sister city across the Rio Grande. A road trip there used to be a standard excursion for anyone living in South Texas. On my first trip there I tasted this incredible chicken and chickpea soup. It arrived with several garnishes that made the combination even better—chunks of creamy avocado, lime wedges, chopped cilantro, and chopped chipotle chiles in adobo sauce. I came up with my own version as soon as I returned home.

CHICKEN STOCK **Makes about 10 cups**

1 whole young **CHICKEN** (about 4 to $4\frac{1}{2}$ pounds)

1 **ONION**, quartered

1 **CELERY STALK**, chopped

1 **CARROT**, chopped

2 fresh **BAY LEAVES**

6 **PEPPERCORNS**

2 to 3 **CLOVES**

1 tablespoon **KOSHER** or **SEA SALT**

SOUP

2 tablespoons **OLIVE OIL**

1 large **ONION**, chopped

1 **LEEK**, thinly sliced

2 **CELERY STALKS**, finely chopped

1 medium **CARROT**, chopped

10 cups **CHICKEN STOCK**

Two 15-ounce cans **CHICKPEAS**, drained and rinsed

3 cups shredded **CHICKEN BREAST** (about 1 whole breast)

Freshly ground **BLACK PEPPER**

FOR GARNISH

**LIME WEDGES**

Chopped **AVOCADO**

Chopped **CILANTRO**

Chopped **CHIPOTLE PEPPERS** in adobo sauce

1. Rinse the chicken, place in a large pot or Dutch oven, and add water to cover (about 10 cups). Bring to a boil over medium-high heat and skim any fat that rises to the top. Add the onion, celery, carrot, bay leaves, peppercorns, cloves, and salt. Reduce the heat and gently simmer, partially covered, for 1 hour. Remove from the heat and allow the chicken to steep for an additional hour. If serving immediately, remove the chicken and skim and strain the stock. If not, refrigerate the chicken overnight, then skim the fat the next day (it will be easier to remove) and strain.

2. Remove the chicken meat from the carcass. Use a fork to shred the breast meat for the soup and reserve the dark meat for another use.

3. To prepare the soup, heat the olive oil in a large pot or Dutch oven. Add the onion and leek, stir to coat with oil, and then cover and allow them to steam for about 3 to 4 minutes, until softened. Add the celery and carrot and cook, stirring, for a few more minutes. Add the chicken stock and bring to a boil. Reduce the heat and simmer for 20 minutes. Add the chickpeas and chicken and simmer another 5 minutes. Taste for seasoning and add salt and pepper to taste. To serve, ladle the soup into large, wide bowls and garnish with lime wedges, chopped avocado, cilantro, and chopped chipotle peppers in adobo.

# Border Town Hunter's Stew with Poblanos, Pumpkin, and Hominy

**Serves 6 to 8**

In our part of Texas, the winter season is brief, so as soon as the temperature drops I seize the opportunity to wear cashmere, light campfires, and simmer stew. Venison has a fraction of the fat of beef, so it will never become as buttery. But once the cubes are browned and simmered for a couple of hours, the meat softens beautifully. I have made this stew with both deer and antelope stew meat. The venison tastes slightly richer; the latter has a milder taste and a texture that suggests veal. I prefer using chicken broth for venison stews, as beef broth can overpower the meat. The subtle sweetness of hominy and pumpkin, and their melting textures, are delicious partners for the meat and spice. Serve it with the same beer you add to the pot and garnish with lime wedges.

3 pounds **ANTELOPE** or **VENISON STEW MEAT** (see Note), cut into 2-inch cubes

**KOSHER SALT** and freshly ground **BLACK PEPPER**

2 tablespoons **OLIVE OIL**

2 medium **ONIONS**, chopped

2 **POBLANO CHILES**, chopped

6 **GARLIC CLOVES**, minced

1 small **SUGAR PUMPKIN** (or 1 medium butternut squash), peeled and cubed (about 3 cups)

3 tablespoons **NEW MEXICO CHILE POWDER** (less for a milder heat)

1 tablespoon plus 1 teaspoon dried **MEXICAN OREGANO**

2 **BAY LEAVES**, preferably fresh

1 **CINNAMON STICK**

One 12-ounce bottle **AMBER BEER**, such as Shiner Bock, Bohemia, or Dos Equis Amber

4 cups **CHICKEN STOCK**

Two 15.5-ounce cans **WHITE HOMINY**, drained

**LIME WEDGES**, for garnish

1. Place the venison in a large bowl and generously season the meat with salt and pepper; set aside for 30 minutes while you chop the vegetables.

2. Heat the olive oil in a large, heavy-bottomed pot or Dutch oven over medium-high heat until very hot but not smoking and swirl to coat. Add the meat, in batches if necessary to avoid overcrowding the pan, until browned and crusty on all sides. Using a slotted spoon, transfer the meat to a bowl and set aside. Add the onions and poblanos to the pan, reduce the heat to medium, and cook, stirring occasionally, until softened, about 5 minutes. Add the garlic and sauté for another 2 minutes.

3. Add the pumpkin, chile powder, oregano, bay leaves, and cinnamon stick and sauté until the spices thicken into a paste and evenly coat the vegetables, about 2 minutes. Pour the beer into the pan and scrape up any browned bits. Return the beef to the pan, add the chicken stock and hominy, and bring to a boil. Reduce the heat and simmer, stirring occasionally, for 2 hours, until the meat is tender. (If the meat is still tough, simmer an additional 30 minutes, adding more stock or water as necessary to prevent the stew from becoming too thick.)

4. Remove the bay leaves. Taste the stew and add more salt, as desired. Serve garnished with lime wedges.

NOTE: I purchase my venison and other wild game, including smoked venison sausage, ground venison, axis chops, and antelope stew meat from Broken Arrow Ranch in Ingram, Texas (800-962-4263 or *www.brokenarrowranch.com*).

# LOVE AMONG THE RUMINANTS

G iven my proclivity toward indulgence, it's no surprise our menagerie continued to grow. We started with a couple of kittens, and eventually acquired three dogs, three horses, several goats, a donkey, and chickens galore. The seemingly endless space to raise animals and the affection they returned were addictive. Ranch life was a childhood fantasy realized. What's to stop you from raising the petting zoo of your dreams? Which got me thinking about lambs. Our neighbor Willis Springfield raises angora goats and sheep. I told him to put me on the list if he needed help with an orphan.

A few days later Willis called and said he had a lamb that was so weak he needed to prop it in a hamper to stand. It was February and the nights were bitter, so I couldn't refuse.

Elvis, as I named him, was a Suffolk or "black-faced" lamb. As a baby, his coat was pure black, but as he grew, the wool around his body would turn a sooty beige. When we got him

he was so skinny that I could effortlessly lift him with one hand. But he took to the bottle right away. He started to fatten up and gain strength, making him more fun to scoop up and nuzzle. I loved to bury my nose in his soft, nubby coat, particularly after he was warmed from the sun and had napped under the rosemary bushes.

Beginner's luck gave me the deceptive notion that lambs were easy. Our next adoptee would change all that. One sunny afternoon, Willis's pickup appeared again. With exaggerated drama that suggested an episode of *Bonanza*, he pointed to a dark bundle on the floor and said, "She needs milk." I was eager for Elvis to have a girlfriend, but that night we had a rare social invitation. Pete, our horse vet, was having his annual party—a crayfish feast called the Big Suck.

"We'd love to help, but we have plans tonight," I explained. "It will be a late night, so we have a hotel reserved in Uvalde."

"Well," Willis said, ignoring the hint, "good luck." Then he unloaded Dolly and sped off.

Dolly needed nourishment every few hours, so we wrapped her in old towels, packed her in a dog kennel, and took her to the party. "We've got a baby lamb in our truck and we're gonna sneak her into the Holiday Inn," we told people at the party. But no one was impressed. Here in the land of ranches and rivers, almost everyone had bottle-fed something and made similar concessions. We even met folks who had slept in the barn to keep predators away.

It became painfully clear why Dolly couldn't survive in the pasture. She never got the knack of sucking. I'd prop her in my lap and gently pry her jaw open with my fingers, then slip the nipple into her mouth and hold her head upright. But she wouldn't cooperate. Despite our diligence, she deteriorated. She grew so weak that she couldn't stand for a couple of weeks and her eyes grew cloudy.

So we got resourceful. We used a dish towel as a sling under her stomach and walked her around to force her legs to move. We wrapped her in blankets, placed her in our red Radio Flyer wagon, and wheeled her into the sunshine. She looked like a tragic invalid, but eventually she got stronger. I got choked up the first time she stood up on her own. She started draining bottles of formula and she even got frisky.

We had just moved Dolly out of the kitchen when Sharon called and said, "I've got a little friend for you. . . ."

"I can't do it," I said. "It's too much." I'd had enough of sporadic sleep, bottle washing, and changing bed linens for ruminants.

"This one is different," Sharon argued. "He's exotic."

Against my better judgment, I went to take a look, and that's when I met Max, an ibex goat. He was tan with black markings and large bug eyes that made him look like a cartoon character. Max had endured a cruel beginning—a local rancher had rescued him from a buzzard (his mother and sister hadn't been so lucky). Max had an alert, intelligent expression, and he was affectionate when I picked him up. "One night," I told Sharon as I carried him out the door, "then I'll find a home for him." By the next morning I was smitten.

Our growing herd put fences to the test and landscaping fantasies to an end. As the lambs and goats grew stronger, they found holes and created new ones. Max was an awesome leaper and couldn't be confined by anything. Over time, they cleaned out my flower boxes, stripped the leaves off my fig trees, and ate the jasmine that had been growing up an arbor.

But I like to think the ruminants went on to greatness. Max ended up in the *New York Times,* and he still accompanies me on daily hikes. Elvis grew into a large and feisty buck. Dolly had twins that we named Lyle and Loretta, after two of our favorite singers.

Still, there were times when I lost it. Once after returning home to find muddy boot tracks through the house and a train wreck of potting soil and ruminants on the porch, I hollered at everyone like a crazed mother. I locked the ruminants in the back and took off to go running. I was bound and determined to escape the mess makers in my life. I made it about a half mile before I heard the thunder of hooves behind me. I turned to see Elvis, Dolly, Max, and the dogs happily bounding after me. They nudged my calves and Max leapt and twirled in animated circles around me. I had to run zigzag to avoid being tripped, but I laughed most of the way home. This mess of a family was my doing, after all.

Awesome Appetizers
Kicking Off a Great Meal

*L*ike the goats in our field, I'm a grazer at heart. I love nothing better than nibbling on a few savory snacks (pass the spicy nuts, toasted bread slathered with a pungent purée, hot salsa and guacamole with tortilla chips) in the early evening, preferably while sipping a cold beer or a glass of crisp sauvignon blanc. It's the time of day when I'm most hungry, and dinner can rarely compare to those first bites. For me, enjoying appetizers signals both the close of a day (time to relax!) and the beginning of something wonderful: an evening meal. Then again, two or three appetizers, like Crostini with Lima Bean and Pecorino Purée, Manchego-Stuffed Seckel Pears with Prosciutto, and Boiled Shrimp with Mayo Verde, could easily make a meal (and a grazer's paradise).

# Spicy Mixed Nuts

**Makes about 5 cups**

These nuts have the perfect mix of heat, salt, and sweetness. They are beautiful to serve–and dangerously addictive. I make big batches for the holidays to give away as gifts and pull out when friends stop by. They complement any cocktail, but they're especially good with something bubbly. If you double the batch, divide the mixture between two cookie sheets: The nuts will crisp up better if they roast in a single layer.

1 large **EGG WHITE**

½ cup **SUGAR**

2 teaspoons **KOSHER SALT**

1 tablespoon ground **CUMIN**

1¼ teaspoons **CAYENNE PEPPER**

1 teaspoon ground **CINNAMON**

8 ounces **PECAN HALVES**

4 ounces **SALTED CASHEWS**

4 ounces **ROASTED ALMONDS**

**1.** Preheat the oven to 250°F.

**2.** Whisk together the egg white, 1 tablespoon water, sugar, salt, and spices in a large mixing bowl. Add the nuts and use a rubber spatula to mix well. Pour the nut mixture onto a cookie sheet. Bake 40 minutes, stirring occasionally with a metal spatula. Reduce the heat to 200°F and bake another 30 minutes. Remove the nuts from the oven, use a fork to loosen them from the baking sheet, and cool. Stored in a metal container with a tight-fitting lid, the nuts will last up to 2 months.

## THE BEST TEXAS MUSIC

*W*hether we're sipping cold beers at Floore's Country Store in Helotes, watching old-time cowboy couples twirl at the Broken Spoke in Austin, or requesting "El Rancho Grande" from mariachis at La Fogata in San Antone, Texas is paradise for a music freak like me. I'm constantly finding new artists that I'm crazy about. For instance, when I went to hear one of my heroes, Guy Clark, I fell for his opening act, the McKay Brothers. Noel and Hollin McKay, brothers from Bandera, Texas, sing toe-tapping Tejano songs in perfect Spanish and rich, melancholy ballads about Texas. When I did an article on them for the *New York Times*, we spent several days talking music and eating Mexican food–my two passions. Since then we've become friends, and when we're lucky we can convince them to bring their guitars to the Frio River.

Here's a short list of my favorite musicians—their CDs belong in any cowgirl's kitchen: Hank Williams, Willie Nelson, Waylon Jennings, Johnny Cash, Rosanne Cash, Guy Clark, Townes Van Zandt, Bruce Robison, Kelly Willis, Lyle Lovett, Robert Earl Keen, Joe Ely (and the Flatlanders, the band he plays in with Jimmie Dale Gilmore and Butch Hancock), the McKay Brothers, Dwight Yoakam, Freddy Fender (and the Texas Tornadoes), Billy Jo Shaver, Don Walser (known as the yodeling cowboy!), Slaid Cleaves, the Dixie Chicks, Patty Griffin, Dolly Parton, George Jones, Gram Parsons, Emmylou Harris, and Lucinda Williams.

# Guacamole with Serrano and Lime

**Serves 4 to 6 as a nibble (or 2 for lunch!)**

**(Makes about 2½ cups)**

Guacamole is one of the few things that's hard for me to order in a restaurant—unless it's a very good Mexican restaurant—because it's almost always disappointing. It's either too expensive for a baseball-sized scoop (I'm greedy when it comes to avocados), or it's that strange puréed version that looks like pale green baby food. Even when guac is prepared tableside it's often combined with tomatoes and onions that have been macerating in liquid for too long—the results are less than fresh tasting.

Guacamole is perfectly simple to do well, and it will never taste better than the minute after it's made, which is all the more reason to make it yourself. I like guacamole bright green and chunky, without tomato. To my taste, all it needs is onion, serrano chiles, cilantro, a hit of lime, and salt. I always add a dash or two of hot sauce, not just for heat, but for the vinegary tang that acts as a seasoning and lights up other flavors. It's easy to use a fork to mash the buttery avocado into the other ingredients. If you can find the small Mexican Key limes, use them. In true Texas fashion, serve with plenty of tortilla chips (blue corn or regular) and a cold margarita.

1 small **YELLOW ONION**, finely chopped

½ teaspoon **KOSHER SALT**

1 **GARLIC CLOVE**, finely chopped

2 **SERRANOS** or 1 to 2 **JALAPEÑOS**, stemmed, seeded, and finely chopped

4 medium or 3 very large **AVOCADOS**

⅓ cup coarsely chopped fresh **CILANTRO**, leaves and tender stems

1 to 2 tablespoons fresh **LIME JUICE**

Dash or two of **HOT SAUCE**, such as Crystal

Place the onion, salt, garlic, and serranos in a medium glass bowl. Halve and seed the avocados, and use a spoon to scoop their flesh into the bowl. Use a fork to mash them into the other ingredients until well combined but still chunky. Add the cilantro, 1 tablespoon lime juice, and hot sauce and mix again. Taste for balance and add more salt, lime, or hot sauce as desired.

# Devilish Eggs with Texas Tapenade

**Serves 12 or more as a snack, with leftover tapenade**

For me, one of the most perfect flavor combinations is egg and tapenade, the pungent black olive paste made with capers and anchovies. I slather tapenade on hard-cooked eggs for breakfast or lunch, but it's even better on deviled eggs, when the yolks are extra creamy and rich with mayonnaise and Dijon mustard.

I make tapenade with fresh rosemary–the king of my garden–and a pinch of crumbled red chile. The purée is traditionally finished with a bit of Cognac or brandy, which helps temper the sharper flavors. A splash of tequila or triple sec would also do the trick (tapenade can also be made with orange zest). You can make a green tapenade by substituting picholine or lucques olives for the black; both versions are even better the next day after the flavors have mellowed. Serve leftover tapenade on toasted rounds of baguette, sandwiches (like Hill Country Pan Bagnat, page 140, or Herbaceous Egg Salad, page 136), or mixed with mayonnaise as a condiment for lamb burgers.

### TEXAS TAPENADE

1 **GARLIC CLOVE**

$\frac{1}{4}$ teaspoon **KOSHER SALT**

3 tablespoons **CAPERS**

4 **ANCHOVIES**

1 tablespoon finely chopped fresh **ROSEMARY**

2 to 3 crumbled **PEQUÍN CHILES** (or pinch of crushed red pepper flakes)

12 ounces pitted **KALAMATA** (or other black, brine-cured olive), drained and rinsed

1 tablespoon **COGNAC** or **BRANDY**

$\frac{1}{2}$ cup **EXTRA VIRGIN OLIVE OIL**

### DEVILISH EGGS

1 dozen large **EGGS**

3 tablespoons **MAYONNAISE**

2 generous tablespoons **DIJON MUSTARD**

Pinch of **SALT** and freshly ground **BLACK PEPPER**

Dash or two of **HOT SAUCE**

1. Place the garlic and salt in the bowl of a food processor and pulse until chopped. Add the capers, anchovies, rosemary, pequín chiles, olives, and Cognac and pulse to form a rough paste. With the motor running, add the oil in a steady stream and blend until completely smooth. Transfer the tapenade to a container, cover, and refrigerate for up to 1 week. Bring to room temperature and stir again before serving.

2. Bring a medium saucepan of water to a boil. Using a slotted spoon, gently lower the eggs into the water and simmer for 9 minutes. Reduce the heat if the boil becomes too lively so the eggs don't crack. Drain the water from the saucepan and run cold water over the eggs until they are cool enough to handle. Peel the eggs and split them in half. Carefully remove the yolks (they should be slightly creamy) and place them in a small bowl. Add the mayonnaise, mustard, and salt, pepper, and hot sauce to taste, and whisk until smooth. Taste and adjust the seasonings as desired. Use a small spoon to scoop the yolk mixture back into the whites. (If you want to get fancy, you can also use a pastry bag to pipe the yolks back into their shells.) To serve, top each egg with a dollop of tapenade.

# Manchego-Stuffed Seckel Pears with Prosciutto

**Serves 8**

One of the most sublime things you will ever pop into your mouth is a warm, jammy fig that's been wrapped with prosciutto and stuffed with Manchego cheese.

When figs were out of season and we needed an equally seductive party nibble, David came up with the great idea of using small Seckel pears. No matter which fruit you use, this pretty appetizer is good warm or at room temperature, so feel free to make them in advance. They're stunning on a serving platter and just the thing with a sip of white wine or bubbly. Blue cheese also makes a delicious filling.

8 **SECKEL PEARS**, halved, or 16 whole **FIGS**
**OLIVE OIL**
4 ounces **MANCHEGO CHEESE**, cut into $\frac{1}{2}$-inch cubes
4 ounces thinly sliced **PROSCIUTTO**

1. Preheat the oven to 350°F.

2. If using pears, slice them in half and use a melon baller to scoop out the core. Leave the stem intact. Brush the core side with olive oil and roast, cut-side up, for 7 to 8 minutes, until tender but not overly soft. Remove the pears from the oven and cool slightly. Place a cube of cheese in the core of each pear and wrap with a 1- to $1\frac{1}{2}$-inch-wide strip of pro-scuitto (one half to one third of a normal slice), trying to keep the seam under the pear. Return to the baking sheet. At this point the pears can be baked and served immediately, or covered with plastic wrap and chilled for up to 4 hours.

3. Just before serving, bake the pears about 10 minutes, or until the cheese begins to melt. Serve warm or at room temperature.

4. To prepare the figs, slice a small slit, from the stem to the bottom of the fruit, and insert the cheese through the slit (no need to use olive oil). Gently press the slit closed, sealing the cheese in the fruit. Wrap the fig neatly with a strip of prosciutto and place in a baking dish. Roast until the cheese begins to melt, about 7 to 8 minutes.

# Boiled Shrimp with Mayo Verde

**Serves 6 to 8 as an appetizer or 10 to 12 as a party nibble**

When shrimp are super fresh and sweet, I serve them simply, boiled with a few aromatics until they are just cooked. Cocktail sauce is a natural, but I like this bright green herbaceous mayonnaise even better. Spinach, scallions, serrano chile, and fresh herbs all lend their fresh flavor and color to create a striking condiment. Slather the leftover mayo on grilled chicken, sliced leg of lamb, roast beef, tomato sandwiches, or hard-cooked eggs. For the best results, make the mayo verde a few hours before serving so the flavors have a chance to mingle and bloom.

## MAYO VERDE

1 quart **MAYONNAISE**

1 cup cleaned and finely chopped fresh **SPINACH**

$\frac{1}{2}$ cup chopped **SCALLIONS**

$\frac{1}{2}$ cup chopped fresh **CILANTRO**

1 **SERRANO CHILE**, seeded and minced

2 tablespoons chopped fresh **TARRAGON**

2 tablespoons snipped **CHIVES**

2 tablespoons fresh **LIME JUICE**

1 tablespoon **GRATED LIME ZEST**

$\frac{1}{4}$ teaspoon **KOSHER SALT**

Freshly ground **BLACK PEPPER**

Dash of **HOT SAUCE**

## BOILED SHRIMP

1 medium **ONION**, halved

4 **CLOVES**

6 **PEPPERCORNS**

2 fresh **BAY LEAVES**

1 **GARLIC CLOVE**, crushed

1 tablespoon **KOSHER SALT**

2 pounds (18 to 24 count) large **SHRIMP**

3 **PLUM TOMATOES**, chopped, for garnish (optional)

**1.** In a medium bowl, use a rubber spatula to combine the ingredients for Mayo Verde until well mixed. Taste and adjust the seasonings, adding more lime juice, salt, pepper, and hot sauce as desired. Chill for at least 2 hours or overnight.

**2.** To prepare the shrimp, slice the onion in half and insert 2 cloves in each half. Place the onion, peppercorns, bay leaves, garlic, and salt in a large pot. Fill the pot three quarters full with water and bring to a boil. Add the shrimp and return to a boil. Drain the shrimp and rinse briefly with cold water. Allow the shrimp to cool, then peel and devein, if desired, leaving tails intact. Refrigerate until needed.

**3.** To serve the shrimp as a first course, place 3 or 4 on a small plate and anchor with a generous dollop of green mayonnaise, along with chopped tomatoes, if desired.

# Pickled Shrimp with Beer and Lime

**Serves 8**

A unique combination of beer, malt vinegar, and lime gives these shrimp a distinct flavor. The herbs and spices impart a rich perfume, and the turmeric lends an appetizing golden hue. The tangy marinated vegetables are as good as the shrimp—I fish them out to eat on buttered rounds of bread. These shrimp should marinate at least 8 hours, and they are best if prepared an entire day ahead, making them ideal for entertaining.

BEER AND LIME MARINADE

12 ounces **BEER** (such as Corona or Pacifico)

1 cup **MALT VINEGAR**

$\frac{1}{2}$ cup **VEGETABLE OIL**

$\frac{1}{2}$ cup fresh **LIME JUICE**

2 tablespoons **SUGAR**

2 tablespoons **KOSHER SALT**

4 fresh **BAY LEAVES**

1 teaspoon **PEPPERCORNS**

1 teaspoon **CORIANDER SEEDS**

1 teaspoon **FENNEL SEEDS**

1 teaspoon **MUSTARD SEEDS**

1 teaspoon **TURMERIC**

$\frac{1}{2}$ crushed **RED PEPPER FLAKES**

3 tablespoons **HOT SAUCE** (like Crystal or Louisiana)

2 pounds **LARGE SHRIMP**, shelled and deveined with tails left intact, if desired

2 large **SWEET ONIONS**, thinly sliced

1 medium **CARROT**, thinly sliced on the bias

$\frac{1}{2}$ cup chopped fresh **CILANTRO**

$\frac{1}{4}$ cup chopped **FLAT-LEAF PARSLEY**

1. Bring all the marinade ingredients to a boil in a medium saucepan. Reduce the heat and simmer for 5 minutes, then cool.

2. Bring a large pot of generously salted water to a boil. Add the shrimp and return to a boil, drain immediately, and transfer the shrimp to a bowl of ice water to stop the cooking. Drain.

3. Combine the shrimp, onions, and carrot in a large bowl or plastic container with a tight-fitting lid. Pour the marinade over the top and cover with a lid or plastic wrap. (If using plastic wrap, place a smaller bowl or plate on top to keep the shrimp submerged.) Marinate at least 12 hours or up to 2 days. Just before serving, add the chopped cilantro and parsley and toss to combine.

# Gulf Ceviche with Tequila and Lime

**Serves 6 to 8 as an appetizer or 12 as a party nibble**

**(Makes about 9 cups)**

The most ubiquitous ceviche in Uvalde, thirty miles south of the ranch, is the slightly sweet, tomato variety made with small shrimp and ketchup. It's sold in plastic cups from a cart across the street from my grocery store, and it's good, especially with saltines and an extra dousing of lemon or lime juice. But I've always loved the cleaner taste of ceviche made mostly with lime. It's common to chop the raw shrimp and allow it to "cook" in the lime juice, but I prefer the texture of shrimp that has been boiled briefly and then marinated.

Ceviche is sublime party food and a light, fresh-tasting appetizer. Served with slices of creamy avocado, plenty of salty tortilla chips (which serve as utensils), and a cold Mexican beer, it also makes a dream lunch. For a simpler and equally tasty version of this ceviche, skip the shrimp and scallops and make this recipe with 2 pounds of meaty white fish.

$1\frac{1}{4}$ cups fresh **LIME JUICE**

$\frac{1}{2}$ pound **MEDIUM SHRIMP**

$\frac{1}{2}$ pound very fresh **BAY SCALLOPS**

1 pound very fresh **SKINLESS SNAPPER** (or other meaty white fish like grouper, bass, or halibut), cut into $\frac{1}{2}$-inch cubes

1 large **RED ONION**, very thinly sliced

$\frac{1}{2}$ cup good **SILVER TEQUILA**

1 **RED, ORANGE,** or **YELLOW BELL PEPPER**, finely chopped

2 **PLUM TOMATOES**, diced (see Note)

2 **JALAPEÑOS** or 2 to 4 **SERRANOS**, to taste, stemmed, seeded, and finely chopped

$\frac{1}{2}$ cup chopped fresh **CILANTRO**, leaves and tender stems

$\frac{1}{4}$ cup chopped fresh **FLAT-LEAF PARSLEY** (optional)

1 teaspoon crumbled **MEXICAN OREGANO**

4 tablespoons **EXTRA VIRGIN OLIVE OIL**

**KOSHER SALT**

**CRUMBLED PEQUÍN CHILES** or **HOT SAUCE** (optional)

2 medium **AVOCADOS**, peeled and sliced

**TORTILLA CHIPS**

1. Bring a large pot of generously salted water to a boil. Add ¼ cup lime juice and the shrimp and return to a boil. Drain the shrimp immediately in a colander and cool. Peel and devein the shrimp and refrigerate until needed.

2. In a large glass or stainless steel bowl, toss the scallops, snapper, red onion, tequila, and remaining 1 cup lime juice. Cover and refrigerate for at least 2 (or up to 4) hours, stirring the mixture every now and then so the fish will be evenly "cooked." When the fish is opaque throughout, drain in a colander. In a large bowl, combine the bell pepper, tomatoes, chiles, cilantro, parsley if using, oregano, oil, reserved shrimp, and drained fish and gently toss to combine. Taste for seasoning and add salt and crumbled chiles or hot sauce as desired. Serve immediately in individual cups or on a big platter, with slices of avocado on top and plenty of tortilla chips on the side.

NOTE: For a smokier, sweeter ceviche use roasted tomatoes (page 74) instead of fresh tomatoes.

# SHAKE OUT YOUR BOOTS:

## A GUIDE TO COHABITATING WITH SCORPIONS

*W*hen I moved to Texas, I knew there were scorpions. Early on they fell under the list of "cons" regarding why I shouldn't leave the city. Ultimately, I lumped scorpions (and snakes, tarantulas, black widows, and the like) with muggings or blackouts. They were things to be feared but that I probably wouldn't encounter that often. Both places have fiends that are more infamous than prevalent, I reasoned.

Little did I know that scorpions, specifically Striped Bark Scorpions, the most common species in South Central Texas, would become a part of life. Our house had been vacant for several months before we moved in. Chances are, the scorpions were just starting to get comfy before we showed up and crashed their party.

In the first six months I found twenty, and they almost made me crazy. They hid under jeans, in the dryer, and behind the dog bed. I'd reach for toilet paper and see one crawling up the wall. I'd open the shower curtain and see one prancing across the tub.

I couldn't walk through the house without scanning floorboards. I didn't sit down without lifting cushions and blankets. I wouldn't crawl into bed without shaking sheets and pillows. I was terrified to walk to the bathroom barefoot in the middle of the night. The frequent sightings fueled and validated my paranoia.

Much to my annoyance, David shared none of this anxiety. He plopped down without looking, flopped into bed without rustling covers, pulled on jeans without giving them a shake. As a result, somehow I knew that in the strange and unfair logic of the universe, I would be stung first.

I e-mailed friends dramatic accounts each time I saw one. Perhaps not coincidentally, no one came to visit.

One Sunday evening after a particularly exhausting week, I set the stage for a soothing night. I put clean sheets on the bed and spritzed them with linen spray. I took a hot shower and put on my favorite Bill Evans CD. I started to sink into sleep soon after my head hit the pillow. Sometime later—early into dreaming but before I reached the deepest depths—I became aware of an increasingly hot prick on my cheek. The sensation, as precise as the point of a needle, grew fiery, then intolerable, until I jolted up, brushed something off my face, and screamed. I toppled out of bed and my knee hit the floor hard. I fumbled for the lamp and turned on the switch. David sat up, looking dazed and confused. Then he pointed to where I had been lying and hollered, "Scorpion!" There on my clean sheets was a tan scorpion, its tail curled into a defiant question mark.

I started to sob and a string of colorful words spilled from my mouth. David whacked the scorpion off the bed. I screamed at him not to lose it. He jumped down and smashed it with the heel of a boot. My knee was throbbing and darkening into a plum-shaped bruise, and my face stung. "I'm checking into the nearest Four Seasons," I bawled. "How can we live here?" A scorpion had stung my face while I was sleeping. Replaying these facts only made me sob harder.

David looked panicked. He was pretty sure that this was my breaking point and we'd be moving by the end of the week. "My cheek hurts," I repeated, not wanting him to move past how upset I was.

"I know," he said empathetically, unsure of what else to say.

Despite a hefty glass of Scotch and a few painkillers, I barely slept that night. The next day, I tried to talk myself past the fear. Why is a scorpion—a small insect, really—so frightening? Its sting is more intense than a wasp's, but I can deal with pain. The real fear, I reasoned, stemmed from the anticipation and jolt of spotting one. Then there was the unfortunate adage that scorpions travel in pairs. Against my better judgment, I started researching them on the Web. I learned that scorpions are dormant during the day but become active at night. Great. I read that the average litter size is thirty. I bought more Scotch and sleeping pills.

Once stung, I became doubly obsessed. Fueling this neurosis was a lack of sleep (I was certain that dozing off meant certain attack). The more restless nights that ensued, the more irrational I became. I started snapping. I was afraid of my own house. After all, I had been sleeping with the enemy.

One of the first bits of Texas wisdom imparted to us was to shake out our boots before putting them on. Scorpions love to hide in them. Needless to say, I did this religiously. But one Saturday morning, as I rushed to get to the post office before it closed, I didn't check. I sat on the end of the couch and started to push my foot into my boot. I hesitated. In that fraction of a second, I thought, *Oh, come on, get over it!* So I pushed my foot down and was promptly stung in the tender arch of my foot.

I yanked off my boot and flung it across the room. The cats scattered like billiard balls. Pulling off my sock to confirm that I wasn't having a nervous breakdown, I found a growing welt. I held my throbbing foot and searched for the culprit. I couldn't find a scorpion anywhere—which made the moment all the more surreal.

When my pulse slowed, I drove to the post office and told Sharon everything. "You flung him!" she said.

"I looked everywhere," I argued.

"You flung him," she said again.

When I got home I got down on my knees and searched one last time. Sharon was right. I found the scorpion, curled up and dead, inside one of my kitchen clogs—exactly where I'd flung him.

# Scorpion Tails with Pequillo Pepper Sauce

**Serves 8**

This appetizer is a play on jalapeño poppers, arguably the most beloved bar (or behind-the-wheel) snack in Texas. For poppers, jalapeños are stuffed with Cheddar or cream cheese, dipped in batter, fried, and served with ranch dressing. Sheer genius, especially at two o'clock in the morning.

Most of the time I prefer a lighter, prettier popper that is more about the unique flavor of the chile pepper. I stuff jalapeños with a filling made with two cheeses, corn, garlic, and basil. The jalapeños are broiled until the filling bubbles and the skins blister and soften, and are then served on a bright-tasting pequillo pepper purée.

Sold in jars in most supermarkets, pequillo peppers are from Spain. They have a vibrant flavor—sweet, smoky, and more concentrated than regular roasted red peppers.

The jalapeños will be easier to fill if you allow the cream cheese mixture to chill for at least 30 minutes before assembling. They will hold their shape better under the broiler if they are covered and chilled again before cooking.

For the best flavor the entire jalapeño should be cooked throughout until it's drab—the raw green heat will be too sharp for most and the crunchy texture isn't as pleasant to eat. If the peppers are still too green after they're sufficiently broiled on top, turn the oven down to 200°F and leave them in the warm oven until you're ready to serve them. The egg in the filling is optional, but it will help the other ingredients pull together and result in a more mousselike texture.

16 large **JALAPEÑO PEPPERS**

One 8-ounce block **NEUFCHÂTEL CHEESE**

½ cup **GRATED COTIJA, QUESO AÑEJO**, or another aged **WHITE CHEESE**

½ cup **CORN** (cut fresh from a cob or thawed frozen)

1 **EGG** (optional)

1 **GARLIC CLOVE**, minced

1 teaspoon ground **CUMIN**

2 tablespoons chopped fresh **BASIL**

½ teaspoon **KOSHER SALT**

Freshly ground **BLACK PEPPER**

Dash of **HOT SAUCE**

**PEQUILLO PEPPER SAUCE**
One 8- to 10-ounce jar **PEQUILLO PEPPERS**, drained
1 tablespoon **EXTRA VIRGIN OLIVE OIL**
1 teaspoon **SHERRY WINE VINEGAR**

**1.** Slice the stems off the jalapeños and reserve. Using a paring knife, slice a vertical V-shaped opening into the side of each pepper. Using your fingers, gently spread the opening and use a paring knife to remove the pepper's ribs and seeds. Repeat the process with the remaining peppers.

**2.** In the bowl of an electric mixer fitted with the paddle attachment, whip the Neufchâtel at medium-high speed just to soften. Add the cotija, corn, egg if using, garlic, cumin, basil, salt, pepper, and hot sauce and beat at low speed until blended. Cover the filling with plastic wrap and chill for at least 30 minutes or up to several hours.

**3.** Using a butter knife, fill each pepper with about 2 tablespoons of cheese filling. Top each pepper with the stem (frost the stem with the filling so it will adhere to the pepper, if necessary) and place on a parchment-lined baking sheet. Cover the sheet with plastic wrap and refrigerate the peppers at least 1 hour before broiling.

**4.** Meanwhile, place the drained pequillo peppers, olive oil, and sherry wine vinegar in a blender and purée. Transfer the purée to a small saucepan. Heat gently just before serving the peppers.

**5.** Just before serving, turn on the broiler and place an oven rack at its highest level. Place the sheet of peppers under the broiler and cook until blistered but not overly blackened. If the bottoms of the peppers are still green, reduce the heat to 200°F, place the peppers on a lower oven rack, and finish warming through. To serve, spread a few tablespoons of the warmed pequillo sauce onto a small plate. Place 2 peppers on each plate and serve.

# Texas Sweet Onion Tart with Rosemary and Pequín Chile

**Serves 6 to 8 (Makes one 10-inch tart)**

This tart is a play on pissaladière, with South Texas influences (rosemary, pequín chile, and a rustic cornmeal crust). The cornmeal pastry crust is wonderful to work with—it's soft and pliable but not sticky. Happily the shells do not need to be prebaked. Consider serving this tart, as a first course or special lunch, with a frisée salad tossed with plenty of herbs (e.g., parsley, chives, chervil, and tarragon) and the leftover lardons.

> **CORNMEAL CRUST** (recipe follows)
>  2 strips thick-sliced **APPLEWOOD-SMOKED BACON**
> 1 tablespoon **OLIVE OIL**
> 2 tablespoons **UNSALTED BUTTER**
> 2 pounds (about 3 large) **SWEET ONIONS**, thinly sliced
> **KOSHER SALT**
> 2 teaspoons **SHERRY WINE VINEGAR**
> 1 tablespoon coarsely chopped fresh **ROSEMARY**
> 1 teaspoon crumbled **PEQUÍN CHILE** (see Note)
> Freshly ground **BLACK PEPPER**
> 2 large **EGGS**
> ½ cup **MEXICAN CREMA** (or crème fraîche, sour cream, or plain whole milk yogurt)

1. Prepare the cornmeal crust. While the dough chills, prepare the filling.

2. Slice the bacon into ¾-inch slices. Cut the slices in half crosswise to make lardons. Heat the olive oil in a large skillet over medium-high heat. Add the lardons and cook, stirring, until lightly browned and crisp but still tender. Use a slotted spoon to transfer the lardons to a paper-towel-covered plate. Reserve for the salad.

3. Drain all but 1 tablespoon of bacon fat from the skillet. Add the butter, onions, and salt to taste and cook, stirring, until the onions reduce by about two-thirds, about 10 to 15 minutes. Add the vinegar, reduce the heat to medium-low, and continue to cook, stirring every now and then, until the onions are deeply golden and have a soft, sticky, marmalade consistency. The onions will need almost constant stirring at the end to prevent them from sticking and burning. Stir in the rosemary and pequín chile. Remove from the heat and

season generously with pepper and more salt as desired. Allow the onion mixture to cool. Preheat the oven to 400° F.

4. In a medium bowl, whisk together the eggs and crema. Stir the egg mixture into the cooled onions.

5. Pour the onion mixture into the prepared crust. Bake until the filling and crust are golden (golden brown for the crust) and the filling has set, about 35 to 40 minutes. Serve the tart at room temperature, with a salad tossed with the reserved lardons.

NOTE: Pequín chiles typically crumble easily between your fingers. However, if they're too soft and leathery to crumble, toast the chiles for 2 to 3 minutes in a dry skillet over medium-high heat and then cool and crumble.

## Cornmeal Crust

**Makes 2 10-inch crusts**

11 ounces (2½ cups) **ALL-PURPOSE FLOUR**
3½ ounces (¾ cup) finely ground **YELLOW CORNMEAL**
2 teaspoons **SUGAR**
1½ teaspoons **KOSHER SALT**
2 sticks cold **UNSALTED BUTTER**
⅓ cup **MEXICAN CREMA** or **SOUR CREAM**
¼ cup ice-cold **WATER** (more as needed)

1. Place the dry ingredients in a food processor and pulse to combine. Add the butter in small pieces and pulse until the mixture is coarse and pebbly (do not overprocess). Transfer the dough to a large bowl. By hand, gradually work in the crema and ice water. The dough should be soft and pliable but not sticky. Adjust as necessary with flour. Chill the dough for at least 30 minutes (or up to a day in advance).

2. Divide chilled dough in half (rewrap and chill or freeze other half until needed). Roll out the crust ¼ inch thick on a lightly floured work surface. Carefully roll the crust around the rolling pin (I use a plastic dough scraper to help lift it from the counter) and transfer to the tart pan. Gently press dough into pan, then roll the pin over the top of the pan to trim excess dough and create a smooth surface.

# Beet Greens with Egg, Aïoli, and Rye Croutons

**Serves 4, with leftover aïoli**

During my last year in New York I worked as a bartender at Prune, a wildly popular East Village bistro, where my friend Gabrielle Hamilton is the chef and owner. The job came with a few conditions. I had to go by my alias, Dixie, wear a tight pink T-shirt, and bright red lipstick. Aw, shucks, that was easy. Gabrielle was one of the first friends to visit us in Texas, and it was comforting to have an old friend hiking on my new terrain. When she offered to make the appetizer one night, I eagerly accepted. I returned to find glistening beet greens and stems marinating in oil and vinegar, a vat of thick, fragrant aïoli, a baking sheet of crisp rye croutons, and a few hard-cooked eggs. To serve this dish, give each plate a generous slather of aïoli, top it with a neat magenta pile of greens, a scattering of croutons, and a few wedges of hard-cooked egg. This dish can only be made when both the beet greens and stems are in good shape, so buy a good-looking bunch, ideally from your local farmers' market.

Greens and stems from 1 bunch **BEETS**, thoroughly rinsed
**BALSAMIC VINEGAR**
**EXTRA VIRGIN OLIVE OIL**
**KOSHER SALT** and freshly ground **BLACK PEPPER**
2 to 3 **PEQUÍN CHILES**, crumbled, or pinch of crushed **RED PEPPER FLAKES**
**AÏOLI** (recipe follows)
2 cups **CRISPY RYE CROUTONS** (page 124)
2 hard-cooked **EGGS**, cut into sixths

1. Bring a medium pot of salted water to a boil. Separate the beet stems from the leaves. Coarsely chop the leaves and finely chop the stems into $\frac{1}{4}$-inch dice. Blanch the stems for 2 to 3 minutes, remove from the water with a fine sieve, and rinse briefly with cold water; set aside. Add the greens to the boiling water and boil for 1 minute. Drain in a colander and briefly rinse with cold water. Use a paper towel to pat the stems dry. Use a clean dish towel or more paper towels to squeeze any excess moisture from the greens. Combine the stems and greens in a medium bowl and moisten with a splash of vinegar and a generous drizzle of olive oil. Season to taste with salt, black pepper, and red pepper flakes. Allow the greens to marinate at room temperature while you make the aïoli.

2. To serve, frost four small plates with a generous swirl of aïoli. Top with a small pile of the beet greens, a generous scattering of croutons (about $\frac{1}{3}$ cup per person), 3 wedges of hard-cooked egg, and a final grinding of black pepper.

# Aïoli

1 large **EGG YOLK**, at room temperature

1 teaspoon **DIJON MUSTARD**

$\frac{1}{2}$ cup **GRAPESEED OIL**

$\frac{1}{4}$ cup **EXTRA VIRGIN OLIVE OIL**

1 **GARLIC CLOVE**

2 **ANCHOVIES**, finely chopped (optional)

$\frac{1}{2}$ teaspoon finely chopped fresh **ROSEMARY**

$\frac{1}{4}$ teaspoon **KOSHER SALT**

1 to 2 tablespoons fresh **LEMON JUICE**

Pinch of **CAYENNE PEPPER**

Freshly ground **BLACK PEPPER**

In a medium bowl, whisk together the egg yolk and mustard. In a very slow drizzle, whisk in the grapeseed oil, then the olive oil. Pound the garlic, anchovies, rosemary, and salt together in a mortar and pestle. Whisk the garlic mixture into the aïoli and season with a tablespoon of lemon juice and a pinch of cayenne. Taste the aïoli and add more lemon, salt, or cayenne, and black pepper as desired. If the aïoli is thick and gloppy, whisk in a small amount of warm water to thin it out. Transfer to a container, cover, and refrigerate until needed.

## CRISPY RYE CROUTONS

Preheat the oven to 350°F. Trim the crust from $\frac{1}{2}$ loaf of rye bread (preferably day old). Slice the hunk of bread into $\frac{1}{2}$-inch cubes. Place the cubes on a cookie sheet and drizzle with just enough olive oil to coat, a sprinkling of kosher salt, and herbes de Provence, crumbled between your fingers. Toss the cubes well to coat evenly with the oil and seasonings. Toast in the oven for about 10 minutes, flipping often with a spatula, until evenly golden brown. Use as needed and save leftovers in a plastic bag for green salads.

# QUICK ANCHOVY MAYO

*P*urists are against making mayo in a food processor, claiming the results are thick and gloppy, but I do it when I'm short on time and the results are smooth and luscious. When I use a food processor, I use the same ingredients for Aïoli, with the addition of an extra whole egg to pull the mixture together. To make Quick Anchovy Mayo, place the garlic, anchovies, rosemary, kosher salt, and Dijon mustard in the bowl of a food processor and pulse until the ingredients form a rough paste. Add the egg yolk and 1 whole egg and process until smooth. Add the grapeseed oil in a slow, steady stream, then repeat with the olive oil. Pulse in 2 to 3 tablespoons lemon juice and a pinch of cayenne. Taste for seasonings, adding more lemon or cayenne, and black pepper as desired. If the mixture is too thick, whisk in water as described above. If not using immediately, store in the refrigerator for up to 2 days.

# Smoky Hummus

**Makes about 3 cups**

I hesitated about putting a hummus recipe in the book because the Middle Eastern spread is ubiquitous and there are countless recipes out there. But I like my version very much. It's lighter and more lemony than most. We scoop it up with blue corn chips for a quick snack or slather it over warm whole wheat tortillas for lunch. The biggest mistake people make with hummus is adding too much tahini and not enough olive oil and lemon juice (and in this recipe yogurt) to lighten it up. In my opinion hummus shouldn't be thick and pasty; it should be as light and creamy as buttercream. For a richer (and less pungent) flavor, try using roasted garlic instead of raw.

One of my favorite ways to serve hummus is in a Middle Eastern-inspired salad plate. I partner a generous pool of hummus (drizzled with additional olive oil and sprinkled with Aleppo pepper) with grated organic carrots (dressed with olive or walnut oil and lemon juice), a cucumber and onion salad (tossed with white wine vinegar, olive oil, and crumbled dried oregano), a few cornichons or other small, tart pickles, a couple of kalamata olives, and a few well-blistered whole wheat tortillas. Lean and Green Broccoli Couscous (page 58) or roasted beets in a vinaigrette could easily join the mix.

1 to 2 large **GARLIC CLOVES**, as desired

1 tablespoon chopped fresh **ROSEMARY** (optional)

¾ teaspoon **KOSHER SALT**

Two 15-ounce cans **CHICKPEAS**, drained and rinsed

2 to 3 tablespoons **SESAME TAHINI**

⅓ cup **PLAIN YOGURT**

2 **LEMONS**, for juicing

4 to 6 tablespoons **EXTRA VIRGIN OLIVE OIL**

2 teaspoons ground **CUMIN**

½ teaspoon **SMOKED SPANISH PAPRIKA** or **ALEPPO PEPPER**

**HOT SAUCE** (such as Crystal or Louisiana)

Place the garlic, rosemary if using, and salt in the bowl of a food processor fitted with a metal blade and process until coarsely chopped. Add the chickpeas and process until they are broken down. Add the tahini, yogurt, the juice of 1 lemon, 4 tablespoons olive oil, cumin, and smoked paprika and process until smooth. Taste for seasoning and add more salt and lemon juice, the remaining olive oil, and hot sauce to achieve the desired balance and consistency. Purée until very smooth. Store in a sealed container in the refrigerator for up to 5 days. For the best flavor, bring to room temperature before serving and garnish with an additional drizzle of olive oil and a sprinkling of paprika or Aleppo pepper as desired.

# Crostini with Lima Bean and Pecorino Purée

**Serves 6 to 8 as a first course or more as a party nibble**

**(Makes about 1½ cups purée)**

When I cooked in Tuscany, I fell in love with the green, garlicky fresh fava bean purée that is typically slathered over crispy rounds of crostini and served as an appetizer. Here in Texas, Fordhook lima beans have a similar taste and texture, and most important, they are available year-round in the freezer section of your grocery. This simple, unexpected appetizer is wonderful with a glass of sparkling wine like prosecco, or sauvignon blanc. A scattering of paper-thin radish slices provides a juicy crunch and brightens up the plate. If you don't have mint, you can use flat-leaf parsley or a few tablespoons of chopped fresh rosemary instead.

1 pound frozen **FORDHOOK LIMA BEANS**
2 **GARLIC CLOVES**
**KOSHER SALT**
Pinch of crushed **RED PEPPER FLAKES** or 2 to 3 crumbled **PEQUÍN CHILES**
½ cups **GRATED PECORINO CHEESE**
½ cup coarsely chopped fresh **MINT**
1 to 2 **LEMONS**, for juicing
½ cup **EXTRA VIRGIN OLIVE OIL**
Freshly ground **BLACK PEPPER**

1 loaf **ITALIAN BREAD**, such as ciabatta, thinly sliced and toasted
4 to 6 **RADISHES** (Icicle, French breakfast, or other variety), very thinly sliced

1. Bring a medium saucepan of salted water to a boil. Add the lima beans and cook until just tender, about 7 minutes. Drain in a colander and shock the beans in cold water. Drain again, shaking the colander to remove excess moisture.

2. Place the garlic and ½ teaspoon salt in the bowl of a food processor fitted with an electric blade and process until coarsely chopped. Add the lima beans and process until they form a rough paste. Add the red pepper flakes, pecorino, mint, and 2 tablespoons lemon juice and pulse until combined. With the motor running, add the olive oil in a steady stream until well incorporated. Taste for seasoning, adding more salt or lemon juice, and black pepper as desired.

3. To serve, slather a generous amount of purée on a slice of toasted bread and garnish with a few rounds of radish.

# WILD PIGS THAT GRUNT

**W**e settled into ranch life with an ease and swiftness that surprised me. Sights, smells, and patterns became familiar and our days developed a new rhythm. With each passing week we felt less like we were on another planet and more at home. I became accustomed to checking the rain gauge and I broke in my boots.

On one of our first road trips, we drove to Elgin, a German-settled town famous for its sausage, to buy the bricks for David's bread oven. Using plans from a book, the oven was constructed the following weekend. For several days in a row, David built increasingly large fires to dry and cure the bricks and mortar. When the oven was finally ready, we celebrated with the first batch of pizzas. At 750°F, the crust crisped and the cheese bubbled in just a few minutes, and the pizzas emerged perfectly charred. David's crust was crackly, chewy, and full of flavor, and the pizzas were as good as anything we'd eaten in Italy. Our Texas trattoria, so to speak, was under way, and the results tasted good.

Our menagerie was growing. The baby calves skipped around the pasture, pausing only to ensure that they had an audience. Kit and I drove to a ranch to pick out two bred goats—the beginning of the herd—and bought Tinto and Baguette. David secured the chicken coop behind our house, making it critterproof, so our hens grew fat and happy from carrot peels, coffee grounds, oatmeal, and couscous.

With my parents' help, I planted a spring garden, a small plot enclosed by a high fence to keep deer and other animals out. My mother, a gifted gardener accustomed to rich, midwestern soil, frowned at the pale, rocky dirt that the tiller churned up. "I don't know how you're going to grow anything here," she said. To improve matters, we turned in chicken litter and straw to lighten the soil so it could breathe, ash from the bread oven, and molasses for minerals. We picked out as many stones as possible. I planted my mainstays: rosemary, a few bay leaf trees, and several kinds of thyme. I didn't have room for many vegetables, but I knew I'd visit an herb garden, apron-clad and shears in hand, every day. The garden was attached to a salmon-colored brick potting shed that I adored. Kit outfitted the space with an antique café table and chairs. I planted a row of lavender along the front.

After a few months of cooking with local ingredients, I began to pull together a menu of regional favorites done my way. I simmered pots of pintos with Shiner Bock beer and epazote (a Mexican herb that tastes like a cross between parsley and oregano) and baked bubbling pans of enchiladas verdes. I blended salsas galore, from roasted tomatoes, blistered tomatillos, and toasted chiles and garlic. Heavy pots of beef chili, made from cubes of well-marbled chuck, bubbled on the stove. We rolled out paper-thin spicy ginger cookies and cut them out with goat-shaped cutters.

We were working hard and we were learning—but there was still so much that we didn't know. The ranch had plenty of surprises in store for us.

On a softly colored evening, David and I set out for a hike. Dusk has always been my favorite time of day; on the ranch it became my most cherished time to walk. The sun sinks behind the hills that frame the back of the ranch. The light, unrelenting during the day, fades to shades of gray and purple. The night air smelled fresher, like pine, cedar, and stone.

We took an old Jeep trail that snakes up a long, gradual incline. This hike would become my daily ritual, as calming and restorative as anything I've done. Walking alone was my private thinking time; with David and the dogs, it was a family outing.

Thighs burning and hearts pounding, we reached the summit and walked around the perimeter of the canyon, pausing now and then to take in the dark hills that stretched out from either side. We continued on, past agarita bushes, mountain laurel trees fragrant with white and purple blossoms, and over tiny pink flowers that sprouted from between the stones. We turned right and headed down. At the bottom of the hill, the trail spilled across a different part of the creek and led into a thick, sheltered hollow. Pecan, black walnut, and oak branches filtered the light, which had faded significantly.

Three small black objects moved onto the trail ahead of us. I caught my breath because I was still unaccustomed to the sporadic appearance of wild animals. As my eyes adjusted, I tried to discern the shapes—were they skunks, bear cubs, or black Lab puppies? Then David cooed, "Look, baby pigs!" and ambled happily toward them. I froze.

"Then there's probably a mother," I said tersely. Not a second later, we heard a husky, ferocious growl from behind a cluster of small cedar. The growl was to our left and the piglets were now on our right. If we tried to pass between the two, we were in trouble—that much I knew. Through the branches, I could make out the dark outline of an animal that appeared to be the size of a Volkswagen.

Here wild hogs are the stuff of lore and legend. Most are feral pigs that have grown tusks and hairy hides, but there are also javelinas (smaller and meaner) that have come up from Mexico. Gene, one of George's ranch hands, told us that up in the hills hogs can grow upwards of eight hundred pounds—the size of a small horse. We'd heard conflicting reports about the threat they pose. Some people swore they were harmless, and assured us that the pigs would run away. We heard different stories from a few people who had been chased up trees. But one detail was constant. "The only time you need to worry is if you come between a momma and her babies," George warned us.

The sow's horror-film growl deepened and resonated. She rasped and wheezed—it sounded like this pig smoked a pack of unfiltered cigarettes a day.

Slowly, I took two steps back. I picked up a stone. I picked up a big stick. I looked for a tree to climb.

After several interminable minutes, the piglets circled back to their mother. The harsh growl eased into the sound of a minor irritation, and we knew it was time to make our break. Steadily, we walked in front of the sow. Pack-a-day grunted and wheezed from behind the tree. As we passed, I could see her shape better. "Huge," I whispered to David.

"I know," he answered.

We walked quickly and deliberately, resisting the impulse to break into a run. When we emerged from the hollow, I'd never been so happy to be in a wide-open field, with no places for pigs to hide, in my life.

# Charming Little Sandwiches and a Belt-Busting Burger

*B*lame it on lunchbox nostalgia, mayonnaise-coated memories of deli counter bliss, or memories of perfect picnics. Either way, sandwiches strike me as fun, and inherently satisfying. When they're made with attention to detail and the ingredients are carefully chosen, there are few things more pleasing to eat.

I tuck them into cowboy lunchboxes for picnics eaten high on a hill. I enhance old-fashioned deli staples with my favorite flavors: Chicken salad gets smoke and green chiles; egg salad is perked up with mustard, capers, and fresh herbs from the garden.

Soft flour tortillas have become vehicles for countless wrap sandwiches, the favorite being smoked turkey slathered with a smoky chipotle cream. I also roll them around grated vegetables and sliced avocados, hummus and harissa, and roast beef and horseradish mayonnaise with sharp Cheddar cheese.

At the end of the day, I can't resist a fat, juicy burger and I can throw them together in a flash. I figure that people can get a classic burger anywhere, so I serve venison burgers made from good ground meat that I get from nearby Broken Arrow Ranch (see page 97). The burgers are flavored with a touch of cumin and marjoram and slathered with an insanely good pasilla chile mayo.

Whether these sandwiches wind up in a lunchbox, backpack, or picnic basket, or on a plane ride, they are gutsy, full of flavor, and promise to hold their own in the pantheon of stellar sandwich moments.

# Smoked Turkey Wraps with Chipotle Cream

**Makes 2 sandwiches (with leftover Chipotle Cream)**

These sandwiches are addictive: soft, tender, and chewy from the meat, tortilla, and creamy spread and crunchy from the cool, crisp salad in the middle. They are a snap to assemble and easy to tote anywhere. For the best flavor, blister the tortillas (over a gas flame or in a dry skillet), then allow them to cool a bit before you fill them. Use the best quality turkey (I have mine sliced to order and avoid the watery, tasteless prepackaged slices). Use perfectly crisp and dry leaf lettuce or a scattering of baby greens. A batch of the chipotle cream keeps for up to 5 days in the fridge, so you'll have the makings of quick, easy sandwiches on hand. I used smoked turkey, but this combination is awfully good with smoked ham or slices of leftover grilled steak. I often serve these sandwiches on hilltop picnics with Cumin Chickpeas (page 62), fresh fruit, and granola bars.

### CHIPOTLE CREAM

**Makes about ¾ cup**

8 ounces **NEUFCHÂTEL** or **LIGHT CREAM CHEESE**

2 canned **CHIPOTLE CHILES** in adobo, chopped

4 **SCALLIONS**, minced

### FOR EACH SANDWICH

1 **FLOUR TORTILLA**

**WHOLE GRAIN MUSTARD**

2 to 3 slices **SMOKED TURKEY**

1 **LEAF OF LETTUCE** or **MIXED GREENS**

Thinly sliced **CUCUMBER**

**1.** Combine the Neufchâtel, chipotles, and scallions in the bowl of an electric mixer fitted with the paddle attachment. Beat at medium speed until light and fluffy. Alternatively, combine the ingredients in a medium mixing bowl and beat by hand with a wood spoon.

**2.** To assemble each sandwich, heat the tortillas directly over a gas flame or in a dry skillet over medium heat, until softened and blistered with light brown spots. Allow the tortillas to cool, then slather with chipotle cream, a small amount of mustard, smoked turkey, a leaf of lettuce, and a few slices of cucumber. Roll the wrap into a snug cylinder and slice in half, on the horizontal. Serve immediately, or wrap in plastic and refrigerate until needed.

**CHIPOTLE CREAM** is also good with many other combinations. Try it with sliced grilled chicken and shredded cabbage, smoked ham and white Cheddar, or my favorite—a veggie wrap with grated carrots and grated cooked beets, julienned red pepper, sliced avocado, and cucumber. I also make tortilla wrap sandwiches with Smoky Hummus (page 126), harissa (or other hot sauce), and cucumber, or leftover sliced ribeye and guacamole.

# Herbaceous Egg Salad

## Makes 2½ cups (enough for 4 sandwiches)

My egg salad is always made with fresh ranch eggs and plenty of herbs. Capers and shallots make this salad more piquant than deli varieties. This salad is very good on soft slices of multigrain bread with a leaf of ruffled lettuce and a seasoned slice of ripe tomato. I also like to add a slather of tapenade or even sliced green olives.

6 large **EGGS**
⅓ cup **MAYONNAISE**
2 teaspoons **DIJON MUSTARD**
¼ teaspoon **SALT**
Freshly ground **BLACK PEPPER**
2 teaspoons chopped fresh **TARRAGON**
1 small **SHALLOT**, finely chopped
1 **CELERY STALK**, finely chopped
1 tablespoon **CAPERS**
1 tablespoon chopped fresh **TARRAGON**
1 tablespoon chopped fresh **CILANTRO**

Bring a medium saucepan of water to a boil. Gently add the eggs and cook 9 minutes (the center of the yolk will still be slightly creamy). Carefully pour off the hot water and rinse the eggs with cold running water to cool. Peel the eggs and roughly chop. Meanwhile, in a large bowl, combine the mayonnaise, mustard, salt, and pepper to taste. Add the remaining ingredients. Gently fold in the eggs. Prepare the sandwiches as desired and serve immediately.

# Smoked Chicken Salad with Green Chiles and Tarragon

**Serves 4**

Whenever grilled meat of any kind is on the menu, I season extra chicken breasts or thighs to smoke after the fire has burned down. The rich, smoky meat is a luxury to have on hand for lunches. I use the meat in all sorts of salads and sandwiches, especially this delicious chicken salad, flavored with green chiles and fresh tarragon.

Nothing tastes better than meat slow-grilled over a wood fire or charcoal, but store-bought smoked chicken would also work in this recipe. If you use canned green chiles, try to find Hatch chiles from New Mexico or a variety that has been fire roasted. They will have a deeper, more complex flavor. This salad is delicious on a crusty baguette or slices of soft white sandwich bread. It's also great tossed with baby spinach, arugula, or mixed greens.

4 cups chopped **SMOKED CHICKEN** (about 3 breast halves or 4 to 5 thighs)
**KOSHER SALT** and freshly ground **BLACK PEPPER**
¾ cup **MAYONNAISE**
1 tablespoon **DIJON MUSTARD**
2 teaspoons **LIME JUICE**
1 teaspoon finely grated **LIME ZEST**
Dash of **HOT SAUCE**
2 large **CELERY STALKS**, finely chopped
1 medium **ONION**, finely chopped
4 **SCALLIONS**, finely minced
2 **HATCH** (or Anaheim) **GREEN CHILES**, roasted, peeled, and chopped (or a 4-ounce can of green chiles, drained)
¼ cup chopped fresh **TARRAGON** (or cilantro or parsley or a combination)

Lightly season the chicken with salt and pepper to taste and set aside. In a large bowl, whisk together the mayonnaise, mustard, lime juice, zest, and hot sauce. Add the chicken, celery, onion, scallions, green chiles, and tarragon and toss well to combine. Serve immediately or store in the refrigerator for up to 3 days.

## SMOKING/SLOW-GRILLING CHICKEN

*S*eason 4 bone-in chicken breast halves or 8 skinless and boneless thighs (trimmed of excess fat) generously with salt and pepper. Heat a gas grill to medium-high, or light a wood or charcoal fire and let it burn until the coals are hot and covered with gray ash. To cook the meat, turn the burner in the center to medium-low, or push the coals or wood to the sides for indirect cooking. Place the meat on the grate and close the grill cover. Grill until the meat is tender, about 2 to 2½ hours. If your grill has a thermometer, keep the temperature between 250°F and 300°F. (To maintain an even temperature with wood or charcoal you will need to add a few pieces every hour or so.)

# Hill Country Pan Bagnat

**Makes 4 sandwiches**

This Niçoise sandwich, which translates to "bathed bread," is a remnant from my South of France days when I cooked at a château just west of Cannes. But it suits the Hill Country weather and I crave the pungent, salty flavors of tuna, capers, anchovies, and olive paste. I often make a big sandwich on one long loaf, then place a cutting board topped with a cast-iron skillet on top so the ingredients and the vinaigrette meld with the bread.

A pan bagnat begins with good tuna packed in olive oil. The tuna should be tossed in a Dijon vinaigrette made with shallots (or scallions) and the best olive oil and vinegar. Because I love herbs I add plenty—parsley, chervil, and basil—but all three aren't essential. Be sure to season the egg and tomato. A pretty leaf of ruffled lettuce and even grated carrots or thinly sliced radishes will add crunch and balance out the salty flavors.

Choose sturdy bread with a nice crackly crust so it can absorb some of the dressing, hold up to being pressed, and still retain a crunch.

2 medium **SHALLOTS**, finely chopped

1 teaspoon **DIJON MUSTARD**

2 tablespoons **LEMON JUICE**

1 tablespoon **RED WINE VINEGAR**

3 tablespoons **EXTRA VIRGIN OLIVE OIL**

**KOSHER SALT** and freshly ground **BLACK PEPPER**

Two 6-ounce cans **TUNA** in olive oil, drained

2 tablespoons **CAPERS**, rinsed

6 **ANCHOVIES**, finely chopped

Pinch of crushed **RED PEPPER FLAKES** or a few crumbled **PEQUÍN CHILES**

1 teaspoon finely grated **LEMON ZEST**

2 tablespoons chopped **FLAT-LEAF PARSLEY**

2 tablespoons chopped fresh **CHERVIL** (optional)

2 tablespoons **CHIFFONADE OF BASIL** (optional)

4 crusty **SANDWICH ROLLS** or 1 loaf **CIABATTA**, cut into 4 squares

3 tablespoons **TAPENADE** (see page 106)

4 pretty **LETTUCE LEAVES**, or a handful of **MIXED GREENS**

1 large ripe **TOMATO**, thinly sliced

2 hard-cooked **EGGS**, sliced

1 small **CARROT**, grated (optional)

2 to 3 **RADISHES**, thinly sliced (optional)

In a medium bowl, whisk together the shallots, mustard, lemon juice, vinegar, olive oil, and a small amount of salt (the other ingredients are very salty) and a generous grinding of pepper. Add the tuna, capers, anchovies, pepper flakes, zest, and herbs and gently combine. Slice the rolls or loaf of bread in half and place on a cutting board. Spread the top half with tapenade (if using rolls, divide evenly). Place the lettuce on the bottom half and top with the tuna mixture, tomato slices, eggs, and carrot and radishes if using. Place the top half of the sandwich over the bottom and gently push together. Place another cutting board on the sandwich and another weight (such as a cast-iron skillet or Dutch oven), and press the sandwich for about 30 minutes. Slice the loaf into squares and serve immediately, or wrap in parchment paper and refrigerate for up to 4 hours.

# THE GREAT ESCAPE

## THREE HORSES AND A DONKEY PAINT THE TOWN

On a warm afternoon in late autumn, Angela, our first and finest fitness director, and I set out for a run toward Rio Frio. We crossed 83, a relatively quiet highway, but a favorite with semi drivers on long hauls across South Texas. We ran along the steamy blacktop, past yellow and white wildflowers and purple miele sage growing along the cedar fences, and through the sporadic shadows of the live oaks that arched over the road. We crossed the rushing Frio River, our halfway point. The low bridge is the entry point for tourists who float the river—during the summer there would have been swimsuit-clad kids clutching inner tubes and coolers. After Labor Day, it was quiet. There was a Lab splashing in the water, and a couple maneuvering lawn chairs onto the white rocks. The sun was just starting to sink. I was ready for a break from the glare and the duskier light that made all the colors pop.

We saw a truck coming toward us and recognized it as Sharon's father, so we prepared to take cover. He was in his eighties, and found it hysterical to drive directly toward us and then swerve away at the last minute. Given his questionable response time, we found this less funny. This time, however, he slowed to a stop and rolled down his window. I readied myself for a "hot enough for you?"

Instead, he said, "Know anyone with three horses and a donkey?"

Because the words were unexpected, they took a minute to sink in. Angela and I stared back, panting and sweating, until I connected the details and answered, "Um, we do. We have three horses and a donkey!"

"Well, they got out and they're running around here loose. And if they get hit by a car you're liable," he scolded before speeding off.

As an experiment, we had moved our horses from the back of the ranch to the field in front of our house. There was plenty of good grass there, and we could keep an eye on them, we reasoned. And our neighbor George assured us that the would be fine—there were fences on either side and a cattle guard on both ends of the road. But clearly the horses had gotten curious and gone exploring. I couldn't believe that they had a) jumped the cattle guard and b) crossed the highway. The possibilities made me shudder. The old man was right. By Texas law, the livestock owner—not the driver—is liable if an animal gets hit. I momentarily panicked over how we could afford to pay for a semi, then transferred my worry to the notion of any of them getting hurt.

Angela and I ran back to the house in record time—at least we got in a good workout.

We'd acquired a third horse, Diego, an appaloosa the color of bittersweet chocolate, and a gray donkey named Lefty. We bought Diego because we thought we were ready for a younger, more challenging horse. He was a good choice in that regard since he would just as soon pitch either of us than ride in a direction that was not of his choosing. David loved him and spent plenty of saddle time trying to convince him who was boss. We adopted Lefty when he was weaned from his mother. He was both mischievous and affectionate, and had become very attached to our horses. Since herd animals hate to be left alone, Lefty played an important role in providing company for the third horse when we took two out for a ride. The problem was, Lefty also hated to miss a good time. Once when we returned from a ride without him, he walked up to David, turned around, and quite deliberately kicked him in the knee. I had come to think of our old boys, Django and Dillon, as curmudgeons—the Jack Lemmon and Walter Matthau of horses. When I imagined what Django, the sad-eyed sorrel, might say if he could talk, it was usually along the lines of waiting for his feed bucket and muttering, "This is bullshit."

Back at the house, I yelled for David and changed into dry clothes. We grabbed halters and lead ropes and headed out, windows down and hearts pounding, to find our horses.

Rio Frio, population 75, is a blink of a town. It seemed impossible that three horses and a donkey could elude us, but a stressful game of hide-and-seek ensued. We sped from house to house, hollering at anyone we saw, only to hear, "Why, yes, they were just here . . . and they ran, um, that way." We took gravel roads along the river. We wound through empty campsites. We pulled down driveways that we hadn't noticed before. Nothing. At each turn, it seemed we had missed them by minutes.

It started to get dark. Our leads felt less hopeful and our spirits sank. If we didn't find them before dark . . . I wondered if people still rustled horses. I wondered if we'd be out the money we'd spent on them and never see our boys again. I was tired and hungry and just wanted it to be over. I called George. I called the sheriff. We finally had a stroke of luck.

A stranger waved us down. He told us the horses had been caught and stabled at a house up the way. We zipped home for the horse trailer, then came back and found a small, well-maintained house, illuminated like a lonely Hopper painting, in a serene spot in the middle of a field. We saw a barn and trailer. "They're horse people," I said. "Who else would go to the trouble?" An older couple greeted us, and they were nice enough not to make us feel foolish.

"They loaded up real easily," the woman said. "They're good horses." Strangely, I felt proud, as though it were my doing. They led us out back and there they were. It seemed to me they looked sheepish. *Oh, well*, they must have thought, *it was fun while it lasted*.

When we got home, we fed the horses and savored the relief of having the family accounted for. Since everybody was safe, the search suddenly seemed funny. We cracked open cold beers and I made BLT sandwiches my way—lightly toasted ciabatta, chewy, slightly underdone thick-sliced bacon, perfect leaves of ruffled lettuce, tomatoes generously seasoned with salt and pepper, and a thick slather of mayo. Exhausted and relieved that we had escaped disaster, it seemed like the best thing we had ever eaten.

When it comes to danger and survival, horses have a keen memory. If a horse is stung by a wasp as it passes a pecan tree, for instance, it will forever become skittish when it returns to that tree. A horse remembers places and objects that pose a threat. But I always wondered if horses remember just for the sake of remembering. Do the boys ever stand in the field and reflect? Does one of them start, "Remember that time . . ." only to hear the others snort and laugh.

"It was a hell of a lot of fun," Lefty might say.

"Bullshit," Django would add.

# Venison Burgers with Pasilla Chile Mayonnaise

**Makes 4 burgers**

You can buy venison with 15% beef fat added, but I love the clean taste of the pure grind. As long as the meat is not cooked beyond medium-rare it will still be juicy. I season the patties with a bit of cumin, fresh marjoram or oregano from my garden, and a splash of Worcestershire. Avoid overworking the meat or the burgers will be tough. Pan-sear the burgers in a hot cast-iron skillet or, better yet, grill them over a wood fire. Serve them with toasted buns, lettuce, and a generous slather of pasilla chile mayonnaise—an alarmingly delicious condiment. Nobody would turn down a cold beer either.

Pasilla chiles are long and slender with a dark, blackish skin and a deep, smoky flavor. The chile paste for the mayonnaise is easily mixed in a "mini" food processor; you can also use a mortar and pestle. You will have more mayonnaise than you need, but that's a very good thing. Use leftovers to make a smoked chicken salad, or serve it with boiled shrimp or grilled sausage.

### PASILLA CHILE MAYONNAISE

2 **PASILLA CHILES**

2 **GARLIC CLOVES**, unpeeled

1 teaspoon **SHERRY WINE VINEGAR**

1 tablespoon **HONEY**

1½ cups **MAYONNAISE**

### VENISON BURGERS

1¼ pounds **GROUND VENISON** (see page 97)

**KOSHER SALT**

Freshly ground **BLACK PEPPER**

1½ teaspoons **CUMIN**

2 tablespoons chopped fresh **MARJORAM** or **OREGANO**

1 teaspoon **WORCESTERSHIRE SAUCE**

4 **HAMBURGER BUNS**

**LETTUCE** and **TOMATOES**, as desired

**GRILLED ONIONS** (optional)

1. Cover a medium cast-iron skillet with foil. Place the chiles and garlic on the foil and heat over medium-high heat, turning as necessary to brown evenly, until fragrant and toasted. The chiles will soften and darken a few shades and begin to smell like chocolate and raisins. The garlic will blister and the peel will blacken. Set the garlic aside to cool, then peel. Transfer the chiles to a small bowl of water (use a plate or bowl, if necessary, to keep the chiles submerged). Soak the chiles for 20 minutes.

2. Meanwhile, place the garlic, vinegar, and honey in the bowl of a small food processor fitted with a metal blade. Pulse to combine. Remove the chiles from the water, stem, seed, coarsely chop, and add to the processor. Pulse to chop and then purée until the mixture forms a rough paste.

3. Add the mayonnaise to the processor and pulse to blend evenly, then transfer to a container and refrigerate until needed.

4. Meanwhile, make the venison patties. Gently combine the venison, salt and pepper to taste, cumin, marjoram, and Worcestershire sauce in a large bowl. Do not overwork the meat. Divide the meat into 4 equal portions and shape the meat into patties. Sear or grill the patties to the desired doneness (for a juicy burger, do not cook beyond medium-rare). Serve on toasted buns with lettuce, tomatoes, grilled onions if you like, and a generous slather of pasilla chile mayonnaise.

Ring the Dinner Bell

O n any given day there is, inevitably, a familiar question that must be answered: "What should we do for dinner?" Happily this part of the world—where great ingredients flourish and feisty flavors abound—provides plenty of inspiration.

Living in the land of Stetsons and big belt buckles, there has to be beef, of course. I serve fat ribeyes (with spicy and subtly sweet glazes) grilled over a wood fire, tender pot roast, and meatballs in chipotle tomato sauce. There are simmering pots of spicy chili, bubbling pans of enchiladas, crispy grilled quail, and juicy venison chops. When it comes to seasonings and aromatics, I reach for Mexican influences (fresh and dried chiles, annatto, oregano, and tomatillos) and cowboy flavors like coffee, whiskey, and beer. I use the herbs that thrive in my garden—rosemary, thyme, parsley, oregano, marjoram, and cilantro—and plenty of them.

Cooking in a land-locked region, I don't prepare as much seafood as I would in another locale. Since I love fish, whenever I go to the market, I pick up halibut, wild salmon, shrimp, or snapper from the Gulf if it's available.

Our corner of the Hill Country boasts great produce—heaven for a vegetable freak like me— so I rely on the best local crops ranging from cabbage to pecans. There are also chiles, spinach, leafy greens, sweet onions, figs, pears, and citrus fruits to inspire.

Whether you are feeding ravenous ranch hands, a rowdy bunch of friends, or simply making dinner for your family, I hope these recipes will inspire you to turn up the (Texas) music, and get cooking.

# Creamy Green Polenta

**Serves 6 to 8**

My local market is brimming with piles of Texas-grown greens. I sauté them and serve them as a simple side dish about once a week. When I want to give them a more sophisticated treatment for a first course or vegetarian dinner, I prepare this dish.

The greens make polenta more nutritious of course, but they also lighten the texture, add a sweet, earthy flavor, and make for a striking presentation. For the best results, use greens so dark they are almost black, like cavolo nero or organic kale.

I like to top the creamy green pool of polenta with strips of roasted yellow peppers and carrots, an additional dusting of Parmesan, and crumbled red chile.

> 6 cups coarsely chopped **GREENS**, such as cavolo nero, kale, collards, chard, or a combination, rinsed
>
> 4 **GARLIC CLOVES**
>
> **KOSHER SALT**
>
> 6 **PURPLE OR ORANGE CARROTS**, sliced into batons
>
> 2 **YELLOW BELL PEPPERS**, sliced into strips
>
> **OLIVE OIL**
>
> 1 cup good-quality **ITALIAN POLENTA**
>
> 2 fresh **BAY LEAVES**
>
> 1 cup **GRATED PARMESAN CHEESE**, plus more for garnish
>
> Freshly ground **BLACK PEPPER**
>
> 2 to 3 **PEQUÍN CHILES**, crumbled, or crushed **RED PEPPER FLAKES**

1. Bring a large pot of generously salted water to a boil. Blanch the greens and garlic cloves for 3 to 4 minutes (the greens will be slightly softened and bright emerald). Drain in a colander. Fish out the garlic cloves, transfer them to the bowl of an electric food processor, and pulse until coarsely chopped. When the greens are cool enough to handle, use your hands (or a clean dish towel) to squeeze out any excess moisture. Transfer the greens to the food processor and sprinkle with salt. Process until very smooth, about 2 to 3 minutes. Set aside until needed. (The greens can be puréed a day in advance, covered, and refrigerated.)

2. Preheat the oven to 400°F. Place the carrots and peppers on a baking sheet, drizzle with olive oil, and sprinkle with salt. Use your fingers to toss the vegetables until well coated with the seasonings and oil. Roast the vegetables for about 45 minutes, until tender and

caramelized, flipping with a spatula every 15 minutes or so for even browning. Cover with foil and keep warm in a low oven (place the serving plates in the oven as well).

3. While the vegetables are roasting, make the polenta. Bring 4 cups of salted water to a boil in a medium pot. Slowly whisk in the polenta. Reduce the heat, add the bay leaves, and cook, stirring often with a wooden spoon, until the polenta thickens considerably and begins to pull away from the sides of the pot, about 45 minutes. If the polenta gets too lumpy, use a whisk to smooth it out. If it gets too thick, add more water, as needed, to maintain a creamy texture. When the polenta is cooked, stir in the puréed greens and cook another 6 to 8 minutes, until heated through. Stir in the Parmesan and taste for seasoning, adding salt and pepper to taste. To serve, spoon a generous pool of the polenta onto a warmed plate. Top with equal portions of the roasted vegetables, an additional drizzle of olive oil, freshly grated Parmesan, and crumbled pequín chile or a pinch of crushed red pepper flakes.

# Gazpacho Risotto with Garlic Shrimp

**Serves 4**

In this light and clean-tasting risotto, the rice is cooked in cucumber and tomato juice, which gives the grains a fresh, summery flavor and a pretty pink hue. Roasting tomatoes and yellow peppers gives the dish a rich, smoky depth. Don't be alarmed by the number of jalapeños—they only add a minimal amount of heat. Quickly seared garlicky shrimp are the perfect finish, but this risotto is delicious enough to eat on its own. If you don't have sherry, use dry white wine instead.

12 **PLUM TOMATOES**, halved

**OLIVE OIL**

**KOSHER SALT**

1 pound medium **SHRIMP**, shelled and deveined

2 **GARLIC CLOVES**, minced

3 **YELLOW BELL PEPPERS**

8 large **CUCUMBERS**, peeled and cut into 2-inch chunks

1½ cups **TOMATO JUICE**

1 tablespoon **SHERRY WINE VINEGAR**

2 tablespoons **EXTRA VIRGIN OLIVE OIL**

6 **JALAPEÑO PEPPERS**, seeded and finely chopped

3 tablespoons minced **SHALLOTS** (or ½ red onion finely chopped)

⅛ teaspoon freshly ground **BLACK PEPPER**

1¾ cups **ARBORIO RICE**

½ cup **DRY SHERRY**

2 tablespoons **UNSALTED BUTTER**

¼ cup chopped **PARSLEY**

1. The night or morning before serving this risotto, preheat the oven to 200°F. Place the halved tomatoes, seed-pockets up, on a baking sheet. Drizzle the tomatoes with olive oil and sprinkle with salt. Roast in the oven for 8 hours, until the tomatoes are concentrated and meaty but not dry. If not using right away, place in a sealed plastic container and refrigerate until needed.

2. An hour before serving, toss the shrimp, garlic, a light sprinkling of salt, and a drizzle of olive oil in a medium bowl. Cover and refrigerate.

3. Place the yellow peppers directly on a burner and char over a gas flame, turning as necessary to blacken evenly on all sides. Alternatively, place the peppers on a baking sheet and broil, turning as necessary, until the skins blacken on all sides. Place the peppers in a bowl and cover with a towel to allow them to steam for at least 15 minutes. Using your fingers or a paring knife, peel and seed the peppers, cut into 1/4-inch dice, and reserve.

4. Using a food processor or blender, process the cucumbers until reduced to a smooth purée. Strain the purée through a fine-mesh strainer into a large bowl, stirring and pressing to extract as much juice as possible. Do this in batches if necessary. (An electric juicer makes quick work of this process.) Measure 6 cups cucumber juice (add extra tomato juice if you don't have enough). Combine the cucumber juice and tomato juice in a medium saucepan and bring to a boil; remove from the heat and reserve until needed.

5. Chop each roasted tomato half into 6 pieces. Combine them with the yellow peppers in a medium bowl and toss with the sherry wine vinegar.

6. Heat 1 tablespoon of the extra virgin olive oil in a small skillet over medium-high heat. When the pan is quite hot but not smoking, sauté the jalapeños, stirring constantly, until softened, about 3 minutes. In a 3-quart saucepan over medium-high heat, heat the remaining tablespoon of olive oil. Add the shallots, 1 teaspoon salt, and the black pepper and sauté 2 minutes, until the shallots are soft. Add the rice and stir about 2 minutes, until all the kernels are coated with oil.

7. Lower the heat to medium and add the sherry. Stir until the sherry is absorbed. Begin adding the cucumber-tomato juice, 1/2 cup at a time, stirring constantly. Allow each addition of juice to be absorbed before adding more. Continue until the risotto is creamy and the rice grains are al dente, 25 to 30 minutes.

8. Stir in the jalapeños, tomato-yellow pepper mixture, butter, and half of the parsley. Season to taste with salt and black pepper and cover the saucepan.

9. Heat a medium skillet over medium-high heat. When very hot but not smoking, add the shrimp and sauté, stirring, just until pink and cooked through, about 3 minutes.

10. Serve the risotto in warm shallow bowls, topped with equal portions of the seared shrimp and the remaining parsley.

**PONY EXPRESS:** If you don't have time to roast the tomatoes, use an equal portion of fresh tomatoes plus 2 tablespoons chopped sun-dried tomatoes marinated in olive oil.

# Wagon Wheels with Peas, Green Herbs, and Ricotta Salata

**Serves 6 to 8**

This dish, which can be assembled in the time it takes to boil pasta, is for herb lovers. It's a perfect spring or summer dinner paired with marinated tomatoes and a hearty salad topped with chopped walnuts, but it would also be great as a side dish alongside grilled salmon. Dill and cilantro aren't common partners, but their fresh, fragrant flavors are delicious together. This dish is particularly good if you splurge and use a really great extra virgin olive oil. Ricotta salata (which means "salted ricotta") is an aged ricotta, and one of my favorite cheeses. It can be grated or shaved like Parmesan but it has a creamier texture.

KOSHER or SEA SALT

1 pound WAGON WHEEL PASTA (also called "rotelle del carrello")

⅓ cup EXTRA VIRGIN OLIVE OIL

1 pound frozen PEAS

1 cup chopped fresh CILANTRO

⅓ cup chopped fresh DILL

Freshly ground BLACK PEPPER

6 to 8 ounces GRATED RICOTTA SALATA or PARMESAN

½ teaspoon PEQUÍN CHILE, finely crumbled, plus more as desired

1. Heat a large pot of water over medium-high heat until it comes to a boil. Add salt and pasta and cook according to package directions.

2. Meanwhile, place the olive oil in a large bowl. During the last minute of pasta cooking, add the frozen peas. Drain and briefly rinse with water. Add the hot pasta and peas to the bowl and toss well, until evenly coated with oil. Add the cilantro, dill, and salt and black pepper and toss again. Taste for seasoning and adjust as necessary. Serve immediately, topped with equal portions of grated cheese and crumbled pequín chile.

# Penne with Cilantro Pesto and Grilled Chicken

**Serves 6 to 8**

This feisty and full-flavored pesto relies on cilantro, mint, and pecans. The richness of the pecans plays nicely off the fresh herbs, garlic, and serrano chile. Cotija is Mexican Parmesan—an aged grating cheese with a salty, tangy flavor. If the pesto is too thick for your liking, thin it with a little hot cooking water from the pasta, which will help create a sauce. Grilled chicken and plenty of cherry tomatoes turn this salad into a warm-weather feast.

$1\frac{1}{2}$ cups chopped fresh **CILANTRO**, tender stems and leaves

$\frac{1}{2}$ cup chopped fresh **MINT**

$\frac{1}{2}$ cup **GRATED COTIJA CHEESE**

3 tablespoons toasted **PECAN HALVES**

1 teaspoon **KOSHER SALT**, with more for seasoning

2 **GARLIC CLOVES**

1 to 2 **SERRANO CHILES**, seeded and sliced

$\frac{1}{4}$ cup **EXTRA VIRGIN OLIVE OIL**

1 tablespoon **SHERRY WINE VINEGAR**

12 cups hot cooked **PENNE PASTA** (about 6 ounces uncooked)

2 cups **CHERRY TOMATOES**, halved

Two 6-ounce **CHICKEN BREASTS**, grilled and sliced

Freshly ground **BLACK PEPPER**

Place the cilantro, mint, Cotija, pecans, the 1 teaspoon salt, garlic, and serrano chiles in a food processor and process until well combined. With the processor on, slowly add the olive oil. Transfer the pesto to a large mixing bowl. Add the vinegar, hot pasta, tomatoes, and chicken and toss well. Taste for seasoning and add more salt and pepper as desired.

*F*or a quick appetizer or side dish, spread a few tablespoons of this pesto over halved tomatoes and broil until warm throughout.

# Gulf Seafood Stew

**Serves 8 to 10**

Prepare this fragrant stew while you simmer your fish stock–a satisfying and aromatic production. This is a much simpler version of bouillabaisse, but the flavors are deep and satisfying.

2 tablespoons **OLIVE OIL**

2 large **ONIONS**, chopped

1 large **LEEK**, thinly sliced

1 large **CELERY** stalk, finely chopped

1 large **CARROT**, finely chopped

1 medium **FENNEL BULB**, chopped

**KOSHER SALT**

2 **GARLIC CLOVES**

1 tablespoon chopped fresh **THYME LEAVES**

1 teaspoon chopped fresh **ROSEMARY**

1 teaspoon **FENNEL SEEDS**

$\frac{1}{2}$ teaspoon crushed **RED PEPPER FLAKES**

$\frac{1}{2}$ cup **DRY WHITE WINE**

One 28-ounce can **ITALIAN PLUM TOMATOES** with their juice

1 quart **FISH STOCK** (recipe follows)

2 fresh **BAY LEAVES**, torn

1 pound skinless **SNAPPER** or other meaty **WHITE FISH**, cut into 1-inch chunks

1 pound medium **SHRIMP** with heads, peeled and deveined (reserve heads and shells)

2 tablespoons **PERNOD**

Freshly ground **BLACK PEPPER**

Chopped fresh **FLAT-LEAF PARSLEY** and **FENNEL FRONDS**, for garnish

Heat the olive oil in a large soup pot or Dutch oven over medium-high heat. Add the onions, leek, celery, carrot, fennel, and a pinch of salt and cook, stirring, until softened, about 5 minutes. Add the garlic, thyme, rosemary, fennel seeds, and pepper flakes and cook another 2 minutes. Add the wine and deglaze the pan, scraping up any ingredients that might be sticking to the pot; simmer until the pan is almost dry. Add the tomatoes, fish stock, and bay leaves and simmer for 30 minutes. Just before serving, add the snapper, shrimp, and Pernod and simmer for another 5 to 10 minutes, just until the fish is cooked through. Taste for seasoning, adding more salt and black pepper as desired. Serve in warmed shallow bowls, garnished with chopped parsley and fennel fronds, with plenty of crusty bread on the side.

# Fish Stock

**Makes about 8 cups**

Shells and heads (if possible) from 1 pound **SHRIMP**
2 tablespoons **OLIVE OIL**
Head and bones from 2 **SNAPPER** (or other white fish)
1 bottle **DRY WHITE WINE**
1 **ONION**, diced
1 large **CELERY STALK**, chopped
2 **BAY LEAVES**, preferably fresh
3 **PARSLEY STEMS**
Three 1-inch-wide strips **ORANGE PEEL**

Preheat the oven to 350°F. Place the shrimp shells on a baking sheet and toss with the olive oil. Roast the shells for 3 to 4 minutes, until they crisp up and turn pink. Transfer the shells to a large stockpot. Add the fish head and bones, white wine, 6 cups water, the onion, celery, bay leaves, parsley, and orange peel. Bring to a boil, reduce the heat, and simmer for 1 hour. Strain the stock and use as needed; freeze any leftovers for another use.

# Wild Salmon with Beets and Citrus

**Serves 4**

When I buy salmon, I splurge on the best quality wild salmon from Alaska. I love its clean, watermelonlike flavor and rich orange color. In this striking and brightly flavored dish, a pretty combination of beets and citrus segments provides an acidic balance to the richness of the fish. Roasting salmon gently over moderate heat results in a particularly supple texture.

Four 6- to 8-ounce **WILD SALMON FILLETS**
4 tablespoons **OLIVE OIL**
**KOSHER SALT**
Freshly ground **BLACK PEPPER**

2 roasted **BEETS** (see roasting beets, page 54), thinly sliced into half-moons
1 **VALLEY** (or Meyer) **LEMON**
1 **ORANGE**
1 **RUBY RED GRAPEFRUIT**
1 tablespoon **BALSAMIC VINEGAR**
2 tablespoons **CHIFFONADE OF BASIL**
Freshly ground **BLACK PEPPER**
2 **PEQUÍN CHILES**, crumbled, or a pinch of **CAYENNE PEPPER**
4 **SCALLIONS**, thinly sliced on the bias, for garnish

1. Preheat the oven to 300°F. Rinse salmon fillets and pat dry. Brush lightly with 1 tablespoon of olive oil, then season with salt and black pepper to taste. Set aside.

2. Place the beets in a medium bowl. Using a sharp knife, slice the ends and peel the lemon, orange, and grapefruit, then cut each fruit into segments. Allow the segments and any juice to fall into the bowl with the beets. Add the remaining oil, vinegar, and a sprinkle of salt and toss to combine. Add the basil, toss again, and taste for balance, adding salt, black pepper, or crumbled chile to taste; set aside to marinate while the salmon cooks.

3. Bake the salmon until just cooked through, about 20 minutes. Serve each piece topped with a spoonful of beets and a scattering of scallions.

# Halibut with Salsa Verde

**Serves 4, with leftover sauce**

When my herb garden took off, Italian-style salsa verde was one of the first things I wanted to make. Purists might object to the addition of cilantro and serrano, two of my Texas mainstays, but they add a complementary heat and perfume. It's not essential to use all the herbs in this recipe.

Salsa verde adds enormous charm to a seared fillet of snowy white fish, like halibut. It is also irresistible with slices of boiled and peeled Yukon gold potatoes; consider serving them alongside the fish or the next day with leftover sauce. The Salsa Verde can be made 1 day ahead and chilled, covered.

Four 1-inch-thick **HALIBUT FILLETS**, 6 to 8 ounces each
**KOSHER SALT** and freshly ground **BLACK PEPPER**

**SALSA VERDE**

**Makes about 1 cup**

1 **GARLIC CLOVE**
½ teaspoon **KOSHER SALT**
1 **SERRANO CHILE**, stemmed, seeded, and chopped
4 **ANCHOVIES**, drained, patted dry, and minced
1 teaspoon **DIJON MUSTARD**
2 tablespoons **CAPERS**, rinsed
¼ cup thinly sliced **CORNICHONS**
2 tablespoons **RED WINE VINEGAR**
1 cup young **SPINACH, MÂCHE,** or **WATERCRESS** (leaves and tender stems)
½ cup finely chopped fresh **FLAT-LEAF PARSLEY**
3 tablespoons chopped fresh **CILANTRO**
3 tablespoons finely chopped fresh **MINT**
2 tablespoons chopped fresh **TARRAGON**
½ cup plus 2 tablespoons **EXTRA VIRGIN OLIVE OIL**
⅛ teaspoon freshly ground **BLACK PEPPER**

**1.** Generously season the halibut with salt and pepper. Set aside while you make the salsa verde.

**2.** Place the garlic, salt, chile, anchovies, mustard, capers, cornichons, and vinegar in the bowl of a food processor and pulse until the ingredients form a coarse paste. Add the spinach and herbs and pulse again until they are pulled into the other ingredients and coarsely chopped. With the motor running, add $\frac{1}{2}$ cup olive oil in a slow, steady stream. Scrape down the sides of the bowl as necessary. When the mixture is smooth, taste for seasoning and add salt and pepper as desired.

**3.** Just before serving, heat the remaining 2 tablespoons olive oil in a large nonstick skillet over medium-high heat and swirl to coat. When the pan is very hot but not smoking, sear the halibut until it's cooked through and flaky throughout, about 4 to $4\frac{1}{2}$ minutes on each side. Serve immediately with Salsa Verde on the side.

# Shrimp-Stuffed Poblanos with Walnut Sauce

**Serves 6**

This dish is a speedy take on chiles en nogada, a knockout dish consisting of a poblano chile stuffed with a spicy ground meat, fruit, and nut mixture, then drizzled with creamy walnut sauce and garnished with red pomegranate seeds to honor the colors of the Mexican flag. Order it whenever you find it on the menu of a good Mexican restaurant. Looking for a fetching way to serve a light sauté of fresh shrimp, I followed the same presentation, more or less. Though untraditional, the results are delicious. Serve with white rice (cooked with finely chopped carrot, perhaps), sliced avocados, lime, and cold beer.

6 large **POBLANOS**, for stuffing

3 tablespoons **OLIVE OIL**

1 cup **MEXICAN CREMA** or **SOUR CREAM**

½ cup fresh **BREAD CRUMBS**, toasted until golden brown

¾ cup coarsely chopped **WALNUTS** or **PECANS**

Pinch of ground **CINNAMON**

2 teaspoons **WALNUT OIL** (optional)

2 large **GARLIC CLOVES**, thinly sliced

1 small **RED ONION**, finely chopped

2 medium **TOMATOES**, chopped

2 tablespoons **TRIPLE SEC**

¼ teaspoon ground **CORIANDER**

1 teaspoon finely grated **ORANGE ZEST**

1 pound medium **SHRIMP**, peeled and deveined

½ bunch fresh **CILANTRO**, finely chopped

2 tablespoons chopped fresh **MINT**

1. Preheat the oven to 350°F. Roast the poblanos (see page 80) and remove the skins and seeds. Keeping the stem intact, slice a slit down the length of each chile. Use 1 tablespoon of olive oil to lightly grease a baking sheet. Place the poblanos on the sheet and set aside.

2. Purée the crema, bread crumbs, nuts, cinnamon, and walnut oil if using in a blender until very smooth. Pour the nut sauce into a small saucepan and keep warm over low heat.

3. Place the remaining olive oil and garlic slices in a large nonstick skillet and heat gently over medium-low heat. When the garlic slices turn golden brown and sizzle, remove with a slotted spoon and discard. Add the onion and cook, stirring, until softened, about 5 minutes. Add the tomatoes and triple sec and cook until the juices have reduced so that the skillet is almost dry. Add the coriander, zest, and shrimp and cook, stirring, until the shrimp are just barely cooked (they will finish cooking in the oven), about 3 minutes. Remove the shrimp from the heat and stir in the herbs; cool slightly.

4. Use a spoon to stuff the poblanos with equal portions of the shrimp filling. Place the stuffed poblanos in the oven and heat until just warmed through, about 10 minutes. Use a large spatula to carefully transfer the stuffed chiles to a plate. Pour the warmed nut sauce over the cooked chiles and serve immediately.

**PONY EXPRESS**: If you don't want to bother with stuffing all the peppers, simply roast, seed, and peel two of them and stir them into the shrimp sauté. Serve with warm corn tortillas and a drizzle of the creamy nut sauce.

# Rye-Crusted Snapper with Pink Tartar Sauce

**Serves 4**

Earthy rye bread crumbs, perfumed with a pinch of dried herbes de Provence, provide a crisp and tasty coating for snapper. To avoid masking the fresh flavor of the fish, I only coat one side of the fillet. I first got the idea for pink tartar sauce from my friend Jennifer Rubell, a hotelier from Miami, while we were sitting in one of her hotels in South Beach and brainstorming about food. Sharing her passion for all things pink, I've been making my own version ever since.

½ cup **ALL-PURPOSE FLOUR**

**KOSHER SALT** and freshly ground **BLACK PEPPER**

Pinch of **CAYENNE PEPPER**

1 extra large **EGG**

2 tablespoons **MILK**

¾ cup finely ground **RYE BREAD CRUMBS**

1 teaspoon **HERBES DE PROVENCE**

4 skinless fillets of fresh **SNAPPER** (or other white fish such as bass, grouper, or tilapia), about 6 ounces each

2 tablespoons **OLIVE OIL** (or grapeseed oil), for cooking

1. Use your fingers to combine the flour, salt and black pepper to taste, and cayenne on a plate or pie tin. In a wide, shallow bowl, use a fork to lightly beat the egg with the milk. On a separate plate or pie tin, combine the bread crumbs with the herbes de Provence. Dredge each fillet in the seasoned flour, shaking off the excess, then the egg wash, and then dredge one side in the bread crumbs. Set aside, bread-crumb-side down, on a clean plate or baking sheet. Repeat with the remaining fillets.

2. Just before serving, heat the oil in a large nonstick skillet over medium-high heat. When the pan is very hot but not smoking, sear the fish (2 fillets at a time), until golden brown (about 3 minutes on each side). Serve immediately with Pink Tartar Sauce (recipe follows).

# Pink Tartar Sauce

**Makes about 1¼ cups**

1 cup **MAYONNAISE**
1 **SHALLOT**, finely chopped
1 tablespoon **CAPERS**, rinsed
4 **CORNICHONS**, finely chopped
½ small cooked **BEET** (about ¼ cup), finely chopped
2 tablespoons chopped fresh **PARSLEY** (optional)
Pinch of **SALT** and freshly ground **BLACK PEPPER**

Combine all the ingredients in a small mixing bowl. The color of this sauce will intensify upon sitting. If you want to make it in advance, I'd suggest stirring in the beets about 10 minutes before serving.

# Grilled Chicken Thighs with David's Mop Sauce and Blistered Cherry Tomatoes

**Serves 4 to 6**

A grilled chicken breast is a grilled chicken breast, but a grilled thigh, especially a thigh grilled over the smoke of a wood fire, is a thing of beauty: rich, moist, and meaty. Traditionally mop sauces were used on whole sides of beef barbecued over coals in a large pit dug in the earth—they helped to break down the fat and keep the meat juicy. But mop sauces also enhance a shorter cooking process and simpler cuts, infusing the meat with an appealingly tart, savory flavor and keeping it moist.

Grilled thighs need little adornment, save a vegetable side dish and perhaps a fragrant rice pilaf. I love to serve them alongside cherry tomatoes that have been blistered in a hot skillet just long enough to make their inner juices a bit more sweet and jammy.

8 to 10 **SKINLESS, BONELESS CHICKEN THIGHS**, trimmed of excess fat

2 tablespoons **OLIVE OIL**

**KOSHER SALT**

Freshly ground **BLACK PEPPER**

3 tablespoons chopped fresh **ROSEMARY** or **THYME**, or a combination of both,
   plus 1 tablespoon chopped fresh **ROSEMARY**

1 pint **CHERRY TOMATOES** (you can also use grape or currant tomatoes)

**1.** Gently toss the chicken thighs with a tablespoon of oil, salt and pepper to taste, and the 3 tablespoons chopped rosemary or thyme until they are well coated, then lay them on a plate or baking sheet. Cover and chill until needed (this can be done up to 6 hours in advance). Pull the chicken from the fridge 30 minutes before cooking so it can come to room temperature. Prepare the grill: Preheat the gas grill to medium-high. Or build a wood or charcoal fire and let it burn down to coals. Spread the coals evenly under the grate, allowing the grate to heat up. Meanwhile, make the mop sauce (recipe follows).

**2.** To grill the meat, place on a hot grate over glowing coals or over a low gas flame. Close the grill cover. If using gas and you have a smoke box, fill it with wood shavings per instructions. The meat should be turned often—use tongs so as not to puncture the meat.

After each turn, mop the top of the meat with the sauce. The meat should cook 30 minutes or so, turning and mopping it every 5 minutes. Keep the grill covered in between. The meat should feel firm but not dry to the touch when done. If your grill has a thermometer, keep the temperature around 250°F. When the chicken is done, serve immediately or cover with foil and keep in a low oven.

**3.** While the chicken is cooking, blister the tomatoes. Heat the remaining tablespoon of oil in a large skillet over medium-high heat. Add the tomatoes, the remaining tablespoon of chopped rosemary, and a pinch of salt and cook, shaking the skillet, until the juice released from the tomatoes reduces just a bit, 4 to 5 minutes. Serve with the chicken thighs.

# David's Mop Sauce

**Makes about 2 cups**

> 2 cups **APPLE CIDER VINEGAR**
> 1 tablespoon **OLIVE OIL**
> 1/2 medium **ONION**, chopped
> 2 **GARLIC CLOVES**, sliced
> 1 **ROSEMARY SPRIG**
> 1 teaspoon **SALT**
> 1 tablespoon **WORCESTERSHIRE SAUCE**
> Several dashes of **CRYSTAL HOT SAUCE**

Combine the ingredients in a small saucepan and bring to a boil. Reduce the heat and simmer for 2 minutes. Remove from the heat.

# Braised Chicken with Annatto and Sweet Vegetables

### Serves 4 to 6, depending on the eaters

I rarely use pre-seasoned ingredients, but I was intrigued by the rust-colored bricks of annatto paste sold in the grocery store. The paste is made primarily from ground annatto seed, a spice popular in the Yucatán region of Mexico, but it's also flavored with vinegar and other seasonings. It gives food a one-of-a-kind earthy taste and a bright orange color (the prepared paste, which contains red dye, stains food even more).

Here I've combined the paste with a few brighter flavors to create a marinade (I call for chicken thighs but you can also use drumsticks). The meat is seared and then braised with aromatic vegetables like onions, carrots, and fennel.

If you can find actual annatto *seed*, try the variation below, which has a cleaner spice flavor. Serve this luscious braise with Carrot Cumin Pilaf (page 217), Arroz (Mucho) Verde (page 218), or a simple pilaf scented with a few bay leaves and cloves, to soak up the delicious juices. A last-minute hit of fresh lime juice really perks up the deep, earthy flavors—be sure to serve wedges as a garnish.

8 bone-in **CHICKEN THIGHS**, skin removed

**KOSHER SALT** and freshly ground **BLACK PEPPER**

1 brick (3.5 ounces) **ANNATTO SEED PASTE**

1 tablespoon **APPLE CIDER VINEGAR**

⅓ cup fresh **ORANGE JUICE** (1 medium orange)

3 tablespoons **OLIVE OIL**

1 large **SWEET ONION**, thinly sliced

1 **FENNEL BULB**, cored and thinly sliced

4 large **CARROTS**, sliced on the bias into 2-inch chunks

8 to 10 **GARLIC CLOVES**, peeled and smashed

1 to 2 **JALAPEÑO CHILES** (or 2 to 3 serranos), julienned

2 fresh **BAY LEAVES**, slightly torn to release the flavor

5 **THYME SPRIGS**

2 cups **CHICKEN STOCK**

**LIME WEDGES** for garnish

**FENNEL FRONDS**, for garnish (optional)

Special equipment: an ovenproof skillet or casserole with a tight-fitting lid

1. Trim the chicken thighs of excess fat and generously season with salt and pepper to taste. Crumble the annatto seed paste (it has the texture of packed brown sugar) into a large bowl. Add the vinegar, orange juice, and 1 tablespoon of olive oil and whisk until moist and fairly smooth. Add the chicken thighs and toss until evenly coated. Cover and marinate in the refrigerator for at least 4 hours, or preferably overnight.

2. Preheat the oven to 300°F. Remove the chicken thighs from the marinade, wiping off any excess, and pat dry with a paper towel (the thighs should still have a fairly thick—but not gloppy—coating of the marinade). Heat 1 tablespoon olive oil in a large nonstick skillet over medium-high heat. When the oil is very hot but not smoking, add the chicken thighs (in batches, if necessary, so you don't overcrowd the pan) and brown on all sides. Be sure to have a good plastic spatula on hand to check the thighs after a few minutes to ensure the marinade won't burn. You'll want to flip them more frequently than you normally do so the marinade doesn't get too dark. Add additional oil to the pan for the second batch, if necessary. If the pan gets too hot and there's a risk of the seed paste burning, splash a few tablespoons of water or apple cider vinegar into the pan to deglaze it.

3. Transfer the chicken to a baking dish big enough to just fit the 8 thighs on a single level. Add the remaining tablespoon of olive oil to the skillet and add the onion, fennel, and a pinch of salt and cook, stirring frequently and scraping up any brown bits, until softened, about 5 minutes. Add the carrots, garlic, jalapeño, bay leaves, and thyme sprigs and cook, stirring, for another 5 minutes, until all the vegetables have picked up some of the annatto oil and seasonings. Transfer the vegetables to the baking dish on top of and around the chicken thighs; add the chicken stock to the dish (the chicken should be half submerged in the stock). Cover the skillet, place in the oven, and cook for about 2 hours, gently turning the thighs every 30 minutes or so, until the chicken is tender and pulls away from the bone.

4. Remove the chicken from the oven and cool, covered, for an additional 30 minutes. Serve with hot rice and lime wedges. Garnish with fennel fronds, if desired.

**VARIATION: ANNATTO SEED MARINADE** Heat 2 tablespoons annatto seeds in $\frac{1}{4}$ cup olive oil until the oil is brick red, about 5 minutes. In another small, dry skillet, heat 1 teaspoon fennel seeds, 1 teaspoon cumin seeds, 1 teaspoon black peppercorns, and $\frac{1}{3}$ teaspoon cloves over medium heat until fragrant, about 3 minutes. Strain the annatto seed oil into a large bowl. Grind the annatto and other toasted spices in a coffee grinder. Add the spices to the annatto oil, along with the vinegar and orange juice. Generously season the chicken thighs with salt and pepper to taste, toss with the annatto marinade, and marinate and cook as described above.

# Chicken Sausage with Fennel, Leek, and Cabbage "Kraut"

**Serves 4 to 6**

The Hill Country was settled by German and Czech immigrants, and many of their food traditions, such as beer halls and Bohemian kolaches, are still prevalent. Great sausage is ubiquitous (you can buy smoked links wrapped in foil at many gas stations—I highly recommend them as a road snack). But a few of my local markets also carry great quality chicken sausage (flavored with anything from cilantro to jalapeños), which also appeals to my more health-conscious leanings. Since kraut and slaw are also staples of the area, and I frequently found myself driving past beautiful fields of cabbage, I was inspired to create a lighter kraut made with leeks and fennel to complement the more delicate sausage. Serve the hot grilled links and a big pile of this kraut with a dab of whole grain mustard on the side.

### FENNEL, LEEK, AND CABBAGE "KRAUT"

2 tablespoons **OLIVE OIL**

2 small (or 1 large) **LEEKS**, thinly sliced

1½ tablespoons **MUSTARD SEEDS**

1 small head **GREEN CABBAGE**, cored and thinly sliced

1 medium **FENNEL BULB**, thinly sliced

2 tablespoons **HONEY**

2 tablespoons **RED, WHITE,** or **CHAMPAGNE WINE VINEGAR**

½ cup **RIESLING** (or other dry white wine)

**KOSHER SALT** and freshly ground **BLACK PEPPER**

3 tablespoons chopped fresh **PARSLEY**

6 good-quality **CHICKEN SAUSAGES**

**WHOLE GRAIN MUSTARD**

1. Heat the oil in a large skillet over medium-high heat. Add the leeks and cook, stirring, until softened, about 5 minutes. Add the mustard seeds, cabbage, and fennel and cook over medium-high heat until the vegetables have wilted, about 5 to 7 minutes. Add the honey, vinegar, and Riesling and sauté until the liquid has thickened into a glaze. Season to taste with salt and pepper. Add the parsley and toss to combine.

2. To serve, grill or pan sear the sausages until charred and just cooked through. Serve the sausages with the slaw and a dollop of whole grain mustard on the side.

# Enchiladas Verdes

**Serves 8**

Traditional enchildas verdes, or enchiladas in a tangy green sauce, can be a bit heavy. The corn tortillas are fried in oil, and the chicken filling relies on sour cream and plenty of cheese. This version is lighter and fresher, yet just as satisfying.

This recipe makes a generous batch, perfect for entertaining. But even if you're not throwing a party you'll be happy for the leftovers—David says the best part about enchiladas is heating them for breakfast the next day. You can bake these enchiladas in individual gratins, which make for the prettiest presentation, or a larger baking dish. Serve them with Shiner Bock pintos or black beans (page 210) and/or Arroz (Mucho) Verde (page 218).

## SALSA VERDE

**Makes about 5½ cups**

2 pounds (about 16) **TOMATILLOS**, peeled and rinsed

2 to 4 **SERRANO CHILES**, stemmed (not seeded)

1 medium **ONION**, chopped

3 to 4 **GARLIC CLOVES**, as desired

½ cup chopped fresh **CILANTRO**

¼ cup coarsely chopped fresh **MINT**

2 tablespoons coarsely chopped fresh **TARRAGON**

1 teaspoon **KOSHER SALT**

1 tablespoon **OLIVE OIL**

1½ cups **CHICKEN STOCK**

## CHICKEN FILLING

**OLIVE OIL**, for coating baking dish(es)

4 cups shredded **CHICKEN** (from 3 poached breast halves)

1 medium **ONION**, finely chopped

6 ounces crumbled **GOAT CHEESE**

½ cup plain low-fat **YOGURT**

¾ teaspoon **KOSHER SALT**

¼ teaspoon freshly ground **BLACK PEPPER**

20 small fresh **CORN TORTILLAS** (maseca tortillas, if possible)

¾ cup **GRATED COTIJA** or other **WHITE CHEESE**

1. Bring a medium saucepan of water to a boil. Add the tomatillos and simmer until they turn a drab green color, about 6 minutes. Drain and cool slightly, and trim any long and wiry stems, if necessary. Transfer the tomatillos to a blender and add the serranos, onion, garlic, cilantro, mint, tarragon, and salt. Purée until smooth. Taste and adjust the salt as desired.

2. Heat 1 tablespoon of olive oil over medium heat in a large skillet. When hot but not smoking, carefully add the tomatillo sauce (it will spit and splatter). Reduce the heat and cook, stirring constantly, for 2 to 3 minutes. Add the chicken stock and simmer until the sauce is slightly reduced, about 15 minutes.

3. Meanwhile, make the chicken filling. Heat the oven to 350°F. Lightly coat individual baking dishes (or a 13 × 9-inch dish) with olive oil and a thin layer of salsa verde. If using individual dishes, place them on a baking sheet.

4. In a medium bowl, combine the shredded chicken, onion, goat cheese, yogurt, salt, and pepper.

5. To toast the tortillas, heat them on both sides over a gas flame (or in a hot, dry skillet), until softened and fragrant (the tortillas heated over a flame will blister slightly).

6. Dip each tortilla in the green sauce to coat lightly. Place the tortillas on a work surface in front of you and top with a generous 2 tablespoons of chicken filling. Roll into a snug cylinder and place in the prepared baking dish, seam-side down. Repeat with the remaining tortillas and filling, forming an additional row if necessary. Ladle the green sauce generously over the top of the enchiladas. Top with grated Cotija and bake 35 minutes, until heated through and the cheese is bubbly.

VARIATION: SPINACH AND ARTICHOKES I love adding either spinach or artichoke hearts to the chicken filling. To do this, add 1 pound fresh spinach (blanched and squeezed dry or briefly sautéed in olive oil), a 10-ounce box of frozen spinach (thawed and squeezed dry of excess moisture), or a 10-box of frozen artichoke hearts. To prepare the artichokes, thaw them and sauté in 1 teaspoon olive oil over medium-high heat for 3 to 4 minutes. Coarsely chop and add to the chicken.

## POACHING CHICKEN BREASTS

*T*his is the standard technique I use to poach breasts for chicken salad. Without fail, they are moist and juicy every time. The key is to poach them over a very gentle simmer and allow them to cool for as long as possible in the stock.

Rinse 3 half bone-in chicken breasts to remove any sticky film, and pull off excess strings of fat. Fill a large pot or Dutch oven with water. Add a chopped onion, a celery stalk, and a carrot, along with a tablespoon of salt, a few peppercorns, and a bay leaf. Bring to a boil and add the chicken breasts and a tablespoon of dried Mexican oregano. Return to a boil, reduce the heat to low, and simmer for 15 minutes. Cover the pot, remove from the heat, and allow the chicken breasts to cool for up to two hours in the stock (I often do this step the day before), then refrigerate if not using immediately. When you're ready to use the chicken, remove it from the stock, peel off the skin, and remove the meat from the bones. Use a fork to shred the meat. Strain the stock and refrigerate up to three days, or freeze.

# Cornish Hens with Wild Rice and Pecan Stuffing

**Serves 4**

Cornish hens are plump, meaty little birds that crisp up nicely and are the perfect serving size–split one in half for two, or serve a whole bird to one good eater. This wild rice stuffing is earthy with mushrooms and nuts and fresh tasting with herbs and citrus. Be sure to bake any stuffing that doesn't fit into the birds separately in a covered dish with a little extra chicken stock.

If you have a good-size herb garden, consider roasting the hens atop several thyme branches.

2 **CORNISH HENS**, rinsed and patted dry

4 tablespoons **OLIVE OIL**

**KOSHER SALT**

Freshly ground **BLACK PEPPER**

1 tablespoon fresh **THYME LEAVES**, or 1 teaspoon **DRIED THYME** or **HERBES DE PROVENCE**

### RICE STUFFING

1 small **LEEK**, thinly sliced

1 **CELERY STALK** (including leaves, if nice), finely chopped

1 **GARLIC CLOVE**, finely chopped

6 **SCALLIONS**, minced

1 **SERRANO**, stemmed and sliced into thin half-moons (trim out the seeds for less heat)

$\frac{1}{4}$ cup **DRY WHITE WINE**

8 ounces **CREMINI MUSHROOMS**

1 cup cooked **WILD RICE** (about $\frac{1}{2}$ cup uncooked)

2 teaspoons finely grated **ORANGE ZEST**

2 teaspoons chopped fresh **TARRAGON** (or parsley or basil)

$\frac{1}{2}$ cup coarsely chopped **TOASTED PECANS**

$\frac{1}{2}$ cup **CHICKEN STOCK** or **WHITE WINE**

1. Preheat the oven to 375°F.

2. Rinse the hens and pat dry with paper towels. Drizzle both birds with just enough olive oil to coat lightly (about 1 tablespoon total). Sprinkle with salt, pepper, and thyme and use your fingers to distribute the oil and seasonings. Place the birds in a small baking dish and set aside.

3. Heat 2 tablespoons oil in a large skillet over medium-high heat. Add the leek and celery and a pinch of salt and sauté about 5 minutes, until softened. Add the garlic, scallions, and serrano and sauté another 3 minutes. Add the white wine and simmer, scraping up any browned bits, until the pan is almost dry. In a separate medium skillet, heat 1 tablespoon oil over medium-high heat. When the pan is hot but not smoking, add the mushrooms and a pinch of salt. Sauté for 3 to 4 minutes, stirring or shaking the skillet to flip the mushrooms, until they are crisp and evenly browned. Add the mushrooms to the celery–leek mixture. Remove from the heat and add the rice, zest, tarragon, and pecans. Season with salt and pepper to taste.

4. Spoon the stuffing into the hens, filling the cavity but not packing it too tightly. Place any additional stuffing in a greased baking dish with a little chicken stock. Pour the chicken stock or wine into the pan and roast the hens for about 45 minutes, basting them with pan juices 3 or 4 times, until golden brown and the juices run clear when the inner thigh is pierced with a paring knife. Allow to rest for 10 minutes before serving. To serve, split the hens in half and divide the stuffing among the plates.

# Smoky Red Hens

**Serves 4**

When Robb Walsh, a funny and talented Texas food writer friend, called and said he was tooling around South Texas, letting himself through ranch gates in the hopes of finding good ranch cooks, I tried to hide my concern and told him to swing by for dinner. Since Robb is a macho sort of guy who likes big flavors, I quickly thought of smoked hens rubbed with bold red spices like ground ancho, chipotle chile, and paprika. I add a bit of sugar to the rub, which acts like salt as a seasoning, coaxing a little extra flavor from the meat. You can season these hens early in the day and cook them for dinner, but the flavors will be deeper if you can marinate them overnight.

I love these hens split and slow grilled over a wood fire or coals so they absorb the smoke, but they also are delicious left whole and roasted in the oven. Leftovers might be even better, eaten cold with blanched green beans, mayo spiked with lemon zest, and crusty bread (perfect picnic fare). I served Robb these hens alongside Greens with Red Chile Sauce (page 229), but they're also delicious with Carrot Cumin Pilaf (page 217) and a simple green salad. For dessert, consider ice cream and your favorite chewy gingersnap recipe spiked with $\frac{1}{4}$ teaspoon cayenne pepper.

2 **CORNISH HENS**

1 tablespoon ground **ANCHO CHILE**

1 tablespoon **CUMIN**

2 teaspoons **PAPRIKA**

1 teaspoon ground **CHIPOTLE CHILE**

1 tablespoon **KOSHER SALT**

$\frac{1}{2}$ teaspoon freshly ground **BLACK PEPPER**

$\frac{1}{4}$ teaspoon **ALLSPICE**

1 teaspoon **SUGAR**

2 tablespoons **OLIVE OIL**

4 fresh **BAY LEAVES**

5 or 6 **THYME SPRIGS**

1 small **ONION**, quartered

1 small **ORANGE**, quartered

4 **GARLIC CLOVES**, unpeeled

**1.** Rinse the hens under cold water and pat dry with paper towels. If you are smoking the hens, use a chef's knife to split them in half. If you are roasting them in the oven, leave them whole. Combine the spices and the sugar in a small bowl. Place the hens in a large bowl, drizzle with oil, and sprinkle with the spices. Rub the spices all over the skin and inside the cavity. Gently slip your fingers under the skin of the breast and spice the flesh of the bird as well. The oil will pick up the spices and create a red paste. Roll the hens in the bowl to coat them with as much of the paste as possible.

**2.** Add the bay leaves and thyme sprigs to the bowl, tucking them under the hens. Cover the bowl and marinate at least 4 hours or overnight, turning occasionally.

**3.** To smoke the birds, heat a gas grill to medium-high or light a wood or charcoal fire and burn until the coals or wood are covered with gray ash and very hot. When the grill is ready, either turn the burners in the center to medium-low or bank the coals or wood to the sides for indirect cooking. For the charcoal grill, set the grill grate in place. Place the hen halves on the grill, close the cover, and cook for 2 to 2½ hours, until the juices run clear when a hen's inner thigh is pierced with a knife. If your grill has a thermometer, you will need to add more coals or wood as necessary to keep the temperature between 250°F and 300°F.

**4.** To roast the hens in the oven, take them out of the fridge 30 minutes before cooking to allow them to come to room temperature. Tuck the bay leaves, thyme, onion, orange, and garlic inside the cavity of each bird. Preheat the oven to 425°F. Place the hens in a roasting pan (scraping any marinade from the bottom of the bowl over the hens and onto the pan) and roast for 30 minutes. Reduce the temperature to 375°F and roast another 30 minutes, basting occasionally. The hens are done when the juices run clear when a hen's inner thigh is pierced with a knife.

**5.** Remove the hens from the oven and cover loosely with foil. Cool for 15 minutes. Use a chef's knife to split the hens in half. Remove the filling from the cavity and discard. Serve the hens immediately.

# Canyon Cotechino

**Serves 6 to 8**

Cotechino is a fresh pork sausage that's a specialty of the Emilia-Romagna region of Italy. It's made with various rich cuts, and most often served with lentils from the same region. I've always loved the earthy combination of sausage and lentils—the way the fat from the sausage makes the lentils creamier and more savory. At the ranch I make a quick Hill Country version of this dish with black beluga lentils (so named because they resemble caviar), and a wonderful smoked venison sausage from nearby Broken Arrow Ranch. Beluga lentils create a particularly rich broth, but you can also use green or brown varieties. The smoked sausage is already cooked, but I sear it to crisp up the edges and create a deeper "browned" flavor when they're simmered with the lentils for the last few minutes of cooking. This is a hearty and rustic one-pot meal to savor on a cold evening when the winds are howling outside. Serve it with a big green salad and a full-bodied red wine.

$1\frac{1}{2}$ cups **BELUGA LENTILS**

3 tablespoons **OLIVE OIL**

1 medium **ONION**, finely chopped

**KOSHER SALT**

2 **GARLIC CLOVES**, finely chopped

$\frac{1}{2}$ small **ONION**

2 whole **CLOVES**

2 fresh **BAY LEAVES**, torn

$\frac{1}{4}$ cup **RED WINE**

Freshly ground **BLACK PEPPER**

2 pounds **SMOKED VENISON SAUSAGE** (see page 97) or other
   **SMOKED SAUSAGE**

**HOT SAUCE** or **RED WINE VINEGAR**

Chopped fresh **PARSLEY**, for garnish

1. Rinse the lentils and sort through to remove any small stones. Heat 2 tablespoons of olive oil in a medium saucepan or Dutch oven over medium-high heat. Add the chopped onion and a pinch of salt and cook, stirring, until softened, about 5 minutes. Add the garlic and cook another 2 minutes.

2. Stud the onion half with the cloves, pushing them through the outer skin toward the middle to help keep the onion layers intact, and add to the pot. Add the lentils, bay leaves, red wine, and 5 cups of water. Bring the mixture to a boil, then reduce the heat and simmer, stirring occasionally, until the lentils are tender, about 20 to 25 minutes. Remove

the clove-studded onion and bay leaves. Taste for seasoning and add salt and pepper as needed.

3. Meanwhile, slice the sausages into 2-inch lengths. Heat the remaining oil in a medium skillet over medium-high heat. Sear the sausages until browned and crispy. Transfer the sausages to the lentil mixture and stir to combine. Simmer for 5 minutes. Taste for balance and add salt, pepper, or a splash of hot sauce or red wine vinegar as desired. Serve in warm shallow bowls garnished with chopped parsley.

NOTE: Feel free to add 1 to 2 cups chopped tomatoes (fresh or canned) to the lentils after they have simmered for about 15 minutes. (Don't add the tomatoes at the beginning of the cooking process, their acid will inhibit the lentils from softening.)

# Mustard and Molasses–Marinated Quail

**Serves 4 good eaters**

Quail and dove hunts are big events in South Texas. The meat rivals chicken in popularity at backyard barbecues, so my local meat market is well stocked with flavorful, partially boned farm-raised birds that are easy to cook. The most classic local preparation is to stuff the quail with jalapeño and wrap it with bacon—who can argue with that? My version is perked up with herbs, good olive oil and vinegar, and a hint of spice. Dredging the quail in cornmeal before grilling gives them a wonderfully crisp crust. I like to serve these crispy birds on a big salad made with arugula, watercress, or other peppery greens.

8 partially boned **QUAIL**, breastbone removed
**KOSHER SALT**
Freshly ground **BLACK PEPPER**
3 tablespoons **CREOLE MUSTARD**
¼ cup **MOLASSES**
3 tablespoons **SHERRY WINE VINEGAR**
½ cup **OLIVE OIL**
1 tablespoon **WORCESTERSHIRE SAUCE**
1 tablespoon chopped fresh **THYME LEAVES**
2 **GARLIC CLOVES**, finely chopped
2 to 3 **PEQUÍN CHILES**, crumbled, or a generous pinch of **CAYENNE PEPPER**
½ cup finely ground **YELLOW CORNMEAL** or **POLENTA**

1. Rinse the quail and use a paper towel to pat dry. Generously season the quail, inside and out, with salt and pepper and set aside. In a medium bowl, whisk together the mustard, molasses, vinegar, oil, Worcestershire, thyme, garlic, and chiles. Place the quail in a baking dish or sealable plastic bag and combine with the marinade, tossing to combine. Use your fingers to ensure the inside cavity of the quail gets coated with the marinade. Cover the quail and marinate for at least 1 hour, or up to 8 hours.

2. An hour before serving, prepare the grill. A half hour before serving, take the quail from the fridge so they can come to room temperature. Remove the quail from the marinade, allowing the excess liquid to run off, and dredge in cornmeal. When the grill is hot, grill until crispy on both sides and cooked through, about 10 minutes total. Turn the quail every 2 to 3 minutes. Serve immediately, or place the quail in a baking pan, cover with foil, and keep warm in a low oven.

# Cornmeal-Crusted Quail with Fig-Rosemary Skewers

**Serves 4 good eaters**

One day I got to thinking about some squab I'd eaten in Tuscany that had been roasted on a bed of sturdy thyme branches. The herb flavor really perfumed the rich meat. I had a surplus of herbs from my garden, and lo and behold, this recipe was born.

Sweet, luscious figs complement both the quail and the herbs. Brushing the figs with olive oil and fig vinegar before they're grilled is a nice way to deepen the fruit flavor. However, regular balsamic will work just fine.

This preparation is easier if you have plenty of herbs on hand—and the ability to snip longer branches of rosemary. But it would still be delicious if you stuffed the quail with just one or two herbs, or even rubbed them with dried herbes de Provence and saved the rosemary for the beautiful, show-stealing skewers. The grilled quail are beautiful served on a platter alongside the fig skewers. Serve them with a salad of mixed baby greens, scallions, and goat cheese.

8 partially boned **QUAIL**

**KOSHER SALT**

Freshly ground **BLACK PEPPER**

1/3 cup **OLIVE OIL**, plus more for basting the figs

2 tablespoons **FIG** or **BALSAMIC VINEGAR**, plus more for basting the figs

4 tablespoons chopped fresh **ROSEMARY** (using leaves discarded from skewers)

8 **THYME SPRIGS**

8 fresh **BAY LEAVES**

Four 8- to 10-inch sturdy **ROSEMARY SPRIGS**

12 ripe **FIGS**

1/2 cup **YELLOW CORNMEAL** or **POLENTA**

1. Rinse the quail and pat dry with paper towels. Place the quail in a large baking dish (big enough to hold them in a single layer) and generously season to taste with salt and pepper. In a small bowl, whisk together the oil, vinegar, and chopped rosemary and drizzle over the birds. Use your fingers to rub the oil inside the cavity of each bird. Stuff each quail with 1 thyme sprig and 1 bay leaf. Cover the quail and marinate for at least 2 hours

or up to 8 hours (occasionally basting the birds with the marinade that pools in the bottom of the dish).

**2.** An hour before serving, prepare the grill. About 30 minutes before serving, pull the quail from the fridge to allow them to come to room temperature. Meanwhile, strip all but 1 to 2 inches of rosemary leaves from the 4 branches. Use the branch to skewer 3 figs each. Set the skewers on a plate and brush with additional oil and fig vinegar.

**3.** Before removing a quail from the dish, roll it in the oil so it is evenly moist. Dredge the quail in the cornmeal and place on a baking sheet. Repeat the process with the remaining quail, adding more cornmeal if necessary. When the grill is hot, grill the quail until crispy on both sides and cooked through, about 10 minutes total. Turn the quail every 2 to 3 minutes. Place the fig skewers on the grill during the last 5 minutes of cooking and grill until the figs soften and char, turning them once or twice for even cooking. Serve immediately, or place the quail in a baking pan, cover with foil, and keep warm in a low oven.

# Seared Axis Chops with Cool Canyon Herbs and Crema Grits

**Serves 4**

Meats are often best seasoned with the flavors that flourish around them. So when I think of perfuming axis chops (my favorite variety of venison because the meat is rich, tender, and finely textured), I gravitate to juniper and rosemary, the cool, piney flavors that I hike through each day. As a vehicle for the herbs, I make a paste with shallots and grapeseed oil. When seared in a hot skillet, the shallots crust the meat with a sweet, toasted flavor. I deglaze the skillet with Riesling, which lights up the herbs and reduces to an aromatic pan sauce. I love to drag a forkful of the herbaceous meat through stone-ground grits, their pleasingly coarse texture softened by thick, tangy Mexican crema. You can sear these chops immediately after you coat them with the fragrant paste, but the herbs will better permeate the meat if you chill them for several hours before cooking. Serve this dish with the same wine you use to make the sauce. As an alternative, consider serving the simply seared chops with Dried Cherry and Whiskey Sauce (recipe follows).

4 **VENISON** (preferably axis) **CHOPS**, about 1 inch thick

**KOSHER SALT**

Freshly ground **BLACK PEPPER**

2 tablespoons **JUNIPER BERRIES**, coarsely chopped

1 tablespoon plus 1 teaspoon chopped fresh **ROSEMARY** (about a 6-inch sprig)

2 medium **SHALLOTS**, coarsely chopped

1 teaspoon plus 1 tablespoon **GRAPESEED OIL**

1 cup good-quality stone-ground **GRITS**

2 fresh **BAY LEAVES**

$\frac{1}{4}$ cup **MEXICAN CREMA** (or sour cream or crème fraîche)

$\frac{1}{2}$ cup **RIESLING** or other **WHITE WINE**

1. Generously season the chops with salt and pepper and set aside. Place the juniper berries, rosemary, shallots, and 1 teaspoon grapeseed oil in the bowl of a small food processor fitted with a metal blade. Process until the mixture forms a thick paste. (Alternately, this mixture can be puréed using a mortar and pestle.) Spread the paste evenly over the chops and set aside for at least 1 hour or refrigerate up to 8 hours. If you chill the chops, bring them to room temperature before cooking.

2. About an hour before you are ready to cook the chops, bring 4 cups of water to a boil in a medium saucepan. Whisk in the grits in a slow, steady stream. Switch to a wooden spoon and stir in $\frac{1}{2}$ teaspoon salt and the bay leaves. Simmer until the grits become thick and begin to pull together away from the sides of the pan, about 45 minutes. When the grits are cooked, stir in the crema and taste for seasoning, adding more salt and pepper as desired. Remove the bay leaves before serving.

3. Heat a large nonstick skillet over medium-high heat until hot but not smoking. Add the remaining tablespoon of grapeseed oil and swirl to coat. Add the chops to the skillet and sear until browned, about 4 minutes. Flip the chops and cook for another 3 minutes.

4. Transfer the chops to a warmed plate and cover with foil. Pour the Riesling into the skillet and scrape up any browned bits. Pour any juices that have drained from the chops back into the skillet. Simmer until the liquid is reduced to $\frac{1}{4}$ cup.

5. To serve, place a generous spoonful of grits on each plate, top with a seared chop, and drizzle with a few spoonfuls of the reduced wine. Garnish with a sprig of rosemary and a few juniper berries, if desired.

**DRIED CHERRY AND WHISKEY SAUCE** Season the venison chops with kosher salt, black pepper, and chopped fresh thyme, sear as directed above, and serve with this not-too-sweet sauce.

DRIED CHERRY AND WHISKEY SAUCE

2 large **SHALLOTS**, finely chopped

$\frac{1}{3}$ cup **DRIED TART CHERRIES**

1 cup **RED WINE**

1 cup **CHICKEN STOCK**

1 **STAR ANISE**

$\frac{1}{2}$ fresh **VANILLA BEAN**

2 teaspoons chopped fresh **THYME**, plus a **THYME SPRIG** for garnish (optional)

2 tablespoons **WHISKEY**

1 tablespoon **RED CURRANT JELLY**

1 tablespoon **BUTTER** (optional)

Bring shallots, cherries, red wine, stock, star anise, vanilla, and thyme to a boil in a small saucepan. Reduce the heat and simmer until the liquid is reduced to about $\frac{1}{4}$ cup. Whisk in the whiskey, jelly, and butter if using, and reduce a few more minutes. To serve, top a seared chop with a few spoonfuls of the sauce. Garnish with a sprig of thyme, if desired.

# Iowa Farmhouse Green Beans and Sausage

**Serves 4 to 6**

When I was a kid growing up in Muscatine, Iowa, my mom prepared this dish in the early summer when the green beans were perfect. Now, when David and I need something fast and hearty, and the grocery store (or farmers' market) green beans are firm and velvety, one of us says, "Let's have green beans and sausage!"

You can make this dish simply, with nothing more than your favorite ground pork sausage, green beans, and salt and black pepper. But it's awfully good if you add onion, garlic, and crushed red pepper flakes. Sometimes I'm inspired to throw in a diced bell pepper or chiffonade of fresh basil as well. Either way, serve it with sliced fresh tomatoes and—in honor of the mother state—ears of sweet corn.

1 pound **GREEN BEANS**, snipped at the stem end

8 ounces **GROUND PORK SAUSAGE**

1 tablespoon **OLIVE OIL**

1 large **ONION**, finely chopped

1 large **GARLIC CLOVE**, finely chopped

$\frac{1}{2}$ teaspoon crushed **RED PEPPER FLAKES**

3 teaspoons **CHIFFONADE OF BASIL**

**KOSHER SALT**

Freshly ground **BLACK PEPPER**

**1.** Bring a large pot of salted water to a boil. Add the green beans and cook until just tender, about 5 to 6 minutes. Drain in a colander and briefly rinse with cold water.

**2.** Meanwhile, heat the sausage in a large, deep skillet over medium-high heat, breaking it up with a wooden spoon as it cooks. When it is no longer pink, use a slotted spoon to remove it from the pan and transfer to a plate. Drain all but 1 tablespoon of fat from the skillet and return to the heat. Add the olive oil and onion and cook, stirring, until the onion has softened, about 5 minutes. Add the garlic and red pepper flakes and cook for 2 more minutes. Return the sausage to the skillet and add the green beans. Cook, stirring to combine well. Add the basil and salt and pepper to taste; serve immediately.

# CALF SCRAMBLE

*A*s newly appointed ranch manager, David was charged with the care of three pregnant cows. This was quite something for a professional bread baker who had discreetly been a vegetarian for nine years. The first calf was due in February, a month after our arrival.

The cows were registered Red Angus, the beginning of a breeding stock that belonged to Carlos Detering. It was an experiment, really. His father, Carl, figured he would teach his son how easy it is to lose money in the cattle business. The breed was chosen because they calved easily and were gentler than most. The easy calving was a relief. David was not ready to roll up his sleeves and lube up—that would come later.

As the due date approached, David watched for the telltale signs of an imminent delivery. The heifer would "bag out," meaning that her udder would become engorged and her vulva would swell and secrete a sticky liquid.

One of the most important details, we were told, was to record each calf's weight. Lower birth weights were actually a selling point—it made the cow more desirable because it suggested easier calving. For accuracy, the calf needed to be weighed within twelve hours of being born.

On the cold morning that the ready-to-pop cow didn't come in for breakfast, David suspected what had happened. Just before birthing, the cow tends to seek out a private, sheltered spot, such as a cluster of mountain laurel or cedar trees. He hopped on the Mule, a Kawasaki ATV, went on a search, and found the mother and calf, curled under a tree, still slick with afterbirth. He raced to find me so I could see it too. We called Carlos and told him to pass out cigars.

Moments like these made me realize how much closer I was to the cycle of life and death out here than I was in the city. In New York, people were born and died all around me, of course. But since I was cloistered in my own world, the details had less impact and I never got my hands dirty. The highs and lows of ranch life, I would learn, were extreme. It didn't get any better than seeing a dewy, blinking calf, kid goat, foal, or baby donkey rise for the first time on wobbly, uncertain legs.

There are smart ways to weigh a calf, but we hadn't learned them yet. And David was too proud to ask George how to do *everything*. So when the first one was born, we simply took a small bathroom scale to the wide-open pasture. The sooner we could get there, the better—with each hour, the calf was more agile and able to run away. We approached the new mother slowly and respectfully, but she was in no mood for visitors. She eyed us suspiciously, and started pawing the ground and bawling. The tawny calf was still slick, now neatly groomed by its mother's tongue. The calf regarded us, blinking its big brown eyes and long, thick lashes.

David explained the plan. He would weigh himself, pick up the calf, then step on the scale and

subtract his weight. I was to help him step on the scale, since the scrambling calf would most certainly hinder visibility and keep the mother at bay.

We walked the cows through the pasture until they were backed into a corner. I stood in front of the mother, raised my arms to shoo her, and said, "Hurry." David lunged a few times before he was able to get a good hold of the calf and scoop her up. The calf bawled and the mother bellowed. I scooted the scale in front of his boots. He stepped on and was able to hold just a second ("Got it!" I shouted) before the calf started flailing and he stumbled back. The eighty-four-pound baby, having tolerated the first stressful moment of its life, raced back to the teat.

When the second calf was born a few weeks later, David's arm was in a sling. He'd fractured his shoulder when he had fallen from a horse. Needless to say, he was in no position to hoist a calf, so I got the job.

This time, we had a narrower window. We needed to weigh the calf before dark and dinner service, or we'd miss the twelve-hour deadline. I changed into a nylon parka that I wouldn't mind slicking with mud and manure, and we returned to the pasture with the scale. I started psyching myself right away. "Oh, great," I said, "my calf looks friskier—she'll be harder to catch." Each mother cow had her own parenting style, and I convinced myself that this one was more aggressive. We herded the cows on foot, approaching from separate directions to work them toward the front gate. David moved in front of the agitated mother. I approached the calf, who regarded me with big, wary eyes. I wanted to grab her at just the right moment and make the transaction as efficient as possible. But I'd never handled a newborn calf, and grace was not coming easily. Time and again, I would hesitate and miss my chance. The calf would panic, slip through my fingers, and race back to her mother. They'd both run off and we'd have to start again, masking growing anxiety with slow, steady movements.

The tension provided the perfect opportunity for David and me to start fighting. I'd hear the cow snort and scratch the dirt and yell, "David!"

"I'm watching her!" he'd snap back. "You're *fine*."

But really, what did he know? Just because the first cow didn't charge, we didn't know this one wouldn't. I considered the montage. There would be a sudden commotion, a warning scream, and then I'd be trampled by a 1200-pound beast. It would be a freak accident, the breaking story on the ten o'clock news: "City slicker meets demise in ranch tragedy," the anchor would report with gravitas. In an interview, Carl Detering would shrug and say, "It's a shame. Those cows were supposed to be gentle."

Growing weary from the chase, the calf sat down by a tree, tucking her long, spindly legs under her stout body. Talking in my sweetest voice, I approached her slowly. I tried to ignore the snorts and bawls coming from behind my back. I placed a hand on her neck, squatted down, and wrapped my arms around her sides. Her coat was coarse and moist. The calf scrambled onto her hooves and I pulled her against me. I slipped my arms around her legs and tried to stand, but my positioning was off and I stumbled. Breathing hard, I set her back down and held on tight. "Damn," I said, "she's heavy." I tried again but the calf flailed. I tried again but couldn't hold my balance on the scale.

I expected the calf to be 80 to 100 pounds. From my gym days, I knew I could lift that much. But it was becoming very clear that hoisting a barbell is entirely different than squatting down, getting your arms under a frantic calf, and then standing back up.

"Did you weigh yourself first?" David asked.

"Yes, I did," I snapped. As if the process wasn't humiliating enough.

I was on the verge of giving up, but the tomboy in me didn't want to buckle under the challenge. "One more time," I said. "I'm going to get it." I still had a hold on the calf. Determined, I slid my arms under her, and with all my strength scooped her up and stood. My legs wobbled, then steadied. Feeling that I had a secure grip, the calf relaxed and went limp. It was strangely satisfying to hold her. For this moment, I marveled, I am suspending this calf above the earth. David scooted the scale in front of me. I felt it with my toe and climbed on top.

"Got it!" David said, announcing an impressive number.

I set the calf down. She didn't run. Then I got to do what I'd wanted all along—I petted her. I scratched her ears, the top of her head, ran my fingers along her spine. Satisfied, I backed away and the calf scampered back to its mother.

"Good job," David said.

"Thanks," I answered. We secured the metal gate behind us and headed up to the lodge to clean up and make dinner. "So the calf weighs ninety-three pounds," I said proudly.

A moment later, David quietly added, "Then I know how much you weigh."

"Don't push it," I shot back.

By the time the next round of calves was born, David had become more efficient. He had learned to separate the calf and heifer from the herd, usually securing them in a pen. He used a large electronic livestock scale. He tagged each calf, piercing its soft inner ear with an identifying number. The process was almost a snap. He was becoming skilled at the job, and I was proud of his accomplishments. But part of me missed the earnest chaos of our earliest attempts. There was something pure and poignant in how little we knew and the logic we thought we could apply. And we got the job done after all.

# Porcupine Meatballs with Chipotle Sauce

**Serves 6**

I can't say that I'd crossed paths with many porcupines before moving to South Texas. Seeing the first one is a shock—they are strange, lumbering creatures that resemble miniature, quill-covered bears. All of our dogs had to learn—the hard way—that they are not something to tussle with. They would return with snouts full of quills, and I would have to decide what vet I was going to rouse for yet another (expensive) after-hours visit.

All these prickly episodes got me thinking about one of my favorite lunches from the school cafeteria: Porcupine Meatballs, made with ground beef and rice "quills" and served in rich tomato sauce. I couldn't resist making an undated version with Mexican flavors. Serve these spicy meatballs with thick slices of toasted peasant bread.

1 pound **LEAN GROUND BEEF**
1 pound **LEAN GROUND PORK**
1 small **ONION**, minced
2 **GARLIC CLOVES**, minced
1 cup raw **TEXMATI** (or other long-grain) **RICE**
2 teaspoons **KOSHER SALT**
1 teaspoon ground **CUMIN**
1 teaspoon **DRIED MEXICAN OREGANO**
¼ teaspoon ground **CINNAMON**
½ teaspoon freshly ground **BLACK PEPPER**
½ cup chopped fresh **MINT**

CHIPOTLE SAUCE
Two 28-ounce cans **CHOPPED TOMATOES** in their juice
2 **CHIPOTLE CHILES**
1 cup **CHICKEN BROTH**
Pinch of **SALT**
2 tablespoons **OLIVE OIL**

1. Use a fork or your fingers to combine the beef, pork, onion, garlic, rice, salt, cumin, oregano, cinnamon, pepper, and mint in a large mixing bowl. Blend the ingredients well, but do not overwork the meat. Shape the meat into 1½-inch balls and place on a baking sheet. Cover with plastic wrap and refrigerate while you make the sauce.

2. Combine the tomatoes, chipotle chiles, chicken broth, and salt in a blender (in batches, if necessary) and blend into a chunky purée.

3. Heat the oil in a large, deep skillet over medium-high heat. Brown the meatballs, in batches so you don't overcrowd the pan, and transfer to a large plate or baking dish. Drain the excess grease and return the meatballs to the pan. Pour the tomato sauce over the top. The meatballs should be submerged in the sauce (if necessary add an additional ½ cup water). Bring the tomato sauce to a boil, reduce the heat, cover, and simmer gently for about 1 hour and 15 minutes. (Alternatively, you can cook the meatballs in a low [200°F–250°F] oven for the same time, or up to 2 hours.)

# Cowboy Pot Roast with Coffee and Whiskey

**Serves 6 to 8**

You might call this dish a spaghetti Western, since a rich hunk of beef is flavored with Italian herbs, tomatoes, and two campfire staples: coffee and whiskey. Note the range of serrano chiles. Use one for a mild heat, two or three for a more noticeably fiery flavor, or four to make everyone sit up a bit straighter.

Quick to assemble and heavenly to smell roasting, this is a perfect Sunday meal (particularly with an Ennio Morricone soundtrack playing throughout the afternoon). The meat becomes fork-tender and buttery, and the vegetables absorb the fragrant juices. Slicing the fingerlings helps them soak up the rich broth.

One 4-pound **BONE-IN CHUCK ROAST**
1 tablespoon plus 1 teaspoon **SALT**
½ teaspoon freshly ground **BLACK PEPPER**
1 tablespoon **CUMIN**
2 tablespoons chopped fresh **THYME**
2 tablespoons chopped fresh **ROSEMARY**
2 large **ONIONS**
1 head **GARLIC**, cloves trimmed and peeled (14 to 16 cloves)
1 to 4 **SERRANO CHILES**
2 cups **BEEF BROTH**
2 tablespoons **INSTANT ESPRESSO POWDER**
1 teaspoon **SMOKED SPANISH PAPRIKA**
2 tablespoons **OLIVE OIL**
2 cups **CANNED TOMATOES** with their juice
½ cup **WHISKEY**
2 fresh **BAY LEAVES**, torn
1 pound **CARROTS**, sliced into 4-inch lengths
1 pound **FINGERLING POTATOES**, sliced into 2-inch chunks

1. Preheat the oven to 325°F.

2. Pull the meat out of the fridge an hour before cooking. Combine the salt, pepper, cumin, thyme, and rosemary in a small bowl. Massage the spice-herb mixture evenly over the roast.

3. While the meat comes to room temperature, assemble the other ingredients. Slice each onion into 8 wedges and peel and crush the garlic cloves. Slice each serrano from just below the stem to the tip (so it is split but still intact). In a large measuring cup, whisk together the beef broth, instant espresso, and paprika until blended.

4. When you are ready to cook, heat the olive oil in a large Dutch oven over medium-high heat. When the pan is very hot but not smoking, add the roast and cook until it is crusty and a rich, deep brown on all sides. Transfer the meat to a plate. Lower the heat to medium and add the onions, garlic, and chiles. Cook, stirring frequently, until coated with the beef fat and the onions start to break down, about 4 minutes. Add the beef broth mixture, tomatoes, whiskey, and bay leaves, stirring up any browned bits. Return the roast to the pan and nestle into the liquid.

5. Cover the pot and place in the oven. Roast for 1 hour, then carefully turn the roast over (spooning some broth over the top) and return to the oven to roast for another hour.

6. Remove the pot from the oven, tuck the carrots and potatoes around the meat (into as much juice as possible), cover the pot, and cook for a final hour. Remove the pot from the oven and allow the meat to rest, uncovered, for 30 minutes before serving. Remove the bay leaves.

7. To serve, use a fork and tongs to remove pieces of the meat (it will be quite tender) to plates. Surround with vegetables and a generous spoonful of juice.

# Cowgirl Steaks with Pink Peppercorns and Red Onion Marmalade

**Serves 4**

I like the idea of giving a macho piece of meat a pretty and rather feminine treatment. In this case it's a fragrant coating of pink peppercorns and other alluring spices, like coriander and orange peel. I came across this sticky Red Onion Marmalade, made with red wine reduced into an aromatic syrup, at a restaurant in France. It's the perfect partner for the mildly spicy, rich-tasting meat. Leftover marmalade is delicious on sliced steak sandwiches or burgers, with a slather of mayo.

3 tablespoons crushed **PINK PEPPERCORNS**, plus more for garnish

1 tablespoon **SZECHUAN PEPPERCORNS**

1 tablespoon **CORIANDER SEEDS**

1 teaspoon **FENNEL SEEDS**

1 tablespoon plus 1 teaspoon **KOSHER SALT**

½ teaspoon dried **ORANGE PEEL**

½ teaspoon **CAYENNE PEPPER** (or other ground red pepper)

Four 6-ounce **SIRLOIN STEAKS**, about 1 inch thick

**THYME SPRIGS**, for garnish (optional)


RED ONION MARMALADE

2 tablespoons **EXTRA VIRGIN OLIVE OIL**

2 large **RED ONIONS**, thinly sliced

**KOSHER SALT**

Generous pinch of crushed **RED CHILE FLAKES**

1 **THYME BRANCH** (or 1 teaspoon dried thyme or herbes de Provence)

1 fresh **BAY LEAF**

2 **GARLIC CLOVES**, minced

1 bottle **RED WINE** (such as Côtes du Rhône or a Spanish Crianza)

3 tablespoons **HONEY**

2 tablespoons **UNSALTED BUTTER**

Freshly ground **BLACK PEPPER**


1. Heat the peppercorns, coriander, and fennel in a small, dry skillet over medium heat, shaking the skillet, until fragrant and slightly darkened, 2 to 3 minutes. Combine the

seeds with the salt, orange peel, and cayenne in a mortar (or an electric coffee grinder used for spices) and coarsely grind. An hour before cooking, place the steaks on a baking sheet lined with parchment. Evenly coat the meat with the spice mixture, pressing it gently so it adheres; set aside to marinate at room temperature.

2. Meanwhile, make the marmalade: Heat the olive oil in a large skillet over medium-high heat. Add the onions and a pinch of salt and sauté, stirring, until softened, about 6 to 8 minutes. Add the chile flakes, thyme, bay leaf, and garlic and sauté a few more minutes. Add the wine and honey and bring to a boil. Reduce the heat and simmer, stirring occasionally, until the wine has reduced to about 1 cup (the mixture should be thick and sticky). Stir in the butter, taste for seasoning, and add salt and black pepper as desired.

3. To serve, sear the steaks over a very hot (but not smoking) skillet. Do not flip the steaks until they have browned enough to release easily from the skillet, about 4 to 5 minutes. Cook the other side to the appropriate level of doneness, about 4 minutes for medium rare.

4. Place each steak (whole or thinly sliced) on a warmed plate alongside a generous mound of the marmalade. Drizzle the meat with any remaining liquid from the marmalade. Garnish the plates with a sprig of thyme and additional pink peppercorns, if desired.

# Ranch Hand Ribeyes, Two Ways

**Serves 4**

Few things say "ranch" or "Texas" more than a thick steak sizzling on the grill. When friends visit from out of town, we always make it a point to serve them a fat, juicy ribeye cooked over an oak fire. Few restaurant experiences can come close: The fat crisps and absorbs the smoke, and the thick cut, grilled just to medium rare, stays incredibly juicy. In all its well-marbled glory, a ribeye is as much an event as an entrée. Most of the time I serve them with nothing more than a sprinkling of coarse salt. But here are two variations that add even more flavor. A Mexican candy glaze gives the steak a subtly sweet and spicy flavor; a pat of fresh rosemary butter, flavored with anchovy and red chile, melts decadently over the top of each bite. Either one will please even the toughest of cowboys.

Two 24-ounce bone-in or 20-ounce boneless **RIBEYES**, cut 2 inches thick
Coarse **SEA SALT** and coarsely ground **BLACK PEPPER**

1. Heat the grill to high. Generously season the steaks with salt and pepper. For the Mexican Candy Glaze, grill the steaks until lightly charred and crusty, 4 to 5 minutes. Turn the steaks over, reduce the heat to medium or move to a cooler part of the grill, close the grill hood, and grill until medium rare, 8 to 10 minutes more. Remove the steaks from the grill and let rest for 5 minutes. To serve, cut the steaks into 1-inch-thick slices and drizzle with the glaze.

2. To serve the steaks with the rosemary butter, season with salt and pepper and grill, then top the steaks with the herbed butter. Once the butter begins to melt and distribute itself over the surface of the steak, slice the steak and serve.

## Mexican Candy Glaze

3 ounces **PILONCILLO** (see Note), coarsely chopped
¼ cup **BEEF BROTH**
2 tablespoons **ANCHO CHILE POWDER**
1 tablespoon **INSTANT ESPRESSO POWDER**
1 tablespoon **SMOKED SPANISH PAPRIKA**
1 tablespoon **SALT**

1 teaspoon freshly ground **BLACK PEPPER**

1 teaspoon ground **CHIPOTLE CHILE**

Heat the piloncillo and broth in a small saucepan over medium heat, stirring, until the sugar has melted and the mixture is smooth. Whisk in the remaining spices, remove from the heat, and set aside.

## *Rosemary Butter*

6 tablespoons **UNSALTED BUTTER**, slightly softened

2 tablespoons chopped fresh **ROSEMARY**

3 **ANCHOVY FILLETS**, finely chopped

2 to 3 **PEQUÍN CHILES** or a pinch of **CAYENNE PEPPER**

In a small bowl, use a wooden spoon to combine the butter, rosemary, anchovies, and chiles. Shape the butter into a log, wrap in plastic, and refrigerate until needed.

NOTE: Piloncillo is a raw, molasses-flavored Mexican brown sugar sold in a hard cone. It must be chopped or grated, and dissolved in liquid before using. You can find it in some supermarkets, Latin markets, and specialty stores.

# Texas Beef Chili with Poblanos and Beer

**Serves 8 (about 8 cups)**

Chili making is serious business in Texas—I quickly learned that *nobody* adds beans (if you do, you'd better drive a fast truck). Here, it's all about cubes of well-marbled chuck braised in a spicy chili broth. My version is as rich and thick as a French daube. This chili is best made the day before. This allows the flavors to meld and mellow, and makes it easier to skim the fat from the chili before reheating. Shredding the meat is an important step—it helps to create a thick, luscious texture. Serve big bowls of this chili with hot Corn Bread with Scallions (page 222) and all the traditional condiments. A dollop of Mexican-style crema helps cool the fire.

3 tablespoons **OLIVE OIL**

2 large **SWEET ONIONS**, diced (about 4 cups)

3 **POBLANO PEPPERS**, stemmed, seeded, and diced

5 **GARLIC CLOVES**, minced

1 teaspoon **KOSHER SALT**

$4\frac{1}{2}$ pounds **BEEF CHUCK**, cut into $1\frac{1}{2}$-inch cubes

2 **BAY LEAVES**, preferably fresh

2 **CINNAMON STICKS**

$\frac{1}{8}$ teaspoon ground **CLOVES**

$\frac{1}{4}$ cup ground **NEW MEXICO CHILE POWDER**

1 tablespoon plus 1 teaspoon ground **CHIPOTLE CHILE POWDER**

1 tablespoon plus 1 teaspoon ground **CUMIN**

One 12-ounce bottle **AMBER ALE**, such as Shiner Bock (made in Shiner, Texas), Bohemia, or Tecate Amber

2 quarts **BEEF BROTH**

**FOR GARNISH**

1 medium **RED ONION**, chopped

3 medium **TOMATOES**, cored, seeded, and chopped

$\frac{1}{3}$ cup chopped fresh **CILANTRO**

**SALT**, as desired

12 ounces **MEXICAN-STYLE CREMA** or **SOUR CREAM**, as desired

1. In a large skillet, heat 2 tablespoons of olive oil over medium-high heat. Add the onions and sauté until softened and translucent, about 10 minutes. Add the poblanos and sauté for an additional 10 minutes, reducing the heat if necessary to prevent the onions from sticking to the pan or turning brown. Add the garlic and salt and sauté an additional 5 minutes. Set aside.

2. Meanwhile, heat the remaining tablespoon of oil in a large Dutch oven (preferably a cast-iron pot with enamel coating). Add the beef in batches, as necessary, to avoid crowding the pan, and brown the cubes on all sides until brown and crusty. Remove the browned beef with a slotted spoon and transfer to a plate. Repeat with the remaining beef.

3. Return all the browned beef to the Dutch oven. Add the spices and sauté until they form a thick paste on the meat, about 4 minutes. Watch the pan carefully to avoid scorching the spices. Add the ale to deglaze the pan, and simmer until slightly reduced and the meat mixture is thick. Add the beef broth, reduce the heat to low, and simmer the mixture, partially covered, for 3 hours, stirring occasionally.

4. If not serving immediately, chill overnight. The next day, skim the fat from the top of the mixture. Using a slotted spoon, remove about 2 cups of the beef cubes to a plate. Shred the meat with a fork (it should be very soft) and return to the pot. The shredded meat will help create a thicker-textured chili.

5. Just before serving the chili, combine the chopped onion, tomatoes, cilantro, and a pinch of salt in a small bowl to create a *pico de gallo* to serve as a garnish. Serve the chili in warmed bowls, topped with a dollop of crema and a spoonful of *pico*. Alternately, you can simply offer separate bowls of chopped onion, tomatoes, and cilantro as garnish.

NOTE: If, like me, you prefer to add beans to chili (it can be our little secret), offer them as a garnish. Drain and rinse two 14-ounce cans of kidney or pinto beans. Place them in a glass bowl, cover with plastic, and warm in the microwave. Offer the warm beans alongside bowls of the other garnishes.

# Hearty Sides with a Ranch-Style Kick

One of the first things I knew I had to master when I moved to Texas was how to make a perfectly creamy pot of pinto beans. Traditional recipes are made with pork fat, such as salt pork, ham hocks, or bacon. The pork creates a rich and buttery pot of beans, but I decided to make a lighter version with aromatic vegetables, fresh herbs, and a bottle of beer. The result is so spicy and full of flavor that you don't miss the fat.

That's more or less how I tried to approach most of the sides I served at the ranch. They are simple and healthy—a roasted vegetable to partner with grilled chicken, or a fragrant pilaf to serve alongside a luscious braise. I'm crazy about vegetables, so a side dish provides an opportunity to serve a pile of them in a delicious way. The less complicated, the better—I usually prepare them with little more than olive oil, salt, garlic, and fresh herbs.

And since in Texas "What do you want on the side?" usually means potato salad or coleslaw, I've included my favorite recipes for those too. They're great alongside a rack of ribs, smoked sausage, or grilled steak—but I also love them on their own for lunch, with a crumble of dried pequín chiles over the potatoes.

# Green and White Beans in Herb Oil

**Serves 6 to 8**

Fresh oregano and marjoram are the creeping monsters in my garden—they threaten to take over everything else. So I am always looking for ways to use them both up. Both herbs are great with any kind of bean, so I decided to combine them with garlic and serrano chiles to make an herbaceous dressing for haricots verts and white beans. This salad is great with grilled sausages, roast chicken, or on its own with marinated tomatoes, a few slices of hard salami, and toasted peasant bread. If you don't have access to these herbs, you can make the dressing with ½ cup flat-leaf parsley instead.

12 ounces **HARICOTS VERTS** (or regular green beans), snapped at the stem end
2 **GARLIC CLOVES**
2 to 3 **SERRANO CHILES** (or 1 to 2 jalapeños), stemmed, seeded, and coarsely
    chopped
¾ teaspoon **KOSHER SALT**
¼ cup fresh **OREGANO LEAVES**
¼ cup fresh **MARJORAM LEAVES**
2 tablespoons fresh **LEMON JUICE**
1 tablespoon plus 1 teaspoon good **RED WINE VINEGAR**
½ cup **EXTRA VIRGIN OLIVE OIL**
Two 16-ounce cans **CANNELLINI** (or any other white beans), drained
½ small **RED ONION** (or 2 medium shallots), very thinly sliced
Freshly ground **BLACK PEPPER**

**1.** Bring a large pot of salted water to a boil. Add the haricots verts and blanch them until just cooked through, about 4 minutes (cook regular green beans 2 to 3 minutes longer). Drain the beans in a colander and rinse them briefly with cold water.

**2.** Meanwhile, make the herb oil. Place the garlic, chiles, and salt in the bowl of a food processor and pulse until chopped. Add the oregano, marjoram, lemon juice, and vinegar and pulse until the mixture forms a rough paste. With the machine running, add the olive oil in a steady stream and process until smooth.

**3.** Transfer the haricots verts and beans to a large bowl (use a paper towel to pat the beans dry, if necessary). Pour the herb oil over the beans and toss well. Add the onion and a generous grinding of black pepper and toss again. Taste for balance and add more salt, pepper, or vinegar as desired. Serve immediately or cover and refrigerate for up to 8 hours. Bring to room temperature and toss again before serving.

# Shiner Bock Beans with Epazote

**Serves 6 to 8**

I used to simmer beans uncovered, very gently, treating them like fragile shells rather than the hearty legumes they are. Then a handsome old man named Dorsey came to the ranch to cook for the deer hunts in December. Dorsey makes insanely good Southern fare: barbecued chicken and the best grits with giblet gravy and "floaters" (eggs fried in a vat of oil) you will ever taste. He also makes great pinto beans. Dorsey added little more than salt pork, but he covered the beans and boiled the hell out of them, checking to see if they needed more water every now and then.

So that's how I started making my beans, and the results are perfectly creamy every time. I flavor mine with Shiner Bock beer, a local variety from Shiner, Texas, but any amber beer will work just fine. If you can't find epazote, feel free to use cilantro, parsley, or leave it out altogether. These beans thicken upon standing and taste even better the second day (with huevos rancheros or in warm flour tortillas with shredded cheese and salsa).

2 cups **PINTO BEANS**, sorted, soaked overnight, or quick soaked (see Note)

1 medium **ONION**, chopped

4 **GARLIC CLOVES**, crushed

1 **JALAPEÑO** (or 2 serranos), seeded and finely chopped

2 fresh **BAY LEAVES**, torn

1 bunch fresh **EPAZOTE**, stemmed and chopped (about ½ to ¾ cup)

1 bottle **SHINER BOCK BEER** or other **AMBER ALE**

2 to 4 tablespoons **CHIPOTLE CHILES IN ADOBO**

2 tablespoons **SHERRY WINE VINEGAR**

**SALT**

½ cup chopped fresh **CILANTRO**

1. Drain and rinse the soaked pinto beans, and place in a pot with fresh water to cover by 1½ inches. Add the onion, garlic, jalapeño, bay leaves, and epazote to the pot and bring to a boil. Reduce the heat and simmer the beans, covered, for 1 hour, stirring occasionally.

2. Add the beer and continue to simmer until the beans are tender and creamy, 30 to 45 additional minutes. When they have reached the right texture, remove the bay leaves and flavor with the chipotle chile purée, vinegar, salt to taste, and cilantro. Taste and add more salt or vinegar, if necessary.

**NOTE:** To quick soak beans, place them in a large pot and cover with at least four inches of cold water. Bring the beans to a boil over medium-high heat. Simmer for 2 to 3 minutes, remove from the heat, and cover for one hour. Drain the beans in a colander and cook as directed.

# Roasted Cauliflower

**Serves 4**

This recipe will change the way you think about cauliflower. Roasting the vegetable at a high temperature caramelizes its natural sugar, and it becomes sweet, succulent, and tender. The small dark brown pieces are the best—they'll probably never see the table because you'll eat them in the kitchen.

> 2 large heads **CAULIFLOWER**, cored and trimmed of any brown spots
> **OLIVE OIL**
> 1½ teaspoons **KOSHER SALT** (more or less, as desired)
> Freshly ground **BLACK PEPPER**

Preheat the oven to 400°F. Cut the cauliflower into florets and place them on a baking sheet. The florets will crumble as you cut them and you'll end up with various sizes, but this is of no importance. Toss the cauliflower with just enough olive oil to coat it lightly. Sprinkle with salt and pepper. Using both hands, carefully toss the cauliflower with the oil and seasonings. Place in the hot oven and roast for 45 minutes to 1 hour. Use a metal spatula to flip the cauliflower every 15 minutes or so to ensure that all sides get evenly browned.

# CADILLAC GIG

He called it a Cadillac gig because the pay was steady and the acoustics were good. And unlike the audiences at the barbecue joints and pizza parlors he played in San Antone, this audience was attentive and appreciative. Plus, he said, the food was better.

Rusty Lawrence was an engineer by day and a country-and-western singer on the weekends. His repertoire was a jukebox of chestnuts, old-time ballads usually relegated to crackly stations on the AM dial. His voice was sweet and clear—in the style of Ray Price or Charley Pride—and his rhythm was pleasingly predictable. Whether he sang a sad, rambling ballad by Glen Campbell or a toe-tapping number by Patsy Cline, the song never strayed from a *boom-chuck-boom-chuck* beat. It was an orderly count; there was comfort in its dependability.

Kit discovered Rusty while he was playing in D'Hanis, an old-water-tower kind of town on Highway 90, at a roadhouse restaurant famous for chicken-fried steak. She was so impressed that she convinced him to play at the ranch every Saturday.

Rusty's appearance was welcome in more ways than one. It signaled the close of the week, but it also meant that he—not us—would shoulder the evening's entertainment. As the weeks flew by and the guests blurred, I would imagine our job as it might be dramatized in a Douglas Sirk film. Days of the year as numbers blowing off a wall calendar, a montage of Hill Country seasons witnessed through the fluctuating bounty of branches, a flurry of pearl-clad women in matching gray sweat suits—all set to Rusty's music. My kitchen prep cued to "Gentle on My Mind," "Rose of San Antone," "Pancho and Lefty," and Bobby Goldsboro's "Honey."

"Saturday Night Live with Rusty Lawrence," as his show came to be called, would start around six. But Rusty would typically arrive much earlier. He enjoyed the scenic drive from Castroville, where he lived, and he relished his routines. On the way, he'd stop for a burger in Bandera or a sandwich in Utopia. More often than not, I'd be on my afternoon break, jogging down the caliche road when I'd spot his turquoise Ranger driving toward me at a respectful speed. When he pulled behind the lodge the dogs, roused from a nap under the bread oven, recognized the truck and wagged their tails. When I got back, I'd give him a kiss on the cheek and say, "Sorry, I'm sweaty."

"I don't mind," he would tease. "I like it."

He'd arrive in shorts and T-shirts that had the arms cut out. He'd set up his equipment, then stretch out on the couch and nap (and startle guests emerging from a massage). Sometimes he'd take his guitar to the pasture and play warm-up songs to the goats.

When I returned for dinner service, Rusty would belly up to the bar and we'd chat while I'd chop and peel vegetables. His accent was unlike any I'd heard, and I loved the particular way he pronounced certain words. He'd talk about strumming guitar *cards* rather than chords and said

ambulance in three drawn-out syllables: am-buh-lance.

"It's been quite a week," I told him one Saturday. "We've got seven guests with assorted eating disorders and menu requests. There's a vegetarian, a carbphobe, and someone who can't do shellfish. One woman told me she wanted blended salads for breakfast."

"Blended salads?" Rusty said.

"Yep," I continued, "as in green salads, blended in a blender. Someone else offered a favorite soup recipe that included something called ham dust."

"Oh, my," Rusty laughed, "I've never heard of that."

"To top things off, the ladies from Boston don't particularly like the ladies from Houston. I need a big glass of wine."

Rusty laughed again and shook his head.

Rusty had a small room with a twin bed in the back of the lodge, but he rarely used it. He preferred to brave the curvy roads back to Castroville so he could sleep on his own bed. The prevalence of animals (coons, deer, skunks, and armadillos—aka Texas speed bumps) made it a harrowing drive, but I understood his reasoning. It brought his routine full circle.

The guests trickled in and nibbled snacks at the bar. At showtime, Rusty emerged from the back room in a clean pressed shirt and trousers, winked at me, then walked to his stool with the gravitas of a concert pianist. He began playing "The Yellow Rose of Texas."

As an entertainer, Rusty endured our whims. Kit yelled for "Amarillo by Morning." A bit later, Angela held the phone to Rusty's mic so he could sing "Mr. Bojangles" to her mother in Los Angeles. I begged him to learn "Wichita Lineman." He feigned indifference but secretly did so, then surprised me with a *boom-chuck-boom-chuck* rendition.

Every single Saturday I told Rusty that he sounded great. Embarrassed by the compliment, he unfailingly responded in the same way, "It's not too loud?"

Hours later the guests, now best of friends, crowded around Rusty to belt out a final round of "Puff the Magic Dragon." Then they stumbled off to bed. Rusty pulled a stool up to the bar. David poured us each a glass of wine. Even if we were dead tired, we enjoyed staying up a bit longer to keep him company. We came to know about his job, family, and the fruit trees in his yard. He, in turn, became an integral part of our lives, and a fixture at milestone events. He played on our front porch for David's fortieth birthday and brought his guitar to the river for mine.

Like any native Texan, Rusty was raised on barbecued brisket and sausage. The food I prepared, with its reliance on fresh herbs and olive oil, was outside his realm, but he was an enthusiastic eater and asked about everything. I served him a plate of Ruby Salad, red cabbage and beets topped with crumbled feta and spiced pepitas. "I didn't think I liked beets," Rusty said between bites, "and I sure like this dressing." It was a sherry wine vinaigrette. I pulled a warm plate of grilled quail from the oven. "I've never had quail cooked like this," Rusty said. The quail was stuffed with a fresh bay leaf, and thyme and rosemary branches from my garden, then sprinkled with cornmeal before it was grilled so it got nice and crispy over the fire. Digging into caramelized spears of roasted cauliflower flecked with coarse salt and a pile of greens sautéed with sweet onions, red peppers, garlic, and red pepper flakes, Rusty said, "Tell me again how you cook that cauliflower."

On the last Saturday that Rusty played at the ranch, we talked him into staying and we had a good long visit. Rusty was a Vietnam veteran. During the war he'd worked as a medic in a military hospital in Japan. It was a *M*A*S*H*-type unit: They'd receive badly wounded guys right off the field, bandaged up just enough to stop the bleeding. The stories were gruesome and the things he saw were unimaginable to me. He had witnessed a world that was out of control, which is probably why his routines and restrained rhythms were so welcome to him.

That night, he told us about a young man brought in with a head injury. The guy clearly wasn't going to make it, so Rusty sat with him. Rusty imitated the challenged, raspy breath the soldier made just before he died. He knew the sound well—he'd heard it plenty of times.

That was the last time we saw Rusty—although we glimpsed his Ranger once more. That next week, on an unexpected night off, David and I drove to Floore Country Store in Helotes to see Robert Earl Keen. We passed Grady's, a barbecue restaurant where Rusty played on Fridays, and saw the turquoise pickup parked out front. It would be fun to surprise him, we said, but we were running late for the show.

Like sudden detours in life, unexpected people can enrich the texture of your days. To lose them unexpectedly is to drag a needle across a record. Rusty's music became the soundtrack to our time in Texas. When he died the next night, suddenly and unexpectedly of a heart attack, ranch life never recovered the same rhythm.

Afterward, I found myself thinking about Rusty on his late-night drives home. I imagined the beam of his headlights catching axis and whitetail poised alongside the road, freezing them into still, eerie mannequins. Their unblinking stares suspended, for that moment, until his truck passed and disappeared into the darkness.

# Carrot Cumin Pilaf

**Serves 6 to 8**

This pretty and flavorful pilaf is a staple because it goes so well with so many things— grilled quail, braised chicken thighs, or a succulent pork roast are just a few examples. Sautéing the rice and cumin seed brings out a toasted, nutty flavor. I add a few serranos (sliced in half lengthwise but kept intact), which add less heat than if you were to chop them. We usually fight over who gets to eat the delicious cooked chiles, but leave them out entirely if you prefer. For parties I often double this recipe and cook it in the oven in a covered baking dish or a metal pan covered with foil.

2 cups **CHICKEN STOCK**

2 fresh **BAY LEAVES**

2 **THYME SPRIGS**

2 tablespoons **OLIVE OIL**

1 medium **SHALLOT** (or ½ red onion), finely chopped

1 cup **TEXMATI** (or basmati) **RICE**

1 teaspoon **CUMIN SEED**

1 large **CARROT**, sliced into very thin rounds

½ teaspoon **KOSHER SALT**

1 to 2 **SERRANO CHILES** (optional)

1.  Warm the chicken stock, bay leaves, and thyme sprigs in a small saucepan over medium-low heat.

2.  Meanwhile, heat the olive oil in a large deep skillet over medium-high heat. Add the shallot and cook, stirring, until softened and lightly golden, about 3 to 4 minutes. Add the rice and cumin and cook until the rice is opaque and the seeds are fragrant and slightly darkened, about 4 minutes. Add the carrot and salt and sauté for 2 more minutes. If using, slice the serranos lengthwise, from the end to the stem, keeping the stem intact. Add the serranos and warmed stock to the rice and stir once. Bring the mixture to a boil, cover, reduce the heat, and simmer 18 minutes. Remove from the heat and keep covered for 10 more minutes. Remove the lid and allow the rice to cool for 2 to 3 minutes, then fluff with a fork. Taste for seasoning and add more salt, if desired.

# Arroz (Mucho) Verde

**Serves 6 to 8**

This herbaceous (and very green) rice is incredibly flavorful, and it couldn't be easier to prepare. Everything green (vegetables, chiles, and herbs) is puréed with chicken stock to create an emerald-colored cooking liquid. The parsley is optional, but it imparts the brightest color. If I have mint or tarragon, or even a handful of fresh spinach on hand, I'll throw that in the blender as well—it only deepens the color and flavor. Arroz (Mucho) Verde is delicious with roasted chicken, grilled fish, and Enchiladas Verdes (page 175). It's also extremely satisfying topped with a poached egg and crumbled queso fresco for a quick and easy meal.

1 medium **ONION**, coarsely chopped

2 **POBLANOS**, seeded and coarsely chopped

1 to 2 **JALAPEÑOS** or **SERRANOS**, seeded and coarsely chopped

2 **GARLIC CLOVES**

1½ cups chopped fresh **CILANTRO**

½ cup chopped **PARSLEY** (optional)

4 cups **CHICKEN STOCK**

Scant 1 teaspoon **SALT**

2 tablespoons **OLIVE OIL**

1 bunch (about 8) **SCALLIONS**, thinly sliced

2 cups **TEXMATI** (or other long-grain) **RICE**

1 pound **FROZEN PEAS**

1. Place the onion, poblanos, jalapeño, garlic, herbs, chicken stock, and salt in a blender and purée until smooth.

2. Heat the olive oil over medium-high heat in a large skillet with a tight-fitting lid. Add the scallions and sauté, stirring, until softened and fragrant but not brown, about 4 minutes. Add the rice and sauté until it turns opaque, about 4 more minutes. Add the green stock and stir once, then cover, reduce the heat, and simmer for 20 minutes. Remove the lid (the stock should be absorbed) and scatter the bag of frozen peas over the rice. Do not stir. Cover the pot and let sit for 10 minutes. Remove the lid, cool for 5 additional minutes, and then fluff with a fork. Taste for salt and season as needed.

# Corn Pico de Gallo

**Serves 4 to 6**

Pico de gallo means "rooster's beak," an appropriate title in my world (see below). It refers to the "pecking" sound of a chef's knife chopping up a little bit of everything. When corn is in season I make this dish with sweet kernels cut straight from the cob. But it's also good with thawed frozen corn. The lime and vinegar, along with the fresh flavor of scallions and cilantro, make this particularly bright and fresh tasting. I serve Corn Pico de Gallo with grilled pork chops or chicken thighs, on a bed of greens as a first course, or in warm corn tortillas with black beans (and/or queso fresco) for a quick meal. If you want yours less spicy, go ahead and seed the serranos.

Kernels cut from 6 ears of cooked **CORN** or 1 pound **FROZEN CORN** (about
    $3\frac{1}{2}$ cups) thawed
4 **SCALLIONS**, thinly sliced
2 **SERRANOS**, stemmed and sliced into very thin rounds
1 cup **CHERRY TOMATOES**, quartered
1 tablespoon **SHERRY WINE VINEGAR**
2 tablespoons fresh **LIME JUICE**
2 tablespoons **OLIVE OIL**
$\frac{1}{3}$ cup chopped fresh **CILANTRO**, including leaves and tender stems
1 teaspoon finely grated **LIME ZEST**
$\frac{1}{2}$ teaspoon **KOSHER SALT**
Freshly ground **BLACK PEPPER**
Dash of **HOT SAUCE**

Combine all the ingredients in a medium-sized bowl. Toss well to combine, taste for seasoning, and add more lime, salt, pepper, or hot sauce, as desired.

## TOO MANY ROOSTERS

*O*ne morning Sharon called with a proposition. Did I want more chicks? She had a box of thirteen New Hampshire Reds, a breed prized for delivering big brown eggs, that she was selling for a dollar apiece. Sexing chickens is a famously difficult process, so I should have been suspicious when Sharon showed me the box of identical chicks and said, "They're all hens, except for that one," and pointed to a chick. "That one there is a rooster."

She was close. As the chickens matured, it became painfully clear that we had twelve roosters and one hen. Country Living 101 is not to keep more than one rooster—more than that means certain havoc. Too many roosters means too much testosterone. Our roosters claimed various perches in the backyard and barn to declare their manhood. Then they'd cock-a-doodle-doo at each other, round-robin style, all day long. (I interpreted the dialogue as "I am the man!" "No, I am the man!") There were vicious duels at high noon and possessive squabbles over hens. Sometimes they would fight to the death. Much of the time our barn sounded like a cantina scene during a gunfight in a spaghetti western.

# Corn Bread with Scallions

**Makes one 10-inch round bread**

This corn bread is subtly sweet with a moist, tender crumb. It's a must with Texas Beef Chili with Poblanos and Beer (page 203). It's also good with lentil or tomato soup, Iowa Farmhouse Green Beans and Sausage (page 189), or with fried eggs for breakfast. For a richer, more savory bread stir in two slices of cooked, crumbled bacon when you combine the wet ingredients with the dry.

**CORN OIL** or rendered **BACON FAT**, for greasing the skillet
One 10-inch cast-iron skillet or 10-inch springform pan

1⅓ cups **UNBLEACHED ALL-PURPOSE FLOUR**
1 cup coarse-grind **YELLOW CORNMEAL**
2 teaspoons **BAKING POWDER**
1 teaspoon **SALT**
1¼ cups **LOW-FAT MILK**
2 tablespoons **HONEY**
2 **EGGS**, lightly beaten
⅓ cup **CORN OIL**
8 **SCALLIONS** (white and light green parts only), cleaned, trimmed, and thinly
    sliced (about ½ cup)
A grinding of **BLACK PEPPER**, if desired

1. Preheat the oven to 400°F (425°F for a springform pan). Grease a cast-iron skillet and place it in the oven. Or grease a springform pan and set aside.

2. In a large bowl, use a fork to combine the flour, cornmeal, baking powder, and salt. In a medium-sized bowl, whisk together the milk, honey, eggs, corn oil, scallions, and black pepper until well combined. Add the wet mixture to the dry ingredients and stir with a rubber spatula until the ingredients are just blended. Do not overmix. Pour the batter into the skillet or pan.

3. Bake the corn bread for 30 minutes (40 minutes for the springform pan), or until golden brown and firm and springy to the touch. A toothpick inserted into the center of the corn bread should come out clean. Serve immediately or at cool room temperature, then cover with foil or a dish towel so it doesn't dry out.

# Roasted Mexican Vegetables with Marjoram

**Serves 4**

This is an easy way to prepare some of the more un-usual Mexican vegetables like calabaza, which looks a bit like a grenade-shaped zucchini (it's from the same family), and chayote, a pale green pear-shaped vegetable with a firm texture and a fairly bland taste. Tossed with summer squash, red onion, fresh marjo-ram, and chile, this makes for a colorful, nutritious, and appetizing side dish. The secret is to roast at a high enough temperature to get brown and crisp (not soggy) results. This is by no means a recipe that requires specific measurements or ingredients. If you don't have oregano or marjoram, use parsley or mint—but toss them with the vegetables after baking. Sometimes I scatter a few fresh pequín chiles into the mix—they create a spicy oil as the vegetables roast. But you could also add thinly sliced serranos, jalapeños, diced green chiles, or crushed red pepper flakes.

1 medium **RED ONION**, chopped

1 **CHAYOTE**, peeled, seeded, and chopped

1 **CALABAZA**, stemmed and chopped

1 **ZUCCHINI**, chopped

1 **YELLOW SQUASH**, chopped

3 tablespoons **OLIVE OIL**

**KOSHER SALT**

Freshly ground **BLACK PEPPER**

3 tablespoons chopped fresh **MARJORAM** or **OREGANO**

2 tablespoons fresh **LEMON** or **LIME JUICE**

Preheat the oven to 425°F. Combine the vegetables on a baking sheet, drizzle with olive oil, and sprinkle with salt, pepper, and herbs. When the oven is hot, roast for about 45 minutes, until nicely browned and tender, flipping the vegetables every 15 minutes or so to ensure even browning. When the vegetables are done cooking, toss with the lemon juice, taste for seasoning, and serve.

# Two-Potato Salad with Creole Mustard and Tarragon

**Serves 6 to 8**

Because sweet potatoes are so dense, they take a few minutes longer than regular potatoes, so boil them separately. This salad is easily doubled for a party and goes great with barbecued brisket, roast chicken, or grilled sausage.

1 pound **SWEET POTATOES**

1 pound **YUKON GOLD POTATOES**

1 teaspoon **KOSHER SALT**

4 **SCALLIONS**, trimmed and minced

2 **CELERY STALKS**, trimmed and finely chopped

2 **SERRANO CHILES**, stemmed, seeded, and minced

½ cup plus 2 tablespoons **MAYONNAISE**

2 tablespoons **CREOLE MUSTARD**

1 tablespoon finely chopped fresh **TARRAGON**

**KOSHER SALT** and freshly ground **BLACK PEPPER**

**1.** Place the sweet potatoes and Yukon gold potatoes in two separate saucepans. Cover the potatoes with water by 2 inches, add ½ teaspoon of salt to each pot, and bring to a boil over medium-high heat. Reduce the heat and simmer the potatoes until just cooked through and tender. The sweet potatoes should take 20 to 25 minutes; the Yukon gold potatoes will be finished a bit sooner. Drain the potatoes and allow to cool.

**2.** When the potatoes are cool, peel them with a paring knife and cube them. Place in a large bowl with the scallions, celery, and chiles. In a small bowl, use a spoon to blend the mayonnaise and mustard. Add to the large bowl and use a rubber spatula to fold the ingredients together until the vegetables are well coated with the dressing. Add the tarragon and salt and pepper to taste, and toss again, tasting for seasoning.

# Highway 55 Slaw with Buttermilk Dressing

**Serves 6 to 8**

One of my favorite quirky South Texas experiences is finding myself behind a slow-moving truck of just-picked cabbages. The pile of pale green globes looks beautiful against the cornflower blue trailers. This always happens on Highway 55, when I emerge from the mesquite- and cactus-studded hills of the Nueces Canyon and hit the flat growing region just north of Uvalde. With so much cabbage around, it goes without saying that slaw is a staple. This dressing is slightly sharp from the mustard and hot sauce, and fragrant with herbs. The pumpkin seeds are optional, but they provide a nice nutty crunch. I could easily eat a big pile of this salad for lunch every other day. If you can find savoy cabbage, use it. I love its sweet flavor and slightly ruffled texture.

1 cup **MAYONNAISE**

1 cup well-shaken **BUTTERMILK**

¼ cup **CREOLE MUSTARD**

¼ cup **APPLE CIDER VINEGAR**

Several dashes of **HOT SAUCE**

1 teaspoon **KOSHER SALT**

½ teaspoon freshly ground **BLACK PEPPER**

1 small **GREEN CABBAGE**, very thinly sliced

½ small **RED CABBAGE**, thinly sliced

½ small **RED ONION**, thinly sliced (optional)

2 **CARROTS**, grated

½ cup chopped fresh **PARSLEY** or **CILANTRO**

⅓ cup **TOASTED PEPITAS** (optional)

In a large bowl, whisk together the mayonnaise, buttermilk, mustard, vinegar, hot sauce, salt, and pepper. Add the cabbages, onion, carrots, parsley, and pepitas if using and toss again. Taste for seasoning and add salt or hot sauce as desired.

# Roasted Eggplant and Tomato Gratin

**Serves 4 to 6**

The secret to this dish is well-browned eggplant slices (to ensure a deep, roasted flavor) that cook with sweet, sautéed onions and the best quality Italian tomatoes. This is a delicious side dish with grilled meat, or a light vegetarian entrée with a salad and crusty bread. To make it more substantial, add ½ cup grated Parmigiano-Reggiano to the bread crumbs.

3 medium **EGGPLANTS**, stemmed and peeled

½ cup **OLIVE OIL**

**KOSHER SALT**

1 large **ONION**, thinly sliced

2 **GARLIC CLOVES**, finely chopped

2 tablespoons chopped fresh **THYME**

½ teaspoon crushed **RED PEPPER FLAKES**

⅓ cup fresh **BREAD CRUMBS**

One 28-ounce can **TOMATOES** in juice, drained, reserving the juice (I use San Marzano tomatoes from Italy)

1. Preheat the oven to 425°F. Cut the eggplants into ½-inch slices and place on a cookie sheet. Brush each side with olive oil and sprinkle with salt. Roast until each side is well browned, about 6 to 8 minutes per side. Remove the eggplant from the oven and set aside; reduce the oven temperature to 375°F.

2. Meanwhile, heat 1 tablespoon of olive oil over medium-high heat in a large nonstick skillet. Sauté the onion until soft and golden, about 8 minutes. Add the garlic, thyme, and red pepper flakes and sauté an additional 2 minutes. Remove from the heat.

3. In a separate skillet, heat 1 tablespoon olive oil with the bread crumbs over medium-high heat, stirring constantly, until the bread crumbs are golden brown.

4. Brush a 2-quart gratin dish with olive oil. Line the bottom with a layer of roasted eggplant slices. Top with a third of the onion mixture, then a third of the tomatoes (breaking them apart with your fingers). Repeat the process two more times with the remaining eggplant slices, onion, and tomatoes. Drizzle the reserved tomato juice over the top. Top with the browned bread crumbs. Bake for 25 minutes, until bubbly and browned on top.

# Garlic Greens with Red Pepper and Sweet Onions

**Serves 4**

At the ranch we often serve these greens atop David's toasted pecan sourdough bread and a little shaved ricotta salata. However, they're also delicious on their own, and partner well with grilled chicken or salmon. For the most interesting flavor, use a mix of greens.

3 tablespoons **EXTRA VIRGIN OLIVE OIL**

1 large **ONION**, thinly sliced

1 **RED PEPPER**, thinly sliced

2 to 3 **GARLIC CLOVES**, finely minced

½ teaspoon crushed **RED PEPPER FLAKES**, or more to taste

8 cups **MIXED TEXAS GREENS** (such as Swiss chard, collards, turnip greens, mustard greens, spinach, and kale), stemmed, cleaned, and chopped

**KOSHER SALT**

Freshly ground **BLACK PEPPER**

2 tablespoons fresh **LEMON JUICE**

Heat 1 tablespoon olive oil in a large nonstick skillet over medium-high heat. Add the onion and red pepper and sauté until soft and wilted, about 4 minutes. Scrape the mixture onto a plate and set aside. Add the remaining oil, garlic, and red pepper flakes to the skillet; heat until fragrant. Add the greens, in batches if necessary, and stir until they begin to wilt and turn dark green. Add the reserved onions and peppers to the greens and continue to cook down until the greens are tender, about 5 additional minutes. Season to taste with salt and pepper and finish with lemon juice. Taste and adjust the seasoning if necessary.

# Greens with Red Chile Sauce

**Serves 4**

The spicy, complex, and smoky sauce is a wonderful complement to the sweet, earthy flavor of the greens. These greens would also be delicious in a warm corn tortilla with scrambled eggs or queso fresco—or any other white cheese.

1 dried **ANCHO** or **PASILLA CHILE**

2 unpeeled **GARLIC CLOVES**

2 medium **TOMATOES**

**KOSHER SALT**

2 tablespoons **SHERRY WINE VINEGAR**

1 tablespoon **HONEY**

2 tablespoons **OLIVE OIL**

1 medium **ONION**, thinly sliced

8 cups **MIXED TEXAS GREENS** (such as Swiss chard, collards, turnip greens, mustard greens, spinach, and kale), stemmed, cleaned, and chopped

Freshly ground **BLACK PEPPER**

1. Line a 12-inch cast-iron skillet with foil. Heat the chile, garlic, and tomatoes over medium-high heat, turning as necessary, until evenly blackened and charred. The chile will puff and darken and the garlic and tomatoes will soften and blister. Soak the chile in hot water for 15 to 20 minutes, until softened. Stem, seed, and chop the chile and place in the bowl of a food processor with the peeled garlic and cored tomatoes. Sprinkle with salt, add the vinegar and honey, and process until smooth.

2. Heat the olive oil in a large skillet over medium-high heat. Add the onion and a pinch of salt and cook, stirring, until soft and golden, about 6 to 7 minutes. Add greens (in batches if necessary, to allow them to shrink and wilt) and cook, tossing, until softened, about 4 minutes. Add the red chile sauce and continue to cook for about 10 minutes. Taste for seasoning and add salt and pepper as desired.

# Simple, Seductive Desserts

*I* love a little something sweet, but after a great meal, I usually don't have dessert on my mind. Most of the time I'm happy with a bite of really good chocolate. I don't like glop, shifting layers of mousse, or an avalanche of sauces. Carefully crafted constructions made by pastry chefs are usually lost on me. I like to keep dessert simple.

One of the things that drive my preferences is timing. I love sweets in the morning and in the middle of the afternoon. I love cookies, dense chocolate cake with a whiff of spice, bright and bracing sorbets, and a big hunk of an old-fashioned, boozy pound cake perfumed with citrus zest.

Many of these desserts are light, for ranch guests who were looking to cinch their belts a bit tighter when they leave. I welcomed the challenge. Vanilla-Painted Pineapple; Candied Grape-fruit Sorbet; Apple, Pear, and Honey Soufflé; or soothing Chamomile Poached Pears end the evening on a sweet note without being too rich.

For those craving more intense flavors, there is Chocolate Whiskey Cake, Espresso Brownies, and a dense, creamy Dulce de Leche Flan, served with a piece of candy as pretty as stained glass.

# Vanilla-Painted Pineapple

**Serves 6**

Inhaling the intoxicating perfume of this light, refreshing dessert is the next best thing to jetting off to a tropical locale—and it's easier to come by than a ticket to Polynesia. This dessert is perfect for people who want a virtuous dessert.

The preparation is incredibly simple. To flavor the pineapple, I simply split a vanilla bean with a paring knife, scrape the fragrant seeds out, spread them onto wedges of fruit, and then broil them until the fruit just starts to caramelize. This is easiest to do with a fresh vanilla bean (it will be soft and pliable) that you can buy in the produce section (they are not cheap), but if you only have a crisp dried one, rehydrate it in warm water, then split it open and scrape out the seeds.

To enhance the vacation flavor of this dessert, splash the pineapple with a bit of dark rum before broiling.

1 large **PINEAPPLE**
1 soft, fresh **VANILLA BEAN**
**DARK RUM** (optional)

1. Preheat the broiler and place the oven rack on its highest setting.

2. Slice the top stem and bottom off the pineapple and slice the fruit into 6 horizontal pieces. Trim the woody middle core from each wedge. Slice each wedge into bite-sized sections by slicing down to, but not through, the skin. This will keep each wedge intact.

3. Place the vanilla bean on a cutting board and use a paring knife to split it in half vertically. Use the knife to spread each half open to reveal the dark seeds. Use the knife to gently scrape the seeds from the pod, then frost each pineapple wedge evenly with the vanilla seeds, spreading in between the wedges and along the entire sides. Drizzle a bit of rum over each wedge, if desired.

4. Broil the pineapple until the top darkens and caramelizes. If the fruit still feels firm, turn down the oven temperature and roast for another 10 minutes or so.

5. After broiling, run a knife under the wedge of fruit, along the peel, to separate the fruit from its skin, keeping the wedge intact. Serve warm. Leftover vanilla pineapple is delicious in fruit salads the next morning.

# Roasted Figs with Honey and Pine Nuts

**Serves 4**

In the late summer and fall, I can buy purple or green figs that are grown in Hondo, a town about an hour from the ranch. Uvalde is the self-proclaimed "honey capital of the world," so the two ingredients, along with a scattering of pine nuts (feel free to use hazelnuts or almonds), came together easily. This simple dish is luscious and satisfying. It's great on its own, but you can also spoon the warm figs over vanilla ice cream.

4 tablespoons **BUTTER**

6 tablespoons **HONEY**

Generous pinch of **KOSHER SALT**

2 tablespoons **STROH RUM**, **COGNAC**, or **BRANDY**

12 fresh **FIGS**

$\frac{1}{3}$ cup **PINE NUTS**

**1.** Preheat the oven to 375°F.

**2.** Melt the butter, honey, and salt in a small saucepan over medium heat. Stir in the rum and set aside. Slice the figs into halves and place in a large baking dish or divide among 4 individual-size baking dishes. Drizzle the butter-honey mixture over the figs and add $\frac{1}{4}$ cup of water to the dish (or a tablespoon of water to each small dish). Scatter the nuts over the figs and bake until tender and the syrup is slightly reduced, about 20 minutes. Use a spoon to baste the figs a few times with the honey-butter mixture. Serve the figs warm, drizzled with the juices that have formed on the bottom of the dish.

# Roasted Plums and Pluots with Amaretti Trail Dust

**Serves 4**

In the height of spring and summer when the market is bursting with stone fruit—gleaming black and red plums and speckled pluots—I use them to make this simple dessert. Pluots are a hybrid, a cross between a plum and an apricot, and they have a pretty perfume and tart-sweet flavor. This recipe requires perfectly ripe fruit—they should be fragrant and yield slightly when gently pressed. Ground Italian Amaretti cookies, walnuts, and a dab of butter create a crunchy, nutty topping. No one will complain if you top each serving with a scoop of vanilla ice cream either.

1 cup **AMARETTI COOKIES**, finely ground (you should have about ¾ cup crumbs)
¼ cup **WALNUTS**
3 tablespoons cold **BUTTER**, cut into small cubes
3 ripe black or red **PLUMS**, halved and seeded
3 **PLUOTS**, halved and seeded

Preheat the oven to 350°F. Place the Amaretti cookies, walnuts, and butter in the bowl of a food processor and pulse until ground into coarse crumbs. Place the plums and pluots, cut side up, in a large baking dish or divide among 4 individual baking dishes. Top each fruit half with a generous tablespoon of the ground cookie mixture, using your fingers to gently press it into the fruit. Bake until the fruit softens and begins to release its juice, about 15 minutes; serve immediately.

# DO I HAVE MY PANTS ON?

## THE LIFE AND TIMES OF COWBOY GEORGE

George Streib has been to New York City—once. Soon after arriving, he sniffed out the hotel bar and ordered up a whiskey. Even though he was without his trademark Stetson, the bartender sized him up and said, "You must be a cowboy." Indeed.

I met George on my first visit to Hart & Hind. In an entrance that would become as familiar as the rumble of his Ford pickup dragging a trail of dust down the road or the rattle of his red horse trailer, he burst into the lodge in the middle of a meal. Sizing up the table of women, he flashed a broad smile that deepened his dimples and the lines around his eyes, and said, "Hello, ladies, I'm George Streib." The ladies beamed back. Part of George's charm was that he fulfilled preconceived notions about Texas—he was just the type of unapologetically Western character you hoped to find on a ranch. And he knew it. The ladies, just back from a hike, were clad in matching gray shorts and T-shirts—the Hart & Hind uniform (that secretly reminded me of women's prison). But there was to be a cocktail party at Kit's that night, did George want to come? He glanced back at the table, grinned, and accepted the invitation.

After several days of trail dust, we were all ready to dress up for the party. I put on animal-striped pants, a black camisole, and my darkest red lipstick. When we arrived at Kit's, she greeted us with a pitcher of her famously lethal margaritas that ensured tall tales, and hilarity ensued. Between bites of guacamole and spiced pecans, we learned that George was newly single. By the time I returned to the ranch as chef he had remarried, but this time he was between wives three and four. Perhaps not coincidentally, his eyes sparkled with possibility. "You look different," he said to me approvingly.

"Well, I saw two cowboy hats over here, so I put on lipstick," I replied.

He shot me a glance, we smiled at each other, and a friendship was born. For the next four years, a benign but entertaining pattern ensued. George tried to catch me off guard with suggestive one-liners, and I'd do my best to fire them back.

George owns Elm Creek Stables, a trail

ride operation that caters to tourists, with his fourth wife, a lovely woman named Beverly who shares his passion for horses. George was born in the Frio Canyon. He went to school in Leakey and spent his summers at the dances at Garner State Park (think jukebox ballads and twinkling strings of light). As a young man, George fought his daddy's wish that he settle down with some horses. Instead, he left for the Gulf Coast to make his fortune in the oil business. Ending up in Wyoming, he made his money, lost it, and then returned to the Frio Canyon to settle down with some horses.

To describe George as a quintessential Marlboro man would be accurate, but too easy. Something about him is undeniably billboard sized. His handsome, sun-weathered face is straight out of central casting—it's a shame he didn't ride across the screen in spaghetti Westerns. He is perpetually clad in Wranglers, round-toe Ropers, a plaid shirt, and a well-worn hat. Not that he was wholly predictable. Every now and then he would appear in a fedora too small for his head. To shake his large, rough hand was to better understand the nature of ranch work.

He has a soft side too. George's most endearing quality is his weakness for kids. "That's the reason I do it," he explained one day, referring to his trail ride business, "the little ones." He stays open an extra hour—or saddles a couple of horses early—if a carload of tiny, enthusiastic riders pulls up. He simply cannot disappoint them or turn them away. In the larger sense, I think he is aware of his power as a creator of childhood memories, and he takes the role seriously. He is also a grandfather of mythic proportions. He frequently has a few "grandbabies" in tow. He brought them on trail rides, and took them hunting, fishing, and swimming in the Frio.

No one has been more important, or more of a fixture in our lives in Texas, than George. During our first few months on the ranch, when we were clearly a crimp in his style (he was used to having the place to himself), he would ask us hopefully, "Do you miss New York?" When he finally realized that we were sticking around, we relaxed into allies and a friendship that made our experience richer. George is the first person we call when we need help: when a pipe bursts or a tractor breaks down, when cows escape through a downed fence or a guest with a sprained ankle needs to be carried out of the woods.

In turn, I sate his sweet tooth with a steady supply of cookies, brownies, and pie. I leave plastic-wrapped hunks of pound cake in his truck.

George taught me how to saddle a horse, load it onto a trailer, and pull one in if it ran away with me. "I just took a seminar to learn that," a jodhpur-clad guest told me. "You're lucky to learn just by knowing him." He also taught me that deer lie down before a good rain, and that if a horse starts stomping it's most likely standing in fire ants. He scolded me if I was too nonchalant in the saddle.

"You think that old horse won't run away with you?" he'd say sternly.

On trail ride picnics he showed me that flour tortilla tacos (stuffed with incredibly spicy beans or vermicelli noodles) are most delicious when they are cooked—not just warmed but blistered and *cooked*—directly against red-hot coals. Before we ate, he'd pull a serrano chile and pocketknife from his jacket, slice a few rounds onto his tacos, and hand the pepper to me to finish.

We accepted that George had the run of the place. In the mornings he'd bust into the lodge and shout, "Got any coffee?" In the evenings, he might burst through our front door and yell,

"Got anything with alcohol in it?" Once I called home looking for David and George mysteriously answered our phone. He was there by himself.

George was always in a "hundred-dollar hurry," hustling to make ends meet. To spend time with him was to hear of a check in the mail or a banknote due. To that end, he was a horse trader in every sense of the word. The next big deal was just around the corner, and just about everything was for sale.

In between his own gigs, George led the trail rides for guests. We couldn't have had a better Hill Country ambassador. "We *love* George!" the women would coo, coming in from their rides. George would sit sideways on the lead horse, light a cigarette, and begin his standard series of questions.

"Where are you from? What do you do? What does your husband do?"

"I'm a nurse and my husband is a psychologist," one guest chirped.

"Well, I could use you both," he said in the next beat.

Whether the guest was a lawyer, politician, film producer, or, God forbid, an investment banker, there just might be a way they could work together, he reasoned. Once he'd quizzed all the riders, he'd light another cigarette and consider the possibilities.

George is a great storyteller, with natural comic timing and an arsenal of one-liners. I saved the best "Georgisms" to recount to my father. Some of my favorites:

On a drive home from Uvalde, David and George went through the beverage barn and bought a six-pack of beer. On the drive home, cans were drained with impressive speed. "I don't drink all the time," George said between chugs, "but when I do—I like to drink a lot."

Once, midproject, David asked George if he had a pocketknife. George frowned, pulled a knife from his pocket, and said, "Have I got my pants on?"

A state trooper pulled George over for speeding. "Do you want to tell me why you were going eighty-four miles an hour?" the officer demanded.

"Because this old truck won't go any faster than that," George shot back.

The officer laughed and sent him on his way.

We gossiped about a local woman known for flirtatious behavior. "I'm sure that's why her husband can't stand me," George said.

"I can't remember, is she a good-looking woman?" I asked.

"Hell, Paula, they're all good looking at my age," he answered.

# Prickly Pear Sorbet

**Serves 6 (Makes about 3 cups)**

Prickly pears flourish on the ranch. In the spring they yield beautiful yellow and orange blossoms, and in late summer and fall they become loaded with bright pink fruit. To pick and juice them yourself is a chore—they are covered with tiny needles that will wind up on your clothes and in your dish towels. But the ones you can buy in the store these days have been washed clean of most—but not all—of the prickly stuff.

The flavor of a prickly pear is tart and sweet—I think of it as a cross between kiwi and raspberry. The color of the skin ranges from green to deep magenta and the flesh is hot pink.

The recipe for simple syrup makes more than you'll need for this recipe, but you'll have it on hand for Candied Grapefruit Sorbet (page 241), iced coffee, iced tea, and more batches of this sorbet, of course.

8 **PRICKLY PEARS**
½ cup **SIMPLE SYRUP** (recipe follows)
¼ cup **TRIPLE SEC** or **COINTREAU**
⅓ cup **WATER**
2 tablespoons **LIME ZEST**

Cut the prickly pears in half and use a spoon to scoop out their bright pink pulp. Save the shells for serving or discard them. Place the pulp in a food processor and pulse until the fruit breaks down and forms a chunky, juicy purée. (Do not process continually or you will chop the seeds.) Push the purée through a mesh strainer. You should have about ¾ cup of juice. Combine the juice with the simple syrup, triple sec, water, and lime zest. Process in an ice cream freezer following the manufacturer's instructions. Transfer to a chilled container, cover, and store in the freezer.

# Simple Syrup     **Makes 2 cups**

2 cups **WATER**
2 cups **SUGAR**

Combine the water and sugar in a small saucepan over low heat. Stir until the sugar has dissolved and the mixture turns clear. Increase the heat and bring to a boil. Remove from the heat and cool. Stored in a clean, sealable glass container, this syrup will keep indefinitely at room temperature.

# Candied Grapefruit Sorbet

**Makes about 3 cups**

I have a standard line that goes something like this: "I'd move to California for the produce," or "I'd move to Seattle for the salmon." Well, I'd stay in Texas for the sweet, ruby red grapefruits. In the winter, I eat one every morning. This bracing, tart-sweet sorbet is the quintessence of the best Texas flavor.

> 3 to 4 large **RED GRAPEFRUITS**, to equal 2 cups (reserve the peels)
> 2 cups **SIMPLE SYRUP** (page 240)
> ½ cup **CANDIED GRAPEFRUIT PEELS** (recipe follows)

Trim the peels from the grapefruits and reserve. Juice the grapefruits to equal 2 cups (if you have extra, combine with vodka and drink immediately). Combine the juice and simple syrup and freeze in an ice cream maker according to the manufacturer's instructions. When the mixture is approximately 5 minutes from the desired texture, add the candied peels.

# Candied Grapefruit Peels

> Reserved **GRAPEFRUIT PEELS**
> 1 pound **SUGAR**
> 1 cup **WATER**
> 2 **STAR ANISE**
> 4 **CLOVES**
> 2½- to 3-inch **CINNAMON STICK**

To candy the peels, trim most but not all of the pith from the skins. Cut the peel into wedges. Bring a large pot of water to a boil and blanch the peels for 1 minute. Drain and repeat the blanching two more times with fresh water each time. In the meantime, bring the sugar and water to a boil in a 2-quart saucepan, brushing down the sides of the pan with cold water occasionally to prevent crystals from forming on the pan. Add the star anise, cloves, and cinnamon stick to the syrup. Add the blanched peel, reduce the heat, and simmer for 15 minutes. Remove from the heat and allow the peel to cool in the syrup. For the sorbet, drain the desired amount of peel and cut into small cubes. The remaining peel can be stored in the syrup in a sealed container in the refrigerator and used to garnish ice cream or other desserts.

# Ginger Goats

**Makes about 72 cookies**

This recipe, a variation on a Swedish pepparkakor recipe, came from Jan Bailey and Emily Eastwood, my Norwegian aunts in Minneapolis—go figure. To give these cookies a Texas twist, we doubled the ginger and added ancho chile, which gives them a warm, tingly heat. David rolls out the most beautiful paper-thin cookies. When I prepare them, the goats tend to be a bit chubbier, but they are just as delicious.

3 cups **ALL-PURPOSE FLOUR**

2 teaspoons **BAKING SODA**

1 tablespoon ground **CINNAMON**

1 tablespoon ground **GINGER**

1 tablespoon **ANCHO CHILE POWDER**

1 teaspoon ground **CLOVES**

1 large **EGG**

1 cup (2 sticks) **UNSALTED BUTTER**

2 tablespoons **MOLASSES**

1½ cups **SUGAR**

**1.** In a large bowl, whisk together the flour, soda, and spices. In the bowl of an electric mixer fitted with the paddle attachment, cream the egg, butter, and molasses, then gradually add the sugar and beat until combined, about 2 minutes.

**2.** Gradually add the dry ingredients to the creamed mixture and stir just until combined. Divide the dough into three equal parts, pat them each out into a rectangle, and wrap in plastic. Refrigerate for at least 30 minutes.

**3.** Place one rectangle of dough on a lightly floured surface (keep the other two in the fridge) and roll out very thin. Cut out goat shapes (or any other shape you have) and place on parchment-paper-lined baking sheets. Bake in a preheated 400°F oven for 5 to 8 minutes. Watch them closely, as they can burn easily.

**4.** Cool on a wire rack and store in an airtight container.

# MY FAVORITE SPOT ON THE FRIO

After enough time passes, it becomes an itch that needs to be scratched: I need to get to the river. I want to see the particular light of the place and swim in its cool, clear water. Luckily my favorite spot on the Frio, a certain point where the beach is wide and the current picks up speed through narrow chutes that rush around rocks, is just a couple of miles away. Sometimes I sneak off with the dogs and go alone. I spend an hour or so throwing them branches to fetch, or I simply stretch out on the rocks and daydream. But mostly I go when I want to have a party. I call friends in Uvalde and we figure out who will bring what. We pick simple foods that are easy to eat. I call my friend Rebecca, who owns Rather Sweet bakery in Fredericksburg. I phone the McKays, musician friends from Bandera, and beg them to bring their guitars. "The beer will be cold and the food delicious," I offer as enticement.

The Frio is one of the most beloved destinations in South Texas. From spring break to Labor Day, families and college kids descend on the area with coolers, kayaks, and charcoal. They rent cabins in Concan and spend afternoons floating down the river on inner tubes. After a good rain the ride is swift and lively. When it's dry, which is most of the time, it's a lazy drift past cedar and cypress roots, and your butt drags every now and then—just like life, I guess.

My favorite stretch of river is more private and not as accessible. Every now and then there will be kids fishing or neon-colored tubes, but usually it's quiet. Heaven is having the place to ourselves, which happens more often than not.

Before a party, I aim to arrive early, so I can have a few minutes to savor the quiet before the fun, frenetic chaos ensues. The dogs can't wait to bail out of the pickup. I grab the cooler and pull a bag of snacks over my shoulder. I sneak past a fence and walk down to the water, negotiating smooth white stones in flip-flops or cowboy boots.

The bank of the Frio is a pale, stark surface of weathered limestone, more reminiscent of a lunar landscape than a beach. I walk a half mile south to the flat rock that we use as a table. I drop my stuff and head to the water, kicking off my shoes. I find a stick to throw to Dilley, my chocolate Lab, who is already swimming. Her wet head is slick as a seal's as she paddles toward me.

I step across slippery, submerged stones until I reach a path of large rocks that jut out of the water and form a dry path to the middle of the river. The biggest stone at the end has a wide, flat top perfect for lounging. I sit down, absorbing the heat of the afternoon sun, hug my knees to my chest, and listen to the rush of water. It occurs to me that it is the sound people pay to have piped into their massage room. I have everything to look forward to. The evening will only get prettier until it is dark, and then the stars will shine and we'll build a fire.

Dilley scrambles onto the rock beside me and leans her full weight against my back, soaking my cover-up. Georgia, our blue heeler, is midstream on a rock. She wants to join us but peers at the swift current that runs between her perch and the next, uncertain about making the jump. Slidell, who hates water, races back and forth on the bank, concealing his embarrassment and hurt feelings with angry, scolding barks.

"*Aiiiyeee!*" I hear Melissa yelp. She and the Uvalde gang are walking toward me in a colorful parade of bowls and blankets. Her husband, Craig, carries a tin tub for beer. I watch them approach and feel lucky to know so many kind people. I leap back across the rocks and step across the stones to the riverbank. We spread out blankets and gather smooth, sun-bleached branches of cedar for a fire.

David picks up a champagne cork and says, "Look, from last time."

I hoist an icy pink jug of watermelon margaritas on a rock and the boys fill a tub of beer bottles with ice. Melissa offers me roasted pecans flavored the way her mother has always done them—moistened with butter, a generous splash of Worcestershire, and plenty of coarse salt.

Finally, when the sun and swimming have made everyone hungry, we are ready to sit down and eat. I use a tortilla chip to scoop up a big bite of guacamole, chunky with onions, serrano chiles, cilantro, and plenty of lime. I pass a plate of deviled eggs slathered with homemade tapenade. Celina unwraps her famous empanadas filled with fresh ricotta and sautéed peppers.

David grills skewers of serrano chiles and smoked Elgin sausages that drip and hiss on the fire. We serve them with tortillas, also blistered on the grill, and whole grain mustard or mayonnaise flavored with a few chopped chipotle chiles. I pass a bowl of green and white beans that have been tossed with an herbaceous oil fragrant with garlic, fresh marjoram, and oregano. Melissa hands me a plate of her perfectly fried chicken flautas. The crisp, tightly rolled cylinders are fun to dip into bowls of smoky red chile salsa.

"Play the river song!" I plead with the McKays, referring to a favorite from their first album.

The brothers reach for their guitars and start to strum. Noel begins, "When I reach the Pedernales . . ."

The dogs settle in close and drift in and out of sleep. The sun sinks so we build up the fire. I try to figure exactly what it is about this place that makes me so happy. Is it the sound of rushing water or the smooth, clean expanse of stone? Or is it the luxury of having an idyllic place to swim, relax with friends, and eat good food? It's all these things. This place, this moment, is the world as it should be. I uncover a tin pail of Milk Chocolate Chip Oatmeal Cookies and pass them around. Perfect.

# Milk Chocolate Chip Oatmeal Cookies

**Makes 36 cookies**

These cookies are a variation on a recipe that I've been making from a church cookbook since I was about fourteen. I love the even ratio of oats to flour, which makes the cookie chewy and substantial. I use two chips, milk chocolate and semisweet, and cacao nibs, roasted cocoa beans that have been crushed into small bits. The nibs add a nice crunch and a unique chocolate flavor, but feel free to substitute chopped pecans or walnuts or leave them out altogether if you prefer.

I take a pail of these cookies to parties at the Frio because they are easy to pass around and everyone loves them—but I confess that my favorite time to eat them is in the morning with coffee. For the prettiest cookies, let the dough chill for at least 30 minutes before scooping out and baking—they'll hold their shape better in the oven.

2 cups **ALL-PURPOSE FLOUR**

2 cups **OLD-FASHIONED ROLLED OATS**

1 teaspoon **BAKING SODA**

1 teaspoon **SALT**

Scant $\frac{1}{2}$ teaspoon **GRATED NUTMEG**

1 cup (2 sticks) **UNSALTED BUTTER**, softened

$\frac{3}{4}$ cup **GRANULATED SUGAR**

$\frac{3}{4}$ cup **DARK BROWN SUGAR**

2 large **EGGS**

2 teaspoons pure **VANILLA EXTRACT**

$1\frac{1}{2}$ cups **SEMISWEET CHOCOLATE CHIPS** or chunks

$1\frac{1}{2}$ cups **MILK CHOCOLATE CHIPS**

$\frac{1}{2}$ cup **COCOA NIBS** (optional)

**1.** Preheat the oven to 350°F.

**2.** In a large bowl, whisk together the flour, oats, baking soda, salt, and nutmeg.

**3.** In the bowl of an electric mixer fitted with the paddle attachment, cream the butter and sugars at medium-high speed until light and fluffy, about 2 minutes. Scrape down the sides of the bowl as needed. Add the eggs, one at a time, beating after each addition. Mix in the vanilla.

**4.** Add half the dry ingredients to the butter-sugar mixture and mix at a low speed until just blended. Add the remaining dry ingredients and mix until no dry crumbs remain.

Add the chocolate chips and cocoa nibs and stir just to combine. Cover the dough with plastic and refrigerate for at least 30 minutes or up to several hours.

**5.** Use a spoon to scoop out golf ball–sized rounds of dough (roll them between your fingers briefly to shape). Place on parchment-lined cookie sheets and bake for 12 to 14 minutes until lightly golden. Cool on the baking sheets for 5 minutes, then transfer to a counter or a cooling rack. Stored in a tightly sealed container, these cookies will keep well for up to 1 week. They freeze beautifully.

# Apple, Pear, and Honey Soufflés

**Makes 8 individual soufflés**

Warm from the oven, this luscious, fragrant soufflé is so satisfying it's hard to believe it's low fat. It's made with homemade apple-pear sauce and whipped egg whites. Dried pears help deepen the fruit flavor. A whisper of butter is used on the ramekins, but other than that it's virtually fat free.

8 individual ramekins

2 to 3 (about 1 pound) **TART-SWEET APPLES**, peeled, cored, and sliced
3 to 4 (about 1½ pounds) **RIPE PEARS**, peeled, cored, and sliced
1 **LEMON**, for juicing
¼ cup **HONEY**
4 dried **PEAR HALVES**, chopped
1 tablespoon **POIRE WILLIAM LIQUEUR** (optional)
**BUTTER**, for greasing ramekins
2 tablespoons **SUGAR**
8 large **EGG WHITES**, at room temperature
¼ teaspoon **CREAM OF TARTAR**

1. Peel and slice the fruit, letting the pieces fall into a large bowl of water acidulated with the lemon juice. When you're finished peeling, drain the fruit and transfer to a 2-quart saucepan. Add the honey and bring to a simmer over medium heat. Reduce the heat to low and cook, uncovered, for 20 minutes, stirring often, until the fruit breaks down and thickens. Add the dried pears and cook an additional 10 minutes. The fruit should cook down into a thick purée. Remove from the heat, stir in the Poire William if using, and cool. Transfer the mixture to a blender and purée until smooth.

2. Preheat the oven to 425°F. Butter the ramekins, then dust the dish with the sugar.

3. In a large bowl, beat the egg whites and cream of tartar until they form stiff (but not dry) peaks. Stir a quarter of the beaten egg whites into the fruit purée. Gently fold in the rest. Transfer to the individual ramekins. Place on a baking sheet and bake for 12 to 14 minutes, until puffed and brown. Serve immediately.

NOTE: You can make the fruit purée several days in advance.

# Drunken Prune Pound Cake

**Makes 1 cake**

**Serves 8 to 10**

If this cake were a car, it would be a 1967 Impala—unabashedly sturdy, built for comfort, and vintage in its flavor and construction. Its bells and whistles are old-fashioned in a poignant sort of way. I'm a sucker for a dowdy Southern pound cake, preferably one made with buttermilk and plenty of eggs, butter, and sugar. In this version, brandy-soaked prunes lend a rich, boozy flavor. A healthy dose of citrus zest balances the sweetness. Serve a big hunk of this cake with strong coffee in the morning, tea in the middle of the afternoon, or a glass of Armagnac at night. The prunes need to be macerated at least one day in advance, but the rest of the cake comes together in minutes. Tightly wrapped in plastic, it keeps well for about 5 days.

One 9 × 3-inch tube or bundt pan

**BUTTER**, for greasing the pan

3 cups **ALL-PURPOSE FLOUR**, plus extra for the pan

1 teaspoon **KOSHER SALT**

$\frac{1}{2}$ teaspoon **BAKING SODA**

1 cup (2 sticks) **UNSALTED BUTTER** (at room temperature)

2 cups **GRANULATED SUGAR**

1 cup **DARK BROWN SUGAR**

4 large **EGGS**

1 cup well-shaken **BUTTERMILK**

1 teaspoon pure **VANILLA EXTRACT**

$\frac{1}{4}$ teaspoon **ALMOND EXTRACT**

Grated zest of 1 medium **ORANGE**

Grated zest of 1 **LEMON**

$\frac{1}{2}$ cup brandy-soaked **PRUNES** (see page 250), chopped

**1.** Preheat the oven to 325°F and position the rack in the lower third of the oven. Butter and flour the pan, shaking out the excess, or spray with nonstick vegetable spray.

**2.** In a large bowl, whisk together the flour, salt, and soda. In the bowl of an electric mixer fitted with a paddle attachment, cream the butter and sugars at medium-high speed until light and fluffy, about 3 minutes. Beat in the eggs, one at a time, mixing well after each addition. Add the flour mixture alternately with the buttermilk. Mix in the extracts and zests and fold in the prunes. Bake for about 1 hour, until the cake pulls away from the pan and a toothpick inserted into the center of the cake comes out clean.

## BRANDY-PLUMPED PRUNES

*P*lumping dried fruit in brandy or another spirit is an old-fashioned way of preserving them. The fruit softens, absorbs the alcohol, and eventually the liquid becomes more of a viscous jelly. I keep a container of them in my pantry, for this cake and a fast topping on vanilla or coffee ice cream. To make them, empty a 16-ounce container of prunes into a clean, sealable glass jar and pour brandy (it doesn't have to be an expensive brand) over the top until it covers them by about an inch. Kept in a cool dark place, the prunes will keep for months.

# Persimmon Pudding with Bittersweet Ganache

**Serves 6 to 8**

Back in New York, David and I belonged to a dining group dubbed the Brooklyn Social Club, which was a pretty refined name for a bunch of friends who liked to eat and drink a lot. At one such dinner my friend April Sachs, a talented and enthusiastic baker of all things sweet, brought this delicious pudding.

With a moist texture somewhere between custard and a molten cake, this pudding needs nothing more than a dollop of whipped cream, but it's really good with an additional drizzle of silky Bittersweet Ganache and a few Spicy Mixed Nuts (page 102) on the plate. I crave it on a cold winter night by the fire, with a glass of something strong nearby.

1½-quart baking dish (such as a ceramic oval-shaped gratin)
**BUTTER**, for greasing the baking dish

1 cup **ALL-PURPOSE FLOUR**
1 teaspoon **BAKING POWDER**
¼ teaspoon **KOSHER SALT**
¼ teaspoon ground **CINNAMON**
¼ teaspoon ground **ALLSPICE**
3 ripe **PERSIMMONS** (see Note)
1 cup **HALF-AND-HALF**
¾ cup firmly packed **DARK BROWN SUGAR**
¼ cup **BUTTER**, melted and cooled
½ cup chopped **WALNUTS** or **PECANS**
8 ounces **HEAVY CREAM**, for whipping
**BITTERSWEET GANACHE** (recipe follows)

**1.** Preheat the oven to 325°F. Butter the baking dish.

**2.** Whisk together the dry ingredients in a medium-sized bowl.

**3.** Blanch the persimmons in a pot of boiling water for 2 to 3 minutes. Drain in a colander, plunge into an ice bath, drain again, and peel. Quarter the persimmons, place them in the bowl of a food processor, and pulse to chop. Add the half-and-half and purée until smooth. Add the brown sugar and melted butter and purée until just blended.

**4.** Fold the wet ingredients into the dry ingredients. Stir in the walnuts and scrape the batter into a buttered baking dish. Bake for 50 minutes to 1 hour, until the pudding pulls away from the sides of the dish (the surface of the pudding should still be fairly soft). Serve warm or at room temperature with whipped cream and/or Bittersweet Ganache.

# Bittersweet Ganache

> 4 ounces good-quality **BITTERSWEET CHOCOLATE**
> 1 cup **HEAVY CREAM**
> ¼ teaspoon ground **CINNAMON**
> 1 tablespoon **COGNAC** or **BRANDY**

Coarsely chop the chocolate and place in a medium bowl. Put the cream in a small saucepan and bring to a simmer over medium-low heat. Pour the cream over the chocolate and let the mixture rest until the chocolate has softened. Stir together with the cinnamon and Cognac. Drizzle the warm ganache over each serving of persimmon pudding.

**NOTE:** I mostly make this with Fuyu persimmons, the smaller variety that look like little tomatoes. You can also use the larger Hachiya persimmons that are shaped like bell peppers with a slightly tapered stem. But the latter needs to be *very* soft and ripe or it will have a harsh, astringent quality that makes your tongue dry up. Fuyu persimmons are sweet even when they're firm.

# Chocolate Whiskey Cake

**Makes a 10-inch cake**

Like spurs, a caliche-dusted pickup, and pearl-snap shirts, whiskey became a way of life when we moved to Texas. It was only a matter of time before it found its way onto the dessert menu. A dark, dense, and superrich chocolate cake was the best choice. The flavor of this cake deepens if it's made at least one day ahead. Because I'm a gingerbread freak, I've added the faintest whiff of ground black pepper and cloves. The chocolate chips dissolve when they're baked, making the texture fudgier and the flavor deeper and more intense.

Need I suggest serving this with a shot of whiskey (preferably a single-barrel bourbon like Knob Creek) or a cup of coffee-spiked whiskey?

12 tablespoons (1$\frac{1}{2}$ sticks) **UNSALTED BUTTER**, cut into 1-inch pieces, plus more to grease the pan

$\frac{3}{4}$ cup plus 3 tablespoons unsweetened (not Dutch process) **COCOA POWDER**

1$\frac{1}{2}$ cups **STRONG BREWED COFFEE**

$\frac{1}{2}$ cup **WHISKEY**

1 cup **GRANULATED SUGAR**

1 cup **DARK BROWN SUGAR**

2 cups **ALL-PURPOSE FLOUR**

1$\frac{1}{2}$ teaspoons **BAKING SODA**

$\frac{3}{4}$ teaspoon **SALT**

$\frac{1}{4}$ teaspoon freshly ground **BLACK PEPPER**

$\frac{1}{8}$ teaspoon ground **CLOVES**

3 large **EGGS**

2 teaspoons pure **VANILLA EXTRACT**

1 cup **MINI CHOCOLATE CHIPS**

**1.** Place an oven rack in the center of the oven and preheat to 325°F. Butter a 10-inch springform pan and then dust with 3 tablespoons cocoa powder, tapping out the excess.

**2.** Heat the coffee, whiskey, butter, and remaining $\frac{3}{4}$ cup of cocoa powder in a heavy medium saucepan over low heat until the butter is melted, whisking occasionally. Add the sugars and whisk until dissolved. Remove from the heat, transfer the mixture to a large bowl, and cool.

**3.** While the chocolate cools, whisk together the flour, baking soda, salt, black pepper, and cloves in a large bowl. In a separate small bowl, whisk together the eggs and vanilla.

Beginning with a slow drizzle, whisk the eggs into the cooled chocolate mixture until combined. Add the flour mixture and whisk until smooth (but don't overmix), then stir in the chocolate chips. Pour the batter into the prepared pan and bake until a wooden pick inserted into the center comes out mostly clean, about 50 minutes to 1 hour.

**4.** Cool the cake in the pan on a rack (if you're going to leave the cake in the pan overnight cover it with a dish towel so it doesn't dry out). Using the tip of a knife, loosen the cake from the pan and remove the outer ring. Wrap the cake in plastic so it doesn't dry out. After 1 day, store it in the fridge, where it will last up to 1 week.

# Chocolate Pecan Squares

**Makes sixteen 2½-inch squares**

The ingredients of these rich, chewy bars are a confluence of my favorite local Hill Country flavors. There are three pecan orchards on the ranch, so we use the nuts in sourdough bread, salads, cookies, and desserts. The secret to the rich, caramel-like filling, made with local honey, is a good amount of salt. Mexican chocolate is typically perfumed with a bit of cinnamon. I've opted for bittersweet chocolate and added the spice to the buttery cookie base.

9 × 9-inch baking pan

## COOKIE BASE

1½ sticks **UNSALTED BUTTER**
2 cups **ALL-PURPOSE FLOUR**
½ cup packed **LIGHT BROWN SUGAR**
½ teaspoon **SALT**
2 teaspoons ground **CINNAMON**

## PECAN TOPPING

10 ounces **PECANS**, toasted
1 stick **UNSALTED BUTTER**
1 cup **DARK BROWN SUGAR**
½ teaspoon **KOSHER SALT**
⅓ cup **UVALDE** (or other) **HONEY**
2 tablespoons **HEAVY CREAM**

3 ounces finely grated **BITTERSWEET CHOCOLATE** (such as Scharffen Berger)

1. Preheat the oven to 350°F.

2. Cut the butter into ½-inch pieces and place in a food processor along with the flour, light brown sugar, salt, and cinnamon. Process until the mixture begins to form pea-sized clumps. Sprinkle the mixture into a 9 × 9-inch baking pan and, using your fingers, pat out evenly into the bottom. Bake the cookie crust in the middle of the oven until golden, about 25 minutes. While the cookie base is baking, prepare the topping.

3. In the bowl of a food processor, coarsely chop the pecans. In a medium-size heavy saucepan, melt the butter and stir in the dark brown sugar, salt, honey, and cream. Simmer the mixture for 1 minute, stirring occasionally, then stir in the pecans.

4.  When the cookie base comes out of the oven, sprinkle the grated chocolate evenly over the top. Pour the pecan mixture over the chocolate, spreading evenly. Bake in the middle of the oven until the entire filling (not just the edges of the pan) is bubbling, about 18 minutes.

5.  Cool completely in the pan and cut into bars. Tightly covered, these bars will keep about 5 days (though they never last that long!).

# Espresso Brownies

**Makes twenty 2-inch brownies**

Brownies are my kind of dessert, and this recipe is a winner, one that you'll immediately zip off to friends and family members and make for years to come. I bake them in a 9 × 9-inch square pan, so they are particularly thick and chewy, but you can also bake them in a 9 × 13-inch pan for less time and a thinner bar. Wrapped tightly in foil, these brownies keep for up to a week and ship particularly well—send them to kids in college and special friends on their birthdays.

9 × 9-inch (or 9 × 13-inch) baking pan
**BUTTER**, for greasing the pan

1 pound (2⅓ cups) **DARK BROWN SUGAR**
1½ sticks **UNSALTED BUTTER**
2 tablespoons **INSTANT ESPRESSO POWDER**
1 tablespoon hot **WATER**
2 large **EGGS**
1 tablespoon plus 1 teaspoon **PURE VANILLA EXTRACT**
1 tablespoon **KAHLÚA** or other **COFFEE LIQUEUR**
2 cups **ALL-PURPOSE FLOUR**
2 teaspoons **BAKING POWDER**
½ teaspoon **KOSHER SALT**
1 cup chopped **PECANS**
5 ounces good-quality **BITTERSWEET CHOCOLATE**, coarsely chopped into chunks

1. Preheat the oven to 350°F and butter the baking pan.

2. In a medium saucepan or microwave-safe bowl, heat the sugar and butter until the butter melts. Stir well to combine.

3. In a small bowl, dissolve the instant espresso in the hot water. Stir the espresso into the sugar mixture and cool to room temperature. Beat in the eggs, vanilla, and Kahlúa.

4. In a separate medium bowl, whisk together the flour, baking powder, and salt. Stir the dry ingredients into the butter mixture. Stir in the pecans and chocolate chunks.

5. Spread the batter evenly into the prepared pan. Bake 45 to 55 minutes (10 minutes less for a 9 × 13-inch pan), or until a wooden toothpick inserted into the center comes out clean. Cool completely and cut into squares.

# Dulce de Leche Flan with Pepita Brittle

**Makes 6 flans**

Pressed to pick a favorite dessert flavor, I'd have a hard time choosing between caramel and coffee. Needless to say dulce de leche, or sweetened, caramelized cream, is right up my alley. Stirring the thick syrup into a traditional flan creates a dessert that's both dense and silky, with a texture more like sour cream than gelatin. You can make your own dulce de leche (see page 261), but you can also buy it in a can (Nestlé makes a version that tastes exactly like the stuff I make myself). Pretty as stained glass, a shard of Pepita Brittle (made with just a hint of spice) is a striking garnish—but these flans are absolutely delicious on their own.

6 individual 4-ounce flan molds

1 cup **SUGAR**
2 cups **WHOLE MILK**
One 14-ounce can **DULCE DE LECHE** (see page 261)
2 large **EGGS**, plus 2 **EGG YOLKS**
1 tablespoon **PURE VANILLA EXTRACT**
**PEPITA BRITTLE** (recipe follows), for garnish (optional)

1. Melt the sugar in a small saucepan over medium-low heat, stirring occasionally. When the sugar is melted and a deep amber color, quickly pour it into flan molds and set aside.

2. Heat the oven to 300°F. Put on a kettle of water to boil for the water bath. Scald the milk in a small, heavy-bottomed saucepan over medium heat, then stir in the dulce de leche until dissolved and remove from the heat. While the milk is heating, whisk together the eggs and yolks and vanilla, either by hand or in an electric mixer fitted with the whisk attachment, until pale yellow.

3. Very slowly at first, drizzle the milk and dulce de leche into the eggs, whisking constantly. As the eggs become tempered, increase the speed of pouring but keep to a slow, steady stream. When all the milk mixture is incorporated, pour the custard into the molds over the caramel. Place the molds in a high-sided baking pan and carefully pour hot water around them, coming to within an inch of the tops. Bake the flans for 30 to 40 minutes, until set in the center. Remove from the water bath and allow to cool on a wire rack for 20 minutes, then chill. To serve, place each mold in boiling water for 30 seconds (to loosen the hardened caramel), run a knife around the top edge, and invert on a serving plate. Allow the liquid caramel to run over the flan. Garnish with Pepita Brittle, if desired.

## DULCE DE LECHE

*I*'d always heard that the best way to make dulce de leche was to boil an unopened can of sweetened condensed milk for 4 hours. But that method always came with a warning: The milk expands during the cooking process, so there's a risk the can will explode. Luckily my friend Rebecca Rather taught me a faster and safer method that yields equally delicious results.

Remove the wrapper from a 14-ounce can of sweetened condensed milk. Use a can opener to make 2 small punctures on opposite sides of the top of the can. Place the can in a 2-quart saucepan with the punctured side up. Add water to reach two thirds of the way up the can. Cover the saucepan and bring the water to a boil. Lower the heat and simmer until the milk pooled on the can has turned deep golden brown, about 1 hour. Check the water level occasionally to ensure the water level does not drop below halfway. Don't worry if a bit of milk seeps out of the can during cooking.

## *Pepita Brittle*

For the best results, use a candy thermometer to make this brittle. The corn syrup helps keep the candy from crystallizing.

> **COOKING SPRAY** and **VEGETABLE OIL**, for the pan
> ½ cup **PEPITAS**
> ¼ cup sliced **ALMONDS**
> 1½ cups **SUGAR**
> ¾ cup **WATER**
> 1 tablespoon **CORN SYRUP**
> Generous pinch of **KOSHER SALT**
> Pinch of **CAYENNE**

1. Line a 9 × 13-inch baking sheet with aluminum foil. Spray with cooking spray or lightly coat with vegetable oil. Spread the seeds and nuts onto the foil.

2. Combine the sugar, water, corn syrup, salt, and cayenne in a heavy, nonaluminum pan. Stir over medium heat until dissolved—then do not stir again. Bring the syrup to a boil, brushing down the sides of the pan occasionally with water to keep the sugar from crystallizing. Measure the temperature with a candy thermometer, bringing the syrup to 340°F. Carefully pour the syrup over the seeds and nuts and allow to cool completely. Break into shards to garnish the flans.

# Chamomile Poached Pears

**Serves 8**

Displayed alongside the poblanos, tomatillos, and ancho chiles in my supermarket are dried bunches of manzanilla, or chamomile. Tiny yellow flowers still cling to the stems on the freshest specimens. Chamomile is most commonly used for tea, but I wanted to use its floral perfume for something more unique—like scenting a ripe, luscious pear. To make this light and soothing dessert, you simply make a pot of tea, flavored with honey, lemon, vanilla bean, and white peppercorns, then poach pears in the aromatic liquid. I can't imagine a lighter and more soothing way to end a meal.

Be sure to save the fragrant poaching liquid for your next batch. After you poach the first batch of pears, it will sweeten even more. Store it in a clean sealed container in the refrigerator for up to 2 months.

One ½-ounce bunch **DRIED CHAMOMILE** (manzanilla; see Note)
½ cup **HONEY**
2 cups **RIESLING** or other **AROMATIC WINE**
One 3-inch strip **LEMON PEEL** (without pith)
1 **VANILLA BEAN**, split in half
1 tablespoon **WHITE PEPPERCORNS**
6 cups **WATER**
Pinch of **SALT**
8 ripe **PEARS**
1 **LEMON**, for juicing

1. Combine the chamomile, honey, wine, peel, vanilla bean, peppercorns, water, and salt in a medium saucepan and bring to a boil over medium-high heat. Reduce the heat and simmer for 15 minutes. Remove from the heat, cover, and steep for an additional 15 minutes. Strain the liquid and return to the pot.

2. Meanwhile, peel the pears, keeping the stem intact. Drop them directly into a bowl of water acidulated with the juice of 1 lemon to keep them from turning brown.

3. Bring the poaching liquid to a simmer. Drain the pears, add to the liquid, simmer for 10 minutes, and remove from the heat. Cover and allow the pears to cool in the liquid. Serve warm, or chill for several hours or up to 2 days—the pears are delicious warm or cold.

NOTE: If you can't buy dried chamomile by the bunch, use 8 tea bags (with string and paper tag removed) instead.

## S'MORES 101

*W*hen I told my ex-boss, a type A New Yorker of the highest order, that we were serving s'mores one night a week out by the campfire, she said, "Oooh, are you making your own graham crackers and marshmallows? Everyone is doing that in New York." Um, negatory on that. I applaud the bakers who are crafting their own s'more fixings. But if I wanted to do that sort of cooking, I would have stayed in New York and spent most of my time in a toque. With our small staff, we are kept plenty busy getting three meals out a day. Besides, how can you improve on a classic?

S'mores are an interesting study in personality. We quickly observed that all people fall into one of two categories: flamers and slow roasters. The flamers are impatient and aggressive types who want immediate satisfaction. They thrust their marshmallows directly into the fire, where they promptly ignite into flames. This creates a black-crusted marshmallow with a molten center. I fall into this category.

The slow roasters are more cautious and show restraint. For them, it is all about the perfect technique. They hold their skewers gingerly, at a respectable distance from the fire, until the marshmallow puffs, then turns an increasingly deep shade of tan. They rotate the marshmallow so it toasts evenly, for a result that you can only call pretty.

I'm happy to report that both species can exist peacefully around a campfire and in life in general (David is a slow roaster). Beyond that, the process is pretty straightforward. A gleaming slab of Hershey's milk chocolate is placed on a graham cracker half. The two halves are sandwiched around the molten marshmallow and pulled off the skewer. Cassie Detering, Kit's daughter, did teach me the ingenious method of placing the chocolate-topped cracker on a rock near the fire, so it begins to soften in preparation for the sandwich.

There are variations, of course. You can make s'mores with Ginger Goats (page 242), gingersnaps, or fancy dark chocolate. You can forgo the process altogether and simply make S'more Bars (page 265). As long as there's a fire to huddle around and a sky full of stars overhead, I'll take them just about any way they come—as long as I don't have to wait too long and they're well done, that is.

# S'more Bars

**Makes 16 squares**

I tell my friend Rebecca Rather, the chef and owner of Rather Sweet Bakery & Cafe in Fredericksburg, that it's all her fault we moved to Texas. I hadn't heard of Hart & Hind until I came to Hill Country to write a story about her for *Food & Wine*. Since then she's become one of my dearest friends—not just because she always brings me shortbread pig cookies with pink icing (one of her specialties). Whenever we can steal away from our respective kitchens we sneak off to ride horses (a tricky and comical endeavor, since she rides English and I ride Western), hear music in Austin, or meet for an enchilada lunch in San Antonio.

One of Rebecca's most endearing qualities is her generosity: She always shows up with a bakery box of treats. When she brought these sumptuous S'more Bars, a sophisticated take on the campfire classic, to one of our parties at the Frio, the night got even sweeter.

These bars are easy to assemble, but the cinnamon-marshmallow filling needs 4 hours to set up, so plan accordingly.

### GRAHAM CRACKER CRUST

2 cups **GRAHAM CRACKER CRUMBS**

4 cups toasted sliced **ALMONDS**, crushed

2 tablespoons **SUGAR**

1 cup (2 sticks) **UNSALTED BUTTER**, melted

### CINNAMON-MARSHMALLOW FILLING

$1\frac{1}{2}$ envelopes **UNFLAVORED GELATIN**

1 cup **COLD WATER**

$1\frac{1}{2}$ cups **SUGAR**

1 cup **LIGHT CORN SYRUP**

$\frac{1}{4}$ teaspoon **SALT**

$\frac{1}{4}$ teaspoon ground **CINNAMON**

### CHOCOLATE TOPPING

4 cups chopped **BITTERSWEET CHOCOLATE**

1 cup **HEAVY CREAM**

1 teaspoon **PURE VANILLA EXTRACT**

1. Combine the ingredients for the crust in a large bowl and press into a 9 × 13-inch pan.

2. Make the filling. Using a mixer fitted with a whisk attachment, whip the gelatin into $\frac{1}{2}$ cup cold water. In a medium saucepan, heat the sugar, corn syrup, the remaining $\frac{1}{2}$ cup

water, and the salt, without stirring, until it reaches the soft-ball stage, registering 234°F to 240°F on a candy thermometer. Add the warm sugar mixture to the gelatin mixture in a slow, thin stream, stirring continuously on low speed. Increase to high speed and beat about 5 minutes, until the mixture has thickened and cooled. Reduce the speed to low, add the cinnamon, and beat until incorporated. Spread the marshmallow filling over the graham cracker crust. The filling will need about 4 hours to set up.

3. Meanwhile, make the topping. In a saucepan over low heat, melt the chocolate. Off the heat, stir in the cream and vanilla until the mixture is smooth.

4. Once the filling is firm, drizzle with the chocolate topping, cut into 4-inch squares, and serve.

Lethal Libations

*I*n the early days in the Frio Canyon, passing another car on the road was such a rare occurrence that the two vehicles would stop to greet each other. One driver would inevitably pull a bottle of whiskey from under the seat of his car, take off the cap, wipe the top of the bottle on his sleeve, and offer the other driver a sip. After accepting the sip, the driver would wipe the bottle on his own sleeve, and then return it. Apparently never more than a sip or two were taken, but it was a nice greeting and a civilized exchange.

The tradition of cocktails, as both a greeting and form of hospitality, is still alive and well in the Frio Canyon and South Texas. Being in such close proximity to Mexico ensures that margaritas are as ubiquitous at parties as sweet tea is with a meal. Mexico inspires in other ways as well: I love to keep pitchers of agua fresca, or sweetened fresh water, on hand for guests. The following concoctions are my favorites for parties, for friends who happen to stop by on a dry and dusty day, or for a lazy evening on the porch.

# Tamarind-Ginger Agua Fresca

**Serves 8**

Spanish for "fresh water," agua fresca is a ubiquitous south-of-the-border cooler. This preparation is based on Rick Bayless's recipe in *Authentic Mexican*. The ginger is not traditional, but I love its tingly heat.

The dark, sticky pulp underneath the rough exterior of the pod provides the essence of tamarind's flavor. Ice-cold *tamarindo* (tamarind agua fresca) is delicious served with enchiladas verdes, grilled chicken, or simply as a midmorning or midafternoon pick-me-up. It's a welcome thirst quencher for guests when they return from hiking our canyon trails.

8 large fresh **TAMARIND PODS**
One 2-inch piece of fresh **GINGERROOT**, peeled and thinly sliced
$\frac{1}{2}$ cup **HONEY**, or more to taste

1. To clean the tamarind pods, hold a pod in one hand, loosen the stem with the other, and firmly pull out the stem, along with the runners that trail down between the shell and pulp. Peel off the shell.

2. Bring 1 quart of water to a boil, add the tamarind pods, gingerroot, and honey, then boil 1 minute. Pour into a noncorrosive container.

3. Let the mixture stand at least 2 hours (the fresher the pod, the more quickly it will soften up). Using your hand or the back of a wooden spoon, break up the softened pods to free the pulp and seeds; knead the fibrous materials carefully to free all of the pulp.

4. To finish the drink, strain the mixture through a fine-mesh sieve, pressing hard on the seeds and fibers to extract as much of the essence as possible. Adjust the sweetness to suit your taste, then cover and refrigerate until serving. Stir well before pouring.

5. You can also use tamarind paste. Scrape about $\frac{2}{3}$ cup into a blender or food processor with 2 cups water and $\frac{1}{2}$ cup honey or sugar. Pulse until the seeds are dislodged. Strain and stir in $1\frac{1}{2}$ cups water. This drink will keep in the refrigerator for about 5 days.

# Gulf Breeze Bloody Mary

**Serves 4 generously**

When David and I would take road trips along I-10 to visit his parents in Pensacola, we would start daydreaming about these delicious Bloody Marys. David's dad George, an enthusiastic and attentive host, made them with particular flourish.

1 quart **CAMPBELL'S TOMATO JUICE**

3 tablespoons **HORSERADISH**

3 tablespoons **WORCESTERSHIRE SAUCE**

2 tablespoons **TABASCO SAUCE**

1 to 2 tablespoons fresh **LEMON JUICE**

1 teaspoon **CELERY SALT**

8 ounces best-quality **VODKA** (such as Tito's vodka from Austin)

**LEMON WEDGES**

**SALT** (or a salt-herb mixture or Bloody Mary rimmer), for crusting the glasses

4 pretty **CELERY STALKS**

4 fresh **SCALLIONS** (optional)

4 thin **LEMON SLICES**

4 large **PIMIENTO-STUFFED OLIVES**

Chopped fresh **DILL**, for garnish (optional)

Combine the tomato juice, horseradish, Worcestershire, Tabasco, lemon juice, celery salt, and vodka in a pitcher and stir well. Rub the rim of each glass with a wedge of lemon. Dip each glass in salt. Stir each drink with a long celery stalk and garnish with scallions, lemon slices, and large pimiento-stuffed olives on a skewer and chopped dill, if desired.

# Sparkling Verbena Cocktails

**Makes 1 cup verbena syrup, enough for 8 cocktails**

When I still lived in New York, I'd often meet my friend Amanda Hesser for an after-work libation. One hot summer afternoon, we met at the restaurant Verbena (which has since closed). We sat in their garden, under a shady arbor, and sipped their house cocktail, a sparkling elixir made with a sweet lemon verbena syrup and champagne. The combination of bubbles and the lemony, faintly astringent scent of verbena made the sultry weather much more bearable. When I planted verbena in my herb garden, guess what I planned on making?

1 cup **WATER**

1 cup **GRANULATED SUGAR**

20 **VERBENA LEAVES**, plus extra for garnishing the glasses

½ cup **SUPERFINE SUGAR**

**CHAMPAGNE**, **PROSECCO** or other **SPARKLING WINE**

**1.** To make the sugar syrup, combine the water, sugar, and verbena leaves in a medium saucepan. Bring to a boil over medium-high heat and boil for 10 minutes, stirring occasionally, until the sugar is dissolved. Cover the syrup and steep until cool, then strain, cover, and refrigerate until needed (the syrup will last up to a month in the fridge).

**2.** To serve, dip the rims of champagne glasses in water, then in superfine sugar. Place 2 tablespoons of the syrup in each glass and fill with champagne. Float an additional verbena leaf in each glass, if desired.

# AN EVENING RIDE

*I*'d be hard-pressed to pick a favorite ranch experience. The pine-scented canyon hikes were my therapy. The cooking and gardening fed my creative impulses. Having an alfresco lunch with a pasture of goats as entertainment, or lounging on our front porch with the dogs and a margarita, was pretty close to heaven. But if I had to choose one event, one moment that best encapsulated the most intoxicating high of our adventure, it would be an evening horseback ride with David. Even the time to take such a ride was a gift—it meant a break from cooking and guests, and the undeniable pleasure of having the place to ourselves. That we had 5,250 acres of range to ride without having to trailer horses to a state park didn't escape us, and we didn't take it for granted.

When we first arrived, George was nice enough to bring horses over when we wanted to ride. But we hated to inconvenience him and yearned to have horses of our own. But one day, on a trail ride at George's place, I pointed to a bronze-colored gelding that practically sparkled in the afternoon sun, and said, "Tell me about that pretty buckskin."

"You wanna buy him?" George replied. As luck would have it, he had just bought two horses recently retired from working cattle in West Texas. Along with the buckskin, named Dillon, there was a sad-eyed sorrel with a crooked white blaze down his face. The horses were seasoned and "dead broke," meaning they were unfailingly obedient, so they were perfect for us to learn on. What's more, they were old friends—I liked the notion of them staying together. A few nights later, we took them for a test ride across Cactus Flats, a flat, cedar-studded expanse at the front of the ranch. Then we wrote the checks. I'll never forget the thrill—and the fear—that I felt when I walked Django (the sorrel named after Django Reinhardt, the Gypsy musician) to the barn behind our house. I couldn't believe that the very large animal on the other end of the reins was mine, sans owner's manual.

Many guests who came to the ranch had years of equestrian training, but they had rarely left the ring or their trainer's side. We learned to ride on the range, which was more dangerous, given our inexperience, but also I think it helped us learn to listen to the horses.

Catching horses from the field requires a combination of trickery and luck. If you approach them with bridle and reins in plain view, for instance, they are likely to size you up, think *To hell with that*, and run. We learned to conceal the tack behind our backs and approach a horse slowly, as if we are seeking nothing more than mutual regard and affection. Then, talking softly and stroking his supple withers, I slip my arms and the reins around his neck. If this fails, we resort to plan B, which is foolproof: Bring a bucket of sweet feed to the pasture.

After I slide the bit into the horse's mouth and tuck his soft ears into the headstall, I tie him to the fence and brush him down. This is an enjoyable process for both of us. I relish the earthy smell, and the satisfaction of brushing dust and salt crystals from his coat and tangles from his mane, and the horse likes the attention. He offers each hoof to me obligingly, so I can use a pick to work out the mud and manure packed into his shoes. I'm careful not to dig into the "frog," a sensitive black tendon that stretches down the center of the hoof. I slide a saddle blanket just below the slope of his withers. Then, using two hands, I sling the saddle over. I've learned to hook the far-sided stirrup and cinch belt onto the saddle horn so they don't come down and slap his sides, and I pride myself on landing the saddle lightly onto his back.

I don't think I'll ever get over the rush of placing my left boot into the stirrup, swinging my right leg over the top of the horse, and settling into the saddle. When we're both ready, we spin the horses around in unison. I press my heels into his sides and we set out before one of us asks, "Where should we go?" Do we head to the back toward the hills, through the pecan and black walnut trees and up to that pasture where the calf was born? Or should we go through Horse Trap to Wood Hollow, where the sound of the creek makes the horses skittish? How about up front to Cactus Flats, around the big hill where we saw the wild turkeys? As long as there is plenty of light for a good ride, we usually opt for the latter, because it's the longest loop and the flat expanse makes the most of the shifting light.

We've covered most of the ranch on foot and by vehicle, but there is nothing like seeing the property from the top of a horse. As the light fades and the air cools against my skin, shadows stretch across the path and animals start to stir. For that reason, even an easy ride requires attention. There are plenty of things that can spook a horse and cause it to jump several feet sideways in an instant. An axis buck or antelope might dart through the cedar. Wild hogs might rise from the tall grass where they were resting. Once an armadillo ambled out from a cactus and raced right under my horse, prompting him to leap to the side. When David looked up, he saw both horse and rider in midair with startled expressions. I stayed in the saddle—that time.

We gravitate to favorite paths that have become familiar. We know where to find smooth, low grass where it's safe to canter, and thick, enchanted tunnels of oak trees. We discover eucalyptus-scented agarita bushes loaded with red berries, and prickly pear cactus heavy with magenta-colored fruit. The horses pick their way up steep hills, stumbling on stones now and then, that offer the best vistas. On the ride down, we lean back and shift our weight to the stirrups. We trot through creeks and seek out long-forgotten water tanks so the horses can drink.

A couple of hours later, the horses are slick and darkened, their backs and buttocks foamy with sweat. When I run my hand down his neck, whispering "That's a good boy," the salt makes my kitchen nicks sting.

A few times we miscalculate the light and ride out too far, so we return home in the dark. On these nights, I am anxious to get out of the brush, where I can no longer see the stumps and armadillo holes. The chalk-white caliche road glows in the moonlight and provides an easier path home. We walk slowly, not allowing the old boys to indulge in the bad habit of running back to the barn, because we want to stretch out the moment, which is perfect. The only sound is the clip and crunch of horseshoes on gravel and the occasional shriek or bugle of an axis buck. The horses sigh heavily. When we finally reach the house, we are tired and empty. Then it's grains all around—a bucket of feed for the horses and a cold beer for us. I don't know if I've ever enjoyed anything more in my life.

# Cadillac Bar Margarita

### Makes 2 powerful drinks

Before it closed, the Cadillac Bar in Nuevo Laredo was an old-school, border-town watering hole, with waiters in bow ties and belt-busting snacks like "panchos" (fried tortillas fully loaded with smoky refried beans, avocado, cheese, and sour cream). And then there were the libations.

The Cadillac Bar margaritas were made with good silver tequila, Controy, a Mexican orange liqueur with a bracing flavor that is almost silvery, and tart little Key limes. The combination creates my favorite margaritas—but you may have a hard time finding the liqueur. No one will complain if you use Cointreau, Grand Marnier, or triple sec, and regular limes instead.

$\frac{1}{2}$ cup best-quality **SILVER TEQUILA**

$\frac{1}{2}$ cup **CONTROY** or other **ORANGE LIQUEUR**

$\frac{1}{2}$ cup fresh **LIME JUICE**, plus extra for moistening the rims of glasses

**KOSHER SALT**, for crusting the rims of glasses

**LIMES**, for garnish

Combine the tequila, Controy, and lime juice in a shaker with ice and shake vigorously. Dip the rims of the glasses in water or lime juice, then in salt. Serve with a lime garnish.

# Prickly Pear Margaritas

**Makes 4 generous margaritas**

Prickly pears flourish on the ranch. Their brilliant pink juice creates cocktails that are instantly festive. Prickly pears offer a subtle melon, raspberry, and kiwi flavor. Serve these drinks with Spicy Mixed Nuts (page 102) and mariachi music.

3 large **RED-FLESHED PRICKLY PEARS** (about ⅓ cup juice)

1 cup best-quality **SILVER TEQUILA**

½ cup **COINTREAU** or **CONTROY**

⅓ cup fresh **LIME JUICE**, plus extra for moistening the rims of glasses

**KOSHER SALT**, for crusting the rims of glasses

3 cups **ICE CUBES**

1. To peel the prickly pears, slice off both ends and make a shallow cut down the length of each pear. (You may want to wear rubber gloves to avoid getting pricked by the tiny stickers.) Hold the fruit by the ends, and use your thumb and finger to peel off the thick skin. Place the fruit flesh in a food processor and pulse into a purée. Do not blend continuously or you will chop the seeds. Push the purée through a mesh strainer. You should have about ⅓ cup of juice.

2. In a small glass pitcher, combine the tequila, prickly pear juice, liqueur, and lime juice. Taste and add more lime or sugar, as desired. Spread salt on a small plate. Using a lime wedge, moisten the rims of 4 glasses. Dip the rim of each glass in salt. Pour half the margarita mixture and half the ice into a cocktail shaker. Shake with gusto, to allow some of the ice to dissolve into the margarita. Repeat with the second half and distribute evenly among the glasses.

# Watermelon Margaritas

**Makes 8 generous drinks**

**(double or triple the recipe as needed, for a big blowout)**

When I was a little girl, my grandparents took me to Slim's, a local roadside market, to buy a watermelon to celebrate my June birthday. As a teenager, I worked at such a market, and I cracked open melons on the concrete floor and dug the hearts out with my hand. Cold, sweet watermelon remains one of the most festive flavors of summer for me.

When it's mixed with lime, orange liqueur, and no small amount of silver tequila, you'll have a hard time finding a more crowd-pleasing cocktail for a scorching afternoon. Trust me—everybody perks up at the sight of an icy pink jug. This recipe is on the strong side because when I take them to the river (or backyard parties), I pour the margaritas in a big jug and add plenty of ice, which dilutes the drink. When I serve them indoors, in a more formal setting, I'd use ½ cup less tequila (and ¼ cup less orange liqueur and lime), use the frozen watermelon as ice, purée everything in a blender, and serve them straight up. Garnish the glasses with thin slices of lime or melon wedges, if desired. I've called for a seedless watermelon because it's easier. But if seeded watermelons are sweeter, use them instead and remove the seeds.

A 4-pound piece of ripe **SEEDLESS WATERMELON**

2½ cups good-quality **SILVER TEQUILA**

¾ cup **COINTREAU** or other **ORANGE LIQUEUR**

1 cup fresh **LIME JUICE**

Lots of **CRUSHED ICE**

**MEXICAN KEY LIMES** or additional **WATERMELON**, for garnish (optional)

Trim the rind from the melon and slice the fruit into 2-inch cubes. You should have about 8 cups. Place the watermelon in a blender and purée until smooth. Combine the watermelon juice, tequila, Cointreau, and lime juice in a pitcher or jug and add plenty of ice. Garnish with thinly sliced rounds of Mexican Key limes or additional melon cubes or wedges.

# Epilogue
## Ranches and Rivers

After a long day in the kitchen, I grab a bottle of water, slip out the back door, whistle for the dogs, and head out for an afternoon hike. Cooking for people has made private time all the more welcome. It's a chance to take off my game face and be alone with my thoughts. It occurs to me that every place I've ever traveled, I seek out my own time. I choose destinations based on their off-season. I yearn for the chance to soak up a place privately.

I walk toward the back of the ranch and the trail I've come to know intimately. Without thinking about what I am doing, I navigate a series of gate locks, shoo the dogs from the heifers, scold them for chasing three misfit donkeys, empty the rain gauge, and check to make sure the water trough is full. Tasks that were once foreign have become routine.

As I walk, I think about the ironies that have always fascinated me: The brownstone in Brooklyn you walk past on a random day, for instance, where you will later rent an apartment and spend several years of your life. Over forty years ago my father did his basic training at Lackland Air Force Base, just west of San Antone. Now I drive past the exit to that base every week. I came to San Antonio six years ago for a convention and caroused the Riverwalk with margarita-soaked colleagues. Little did I know that a few years later I would become a regular at a few restaurants there, return each Christmas to see the colored lights, or accept a marriage proposal on a bridge that arched over the river.

I descend a steep hill, surprised that I've come this far. It's a hot afternoon and I have this little corner of the world to myself, so I indulge in one of my favorite post-hike pastimes. I stop at a spring-fed pool framed by limestone rocks, slip out of my clothes, and take the stone steps into the cool, green water. The stones at the bottom are slightly slippery from a thin coat of algae. The cool water is welcome against my hot skin. I paddle around and listen to the frogs. I notice the dappled light streaming through the sycamore and oak leaves overhead.

This unfettered time alone, to exercise, to sink into a property and daydream, has been the biggest reward of changing my life and coming to Texas. Life with animals and a beautiful place to walk. Good food to eat and the time to cook and enjoy it. When I think about how I want to spend my future days, I keep coming back to these simple, precious things.

"Can you see yourself back in New York?" people often ask me. The quick answer is yes. In a heartbeat, I can conjure up the dress, lipstick, city girl shoes and scenario—a proper lunch or late nights of bistros and bar stools. Trust me, when I find myself covered with paw prints and soot smudges, I've wished myself back more than once. But the fantasy is fleeting. At this point in my life, urban pangs can be sated with a few visits every year. Besides, where would the ruminants graze?

You know how you can pull on a certain pair of jeans, or connect a bat to the sweet spot of a ball, or kiss someone deeply on the mouth and the fit—the connection—is unquestionably perfect? That's pretty much how this life, with its quirks, rugged beauty, and thorny edges, feels to me. I found a place I didn't know I was looking for.

I moved to Texas because I wanted to learn new lessons. I wanted to become a better cook, to have a garden, and to know what seasons smelled like in a new part of the world. I wanted to learn what it was like to live on a ranch and care for animals. I got what I wanted, with plenty of surprises thrown in.

When it came time to leave the château where I cooked in France, it was the details—and the recipes—that I took away. Those details were what made the experience uniquely mine. I know a loose tile in that château. I know at a certain time each evening the sea and sky fuse into the same shade of periwinkle. I know the string of lights that drape, like icing on a wedding cake, down the hill on the road toward Théoule, and I can still hear the TGV whizzing by in the night.

When I think about the last four years, I cling to the details. I've learned to look for sycamore trees when I want to find a creek. I know the difference in bark between a black walnut and a pecan tree. I know it is impossible to feel sadness in the presence of a baby goat. I know the high-pitched hum armadillos make when they are being chased by a dog. I know the moody groan of the windmills and the salmon color of the brick barn near the house where we lived.

And then there is the food. I no longer use a recipe to make creamy pinto beans, red chile salsa, or enchiladas verdes. I've gotten old enough to cook the food I like to eat without apology. I've learned that cooking for people and seeing them enjoy the meal I've prepared is more rewarding than I could have imagined. The result is this book of recipes, born of this place and time, that I will prepare for the rest of my life. I hope you will too.

I couldn't have enjoyed any of this without a supportive, loving, and talented partner. For that I must again thank David.

As I mentioned in the beginning, I like living life in chapters because the days remain vibrant and dense with learning. But I know a good thing when I find it. For this cowgirl, heaven is a porch with three dogs stretched out on the cool concrete, light fading behind hills and oak trees, a cold margarita, a crackling fire, and the company of a kindhearted, bread-baking cowboy. With a full heart and plenty of gratitude for the rides I've already had, I look forward to adventures yet to come.

# Index

jalapeño chiles (*continued*)
    for scorpion tails with pequillo
        pepper sauce, 118–20

Keen, Robert Earl, 216
King, Angela, 142, 215

Lawrence, Rusty, 214–16
leek, fennel, and cabbage "kraut,"
    chicken sausage with, 172
lentils:
    in canyon cotechino, 182–83
    soup, Mexican, with roasted
        garlic, 86–87
Leskovar, Celina, 245
lime:
    guacamole with serrano and, 105
    Gulf ceviche with tequila and,
        114–15
    Mexican, salad, 62
    pickled shrimp with beer and,
        112–13

McKay, Noel, 245
Manchego-stuffed Seckel pears with
    prosciutto, 109
maple syrup, pepitas, and yogurt,
    17
margaritas:
    Cadillac Bar, 277
    prickly pear, 278
    watermelon, 281
marjoram:
    roasted Mexican vegetables with,
        223
    turkey sausage with, 42
marmalade, red onion, cowgirl steaks
    with pink peppercorns and,
    198–99
maseca tortillas, 26
mayonnaise:
    pasilla chile, venison burgers
        with, 144–45
    quick anchovy, 125
    verde, boiled shrimp with, 110–11
meatballs, porcupine, with chipotle
    sauce, 193–94
meats, *see specific meats*
melon cup with yogurt, 17
Mexican candy glaze, 200
Mexican cheeses, 27
Mexican lentil soup with roasted
    garlic, 86–87
Mexican lime salad, 62
Mexican vegetables, roasted, with
    marjoram, 223
migas, cowgirl, 25–26
muffins:
    blackberry blue corn, 31

spiced pumpkin, with pepitas,
    32–33
mushrooms:
    and corn soup with fresh herbs,
        creamy, 84–85
    in wild rice and pecan stuffing,
        Cornish hens with, 178–79
mustard and molasses-marinated
    quail, 184

New Mexican chiles, 11
*New York Times*, 102
nopalitos (pickled cactus paddles), 25
Norman, David, 21, 38–39, 51,
    116–17, 130–31, 190–92, 238,
    245, 274–75
Norman, George, 271
Nuevo Laredo Tlalpeño soup, 92–94
nuts, spicy mixed, 102

olives, in Texas tapenade, devilish
    eggs with, 106–7
onion(s):
    red, marmalade, cowgirl steaks
        with pink peppercorns and,
        198–99
    sweet, garlic greens with red
        pepper and, 228
    sweet, in pickled shrimp with
        beer and lime, 112–13
    Texas sweet, tart with rosemary
        and pequín chile, 121–22
orange essence, banana bread with
    almonds and, 36

pan bagnat, Hill Country, 140–41
panela cheese, 27
panzanella, ranch, with avocado, 70
Parmesan cheese, in creamy green
    polenta, 148–49
parsley, in potato poblano soup with
    cheese, 80–81
pasilla chiles, 10
    mayonnaise, venison burgers
        with, 144–45
pasta:
    penne with cilantro pesto and
        grilled chicken, 154
    wagon wheels with peas, green
        herbs, and ricotta salata,
        152
pear(s):
    apple, and honey soufflés, 248
    chamomile poached, 262
    Manchego-stuffed Seckel, with
        prosciutto, 109
    -rosemary bread with pine nuts,
        34
    -rosemary preserves, quick, 35

peas:
    in arroz (mucho) verde, 218
    wagon wheels with green herbs,
        ricotta salata and, 152
pecans:
    in canyon granola, 2–3
    chocolate, squares, 256–57
    and wild rice stuffing, Cornish
        hens with, 178–79
pecorino and lima bean purée,
    crostini with, 128
pepitas:
    brittle, dulce de leche flan with,
        259–61
    spiced pumpkin muffins with,
        32–33
    spicy, ruby salad with crumbled
        feta and, 56–57
pequillo pepper sauce, scorpion tails
    with, 118–20
pequín chiles, 10
    in beet greens with egg, aïoli, and
        rye croutons, 123–24
    Texas sweet onion tart with
        rosemary and, 121–22
persimmon pudding with bittersweet
    ganache, 251–52
pico de gallo, corn, 220
pineapple, vanilla-painted, 232
pine nuts:
    pear-rosemary bread with, 34
    roasted figs with honey and, 233
plums and pluots, roasted, with
    Amaretti trail dust, 234
poblano chiles, 10
    border town hunter's stew with
        pumpkin, hominy and, 95–97
    potato, soup with cheese, 80–81
    shrimp-stuffed, with walnut
        sauce, 161–62
    Texas beef chili with beer and,
        203–4
polenta:
    creamy green, 148–49
    eggs over, with serrano-spiked
        tomato sauce, 28–30
pork:
    in porcupine meatballs with
        chipotle sauce, 193–94
    sausage, Iowa farmhouse green
        beans and, 189
    wild rice and chickpea salad with
        smoked ham, 64
potato(es):
    poblano soup with cheese, 80–81
    two-potato salad with Creole
        mustard and tarragon, 224
pot roast, cowboy, with coffee and
    whiskey, 195–97

preserves, quick pear-rosemary, 35
prickly pear:
    margaritas, 278
    sorbet, 240
prosciutto, Manchego-stuffed Seckel
    pears with, 109
prunes, brandy-plumped, 250
pumpkin:
    border town hunter's stew with
      poblanos, hominy and, 95–97
    roasted, soup with red chile
      cream, 82–83
    spiced, muffins with pepitas,
      32–33
Purnell, Sharon, 6–7, 20, 117, 220

quail:
    cornmeal-crusted, with fig-
      rosemary skewers, 185–86
    mustard and molasses-marinated,
      184
queso añejo, 27
queso fresco, 27
quinoa salad with tomatillo
    vinaigrette, 67–68

radishes, for quinoa salad with
    tomatillo vinaigrette, 67–68
Rather, Rebecca, 244, 265
rice:
    arroz (mucho) verde, 218
    carrot cumin pilaf, 217
    gazpacho risotto with garlic
      shrimp, 150–51
    in porcupine meatballs with
      chipotle sauce, 193–94
    Sardinian, salad, 66
    wild, and chickpea salad with
      smoked ham, 64
    wild, and pecan stuffing, Cornish
      hens with, 178–79
ricotta salata cheese, wagon wheels
    with peas, green herbs and, 152
romaine, hearts of, and spinach with
    walnuts and eggs, 47
rosemary:
    butter, 201
    -fig skewers, cornmeal-crusted
      quail with, 185–86
    -pear bread with pine nuts, 34
    -pear preserves, 35
    Texas sweet onion tart with
      pequín chile and, 121–22
Rubell, Jennifer, 163
rye-crusted snapper with pink tartar
    sauce, 163–64

Sachs, April, 251
sage, turkey chili with white beans

and, 90–91
salads, 45–70
    celery root rémoulade with
      arugula, 53
    chicken and citrus slaw tostadas,
      59–61
    cumin chickpeas, 62
    golden beet, celery, and chèvre,
      54–55
    green and white beans in herb oil,
      208
    Highway 55 slaw with buttermilk
      dressing, 225
    lean and green broccoli couscous,
      58
    Mexican lime, 62
    my favorite green, 46
    quinoa, with tomatillo vinaigrette,
      67–68
    ranch dressing, 48
    ranch panzanella with avocado,
      70
    ruby, with crumbled feta and
      spicy pepitas, 56–57
    Sardinian rice, 66
    smoked chicken, with green chiles
      and tarragon, 138–39
    spinach and hearts of romaine
      with walnuts and eggs, 47
    tuna and haricot vert, 69
    two-potato, with Creole mustard
      and tarragon, 224
    wild rice and chickpea, with
      smoked ham, 64
salmon, wild, with beets and citrus,
    157
salsas:
    blistered tomatillo, 9
    horse trader, 14
    smoky red chile, 12
    verde, 8
    verde, for enchiladas verde,
      175–77
    verde, halibut with, 158–59
sandwiches, 133–45
    herbaceous egg salad, 136
    Hill Country pan bagnat,
      140–41
    smoked chicken salad with green
      chiles and tarragon, 138–39
    smoked turkey wraps with
      chipotle cream, 134–35
    venison burgers with pasilla chile
      mayonnaise, 144–45
Sardinian rice salad, 66
sauces:
    aïoli, beet greens with egg, rye
      croutons and, 123–24
    chipotle, porcupine meatballs

with, 193–94
    David's mop, grilled chicken
      thighs with blistered cherry
      tomatoes and, 165–67
    dried cherry and whiskey, for
      seared axis chops, 188
    mayo verde, boiled shrimp with,
      110–11
    pequillo pepper, scorpion tails
      with, 118–20
    pink tartar, rye-crusted snapper
      with, 163–64
    quick anchovy mayo, 125
    ranch hand red, huevos with,
      16–17
    red chile, greens with, 229
    serrano-spiked tomato, eggs over
      polenta with, 28–30
    walnut, shrimp-stuffed poblanos
      with, 161–62
    *see also* salsas
sausage(s):
    canyon cotechino, 182–83
    chicken, with fennel, leek, and
      cabbage "kraut," 172
    Iowa farmhouse green beans and,
      189
    turkey, with marjoram, 42
scallions, corn bread with, 222
scallops, in Gulf ceviche with tequila
    and lime, 114–15
seafood stew, Gulf, 155–56
serrano chiles, 10
    guacamole with lime and, 105
    -spiked tomato sauce, eggs over
      polenta with, 28–30
shellfish, *see specific shellfish*
shrimp:
    boiled, with mayo verde, 110–11
    garlic, gazpacho risotto with,
      150–51
    in Gulf ceviche with tequila and
      lime, 114–15
    in Gulf seafood stew, 155–56
    pickled, with beer and lime,
      112–13
    -stuffed poblanos with walnut
      sauce, 161–62
side dishes, 207–29
    arroz (mucho) verde, 218
    carrot cumin pilaf, 217
    corn bread with scallions, 222
    corn pico de gallo, 220
    creamy green polenta, 148–49
    garlic greens with red pepper and
      sweet onions, 228
    green and white beans in herb oil,
      208
    greens with red chile sauce, 229